A Girl in Paris

Also by Shusha Guppy

The Blindfold Horse
Looking Back

A Girl in Paris

Shusha Guppy

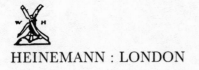

HEINEMANN : LONDON

William Heinemann Ltd
Michelin House, 81 Fulham Road, London sw3 6rb
LONDON   MELBOURNE   AUCKLAND

First published 1991

Reprinted 1991, 1992

Copyright © Shusha Guppy 1991

A CIP catalogue record for this book
is held by the British Library
ISBN 0 434 30852 8

Phototypeset by Intype, London
Printed in Great Britain by
St Edmundsbury Press Ltd, Bury St Edmunds, Suffolk

To my sons Darius and Constantine
and their father Nicholas

Contents

Acknowledgements

I wish to express my gratitude to those friends who helped me during the writing of this book. In particular Yannick Bellon and Aube Breton for their hospitality in France; Loleh Bellon and Claude Roy for their support all along; Sandra Calder-Davidson; Gillon Aitken; Helen Fraser and others at William Heinemann. I also thank Nicholas Guppy for his guidance over the years. And Anthony Smith, always.

Ma jeunesse ne fut qu'un ténébreux orage,
Traversé çà et là par de brillants soleils

CHARLES BAUDELAIRE

I

The Brown Dove

My room is on the top floor of a seven-storey building on the embankment, on the Left Bank. There are nine others like it, strung along a narrow L-shaped corridor beneath the roof. It is tiny and sparsely furnished: a single bed, a bedside table on which stands a wooden lamp with a faded pink shade, a clothes-rack holding a few coat-hangers, a desk by the wide dormer window, and a large antique chest of drawers which looks out of place in so modest a dwelling.

The low ceiling slopes down to the one window. This opens on to the back of the building with its tangle of black metal ledges, rain gutters and pipes, going down vertiginously to a dark square courtyard. But you don't see them unless you lean out. Otherwise the view stretches over the green canopy of trees bordering the Seine to the shimmering roofscape of the Right Bank, as far as the eye can see. Famous landmarks stand out and help gauge distances: the Obélisque in the Place de la Concorde, La Madeleine, Les Tuileries, and on a clear day even the white cupola of the Sacré Coeur. Through the swaying branches in the foreground you can glimpse the river, its green-ish flow hardly perceptible between the steady stream of traffic on its banks, its barges chugging along sluggishly, its cheerful pleasure-boats, and the graceful curve of its bridges, like athletes leaping at intervals, far down river to Notre Dame and the Ile de la Cité.

At dusk the multi-coloured lights of the pier by Alma Bridge are switched on, and the embankment becomes a fairground, with *bateaux mouches* coming and going, their lights ablaze, picking up or disgorging cargoes of tourists and revellers. Your gaze can follow them a mile or two down river, huge dragons blowing the flames of their headlights on to the dark water, pausing at their journey's end, then turning round and slowly coming back. Around midnight, when the last boat has returned and tourists have left the pier, the lights go out, leaving only the glow-worms of cars flashing through the foliage, and you can feel the sleeping giant of the city breathing steadily till dawn.

The trees harbour a large population of pigeons, which fly up and perch on the ledges, window-sills and eaves of the embankment buildings. My friend Violette, who has lent me this room, says that it would be fatal to feed or encourage them, that they would soon invade the room and become pestiferous. During the day they fill the air with the fluttering of their wings, their garrulous cooing and mating, and when night falls they curl up into feather balls dotted along the ledges and the eaves or on the branches. Where are they when it rains? They seem to disappear, but they return as soon as the sky is clear, as if by conjury.

Despite Violette's warning I have befriended one bird, who sits alone outside my window, separate from all the others in pairs or clusters further away. She is smaller than they, and the only one with a different colouring – instead of the usual bluish-grey, her feathers are brown, brushed here and there with thin white lines.

She hops out of my reach as soon as I stretch a hand to touch her, but takes the crumbs I sometimes leave on the edge of the window-sill. 'She'? Only because dove in French is feminine, *la colombe*. And something in her dark colouring, her slight stature, her *farouche* aloofness touches a chord . . .

In the past these tiny rooms, with their narrow stairs, their

2

communal cold water tap at the bend of the corridor, and their one lavatory at the far end, were inhabited by the maids of the wealthy families who occupied the spacious apartments of such residential blocks. But gradually as people ceased to afford living-in staff they were converted into guest-rooms or let to students, artists, and other impecunious solitaries.

Today, even hotels have turned them into extra rooms for long-term residency. They make up in privacy what they lack in comfort: you enter the building through the 'service' door and climb the stairs without being detected by the concierge or the residents; and there is the panoramic view. So when Violette offered me hospitality, I chose this *chambre de bonne* in preference to a room inside her apartment.

What better setting could there be for remembrance? For once I had lived in such a room, a long time ago, when I first arrived in Paris from Persia. How long ago? After a quarter of a century or more, life's colours fade, its contours blur, and even memory mellows. Of the Paris of my youth, as of the Persia of my childhood*, I now mostly remember the sweeter flavours, though I know how cold, grim and lonely life often was. It was a time of wandering and exile, tempered by chance encounters, relationships formed and diffused, sweet dreams and rude awakenings, dire errors and lucky breaks, a couple of significant turnings.

So I have selected much more to assuage than to lacerate nostalgia: there is enough in the present with which to be preoccupied and tormented. What follows is in no chronological order, rather a set of stories, of little currents meandering towards a stream. 'Life as it is', or was, drops remembered from the pool of what is forgotten.

* see: *The Blindfold Horse – Memories of a Persian Childhood* (Minerva)

2

The Flight

La vie est ailleurs
ARTHUR RIMBAUD

In those days only one or two planes left per day for Europe or America – in the 50s Teheran Airport was little more than an earth track surrounded by flat, sun-scorched wilderness, with an asphalt ribbon of runway cutting through it. The air terminal consisted of a squat tin-roofed building divided into arrival and departure halls, with sections for customs and passport control. The huge international airport which became the busiest in the Middle East in the 60s and 70s was then still only a twinkle in the Shah's eyes.

Our plane, a four-engine Air France carrier, stood alone a little distance from the terminal building while we went through the formalities of departure and the convulsions of farewell. Eventually we were escorted aboard by a chic blonde air-hostess and given our seats.

Compared to today's jumbo jets our plane was tiny, and packed mostly with male passengers. I was travelling with Pari, a school friend who was going to a German university and would be changing planes in Paris. As far as I recall we were the only students among the passengers – forerunners of the heavy traffic that conveyed tens of thousands of Persian students to Europe and America in the decades that followed.

For us going to a Western university was a high privilege, possible only for a few, especially if you were a girl. We were

4

lucky, we should be glad, yet we were weeping our eyes out, and I would have given half my life to stay.

I sat by the window and tried to pick out my mother and other members of our household who had accompanied me, but they were too far away, lost in the crowd. As last the motors started and the plane began to move along the runway. Presently we were airborne and over the mountains bordering the city, their higher ridges streaked with the first autumnal snows, glittering in the sun. Soon we were heading south-west over the empty vastness of the Iranian plateau. The city had vanished like a chimera, and the ground was a fawn *moiré* dotted with small oases, – a row of poplars bordering a bluish-green pond, a few goats, a huddle of flat-roofed huts. More often all I saw was the shadow of the aeroplane sliding over the undulating ground like a little kite, and the flawless blue sky above. Exhausted by anxiety and crying, I fell asleep, and woke up to sunset, the horizon a delirium of colours – gold, red, purple, deepening into black. Then darkness fell and we were travelling among the stars.

During my whole short life I had never before spent a day away from home and family. Even in the summer, when we moved from our town house to the country, we were encouraged to ask our friends to stay with us rather than go to their homes. This ensured that we were always chaperoned and did not fall under 'bad influences', which my mother dreaded, ever mindful of our virtue. Against this solid background of protection all my dreams of adventure and romance were woven and embroidered, and all the small dramas of life became aggrandized, and were relished with the intensity of adolescence.

But now the reality was different: ahead lay days, months, years perhaps, alone, far from everyone I loved, and no promise of future happiness and fulfilment could compensate for the loss. What *had* I done? How *could* I leave them all behind? Panic and regret overwhelmed me, and hopeless tears began again to pour down my face.

'If you go on crying, I shall get cross!' Pari nudged me,

turning my face away from the window towards her, and kissing my cheeks. Think how lucky we are, how many of our friends would have given their right arms to be in our place! I'm sad too, but I know that we will get used to it and have a good life. Come, let's go and wash our faces and put on some lipstick!'

Lipstick! My older sister and I were not allowed to wear make-up, short sleeves, flimsy stockings, even scent, lest they were construed as wishing to be attractive to men! Such interdicts and taboos were perhaps trivial in themselves, but imposed from outside, they were part of the lack of personal sovereignty against which I rebelled. I bitterly resented and resisted the family, social and religious rules that hampered the natural flow of life, the soar of the imagination, the aspirations of the soul. My mother's generation of women, not to mention all the others before, had accommodated themselves to these restrictions, but I and my friends had read books and magazines, seen photographs and above all movies, and we knew of other possibilities: a world in which women were seemingly as free as men to shape their own destinies, in which they could choose their own mates, develop their talents. *We* saw no contradiction between freedom and virtue.

I could see no way of breaking free except by leaving the country, indeed as far back as I could remember I had dreamed of being '*ailleurs*' – elsewhere – and that for me meant Europe, and more precisely Paris. Now at last '*ailleurs*' was within reach, and yet I was bereft, devastated by homesickness, wishing to be parachuted down into one of those oases in the desert and never again to dream of escape! It would take me half a lifetime to realize that '*ailleurs*' is unattainable, that it recedes as you approach it, and that whenever you think you have at last reached it, it has gone 'elsewhere'.

I remember those first few hours of our flight as if they were yesterday, such was their emotional intensity. Unconsciously I knew that, whatever the future had in store, nothing could ever be as painful, and that the rest of my life would be played against the backdrop of this first, irreparable *déchirure*.

We went to the rear of the plane and washed our faces. Then Pari took a lipstick out of her handbag, put some on and then some on me. I looked in the mirror at the odd, gaudy result, but did not dare to wipe it off for fear of annoying her. Going back in the cabin I was so shy that I put my hand in front of my mouth while walking down the aisle, as if all eyes were fixed on me with disapproval. As it happens I never did wear much make-up, and hardly ever touched a lipstick after the novelty had gone.

But now let me tell you Pari's story.

Pari had come to our school, The Princess, during my last year, to prepare for taking the Baccalaureat. We were few in the class, as most girls had left school after the diploma exam, usually to get married and have children. (In 1932, Reza Shah had made sixteen the legal age for marriage but many parents updated their daughters' birth-certificates so that they could marry at fifteen or even younger.) Only those planning to go to university stayed on for an extra year, to prepare for their entrance exams. You could choose maths, natural sciences, or literature and philosophy. As not all high-schools had facilities for all three divisions, nor enough applications to warrant setting one up, Pari had come from her own school to ours.

We were a small class of some twenty girls studying for the literature Baccalaureate, and six of us formed a group who went around in a pack, and saw each other outside school as well. We all looked up to Pari, who was not only more grown-up and sophisticated than the rest of us, but 'different'. For she was a foundling – a secret closely guarded by her nearest friends, and unknown even to teachers and the Principal.

Pari's adoptive parents were an elderly doctor and his wife, who had despaired of producing children of their own, and had looked around for a baby to adopt. This was not easy, for there were no adoption agencies, so they had to enquire through family and friends, the grapevine of the *Hammam* (public baths), and among the local bazaar traders. It was rare for parents, however poor and destitute, to consent to part with their babies.

7

'The One who gives the teeth, gives the bread', they quoted the poet, trusting in providence to provide a livelihood for their progeny, no matter how numerous. Illegitimate children were practically unknown: given the traditional family structure and the strict surveillance of women, the price of 'sin' was often death for both the girl and the man who had seduced her. To avenge her honour, her father, or more often her brother, could kill the offender almost with impunity. Besides no one would want to keep a child conceived out of wedlock, who would surely become a thief or a murderer. Gruesome stories were told of how illegitimate babies were killed: pins pushed into their fontanelles, or they were wrapped in rags and put into garbage pits and communal latrines, or even buried alive. Amazingly, this task was usually done by an elderly woman who could be trusted to keep the secret. So the rare adopted child was likely to be an orphan, which was Pari's case. No one knew who her real parents were or how she had come to be adopted, as she had not been told, nor did she ever discuss the subject with her parents. We just knew that Pari had been a foundling, which made her all the more fascinating. Budding feminists *avant la lettre* as we all were, we hoped that she was a 'love child', conceived in a passionate embrace, whose survival and blossoming had belied the common superstitious beliefs. No wonder her name was Pari – Fairy.

Luckily for her parents Pari had turned out an enchanting little girl: pretty and bright, and very affectionate. She had fine features, a tall graceful stature, and a sense of humour. Childhood ailments had kept her away from school for a year, which meant that she was slightly older than the rest of us, and she seemed more precocious, perhaps because her indulgent adoptive parents had allowed her small freedoms that we were denied – she wore short skirts and fitted dresses with bold cleavages that revealed her long neck and shapely figure. Sometimes faint traces of make-up from the previous evening's party could be detected on her face, the soft rosy shadow of rouge enhancing an otherwise pale face, a pinkish line emphasizing

8

the contour of her lips. All of these things were beyond the strict code of conduct to which we had to adhere.

Pari's adoptive parents adored her, and she was devoted to them. In later years she sacrificed her own life to their well-being. After spending a year in Germany learning the language, she entered the university in Tubingen to read psychology, but almost immediately abandoned her studies to return to Persia and look after her aged father, who had fallen ill. It was the beginning of the petrol boom and, in the resulting economic development which brought many foreign firms to Iran, Pari took a job with a German trading company. She lived at home and nursed her parents until they died, within a few years of each other. By then Pari was nearly thirty, and she never married. Too fastidious to compromise, she turned down many advantageous marriage proposals, preferring to follow the vagaries of her heart. She once told me that she had a few 'liaisons' which did not lead to more permanent relationships, but she was too diffident for anyone to be sure.

Another reason why we admired Pari was that she practised what she preached more than we dared to do. While we assuaged our adolescent yearnings with dreams of film stars, she had a real sweetheart: a boy from the American College. Students from male *lycées* and the nearby Faculty of Letters often walked past The Princess to watch us come out at the end of the day. They kept a respectful distance, but they appraised us and picked out their favourites for special attention. Pari's boyfriend had followed her home every day for a long time, and one day, encouraged by a smile from her, he had approached and talked to her. From then on he followed her every afternoon, and once they had left the vicinity of our school he walked her home. Sometimes they stopped at a café for tea and pastries, and once or twice they even managed to go to the cinema together. Our vicarious pleasure at her amorous adventure peaked when she told us that she had allowed him to kiss her good night. And now they were madly in love with one another and we, her closest friends, shared and closely guarded her delicious secret, for if it was known by the school authorities she would surely be expelled, bringing opprobrium onto herself and her parents.

So why were they both leaving the country, Pari for Europe and her boyfriend for America, instead of driving off into the sunset and living happily ever after? Because the decision had been taken by their parents, and at seventeen and eighteen respectively they had to obey. But they had vowed eternal fidelity and would wait for each other, no matter how many years their separation lasted.

On a trip to Persia several years later Pari told me that after a few passionate letters he had stopped writing to her and they had lost touch. She later learnt that he had married an American girl and settled down somewhere in the Mid-West. He never returned home. But at the time of our departure his promise of love and ultimate reunion sustained Pari, which explained why she was less heartbroken than I was.

Later I lost touch with her, as with most members of our group, but I have heard that after the events of 1979, she left Persia for Germany, where she now lives and works.

My mother did not know any of this about my travelling companion, otherwise she would have forbidden me to see her, for fear of contamination. How on earth did she think I would be immune to such 'influences', alone in Paris? She counted on my 'seriousness' and the modesty she had inculcated in us. Above all she believed that hers and my father's prayers would create a screen around me which would protect my life and integrity.

Looking back on the peripeteia of those years I tend to think that perhaps they did. And if they didn't, then what did?

3
Arrival

Do not fight
But help one another
On your way
Dear migrating birds
ISSO − *HAIKUS*

From the air Orly airport seemed a sea of lights, as if Aladdin
had opened his chest of gems and spread its content over
the velvety darkness. The large, luminous terminal building to
which the air-hostess led us was of a palatial splendour compared to the shack from which we had departed. Coloured
pictures of historic sites and natural beauty spots of France
decorated the walls, windows exhibited the latest creations in
couture and jewellery, uniformed staff attended to passengers.
We were being met by Mr Raheem, a councillor at the Iranian
Embassy, who was a friend and senior colleague of my elder
brother. I had heard about him from various members of his
family who came to our house, but had never met him on
account of his being nearly always abroad. Now his presence
at the airport was reassuring, a link with the world I had left
behind. Being a diplomat he was allowed to meet us before we
went through Customs and Immigration formalities and to
smooth our passage. I had always taken such privileges for
granted, not knowing that they would soon disappear, and
that I would become one more lonely foreign student among
thousands.

Mr Raheem explained that he had reserved a room for us in
a fairly grand hotel for the night, but that in the morning when
Pari left he would take me to a smaller one near his home

until permanent accommodation could be found for me. What remains in my memory of the drive to central Paris is a phantasmagoria of flashing lights, tall black buildings, and wide tree-lined boulevards, apprehended dimly through a haze of physical and emotional exhaustion. The flight that today takes five hours had taken twelve, and, racked with sadness and anxiety, we had not touched the alien food of the aeroplane.

The spacious entrance hall of the hotel, lit with huge crystal chandeliers, seemed to quiver like a fairy palace. Mr Raheem registered us and said goodbye, entrusting our luggage to a porter who took us to our room on the third floor. It was a large room with a high ceiling and long windows overlooking the street. The antique-rose and milky white of the walls and furniture, lit by Art-Nouveau shades of coloured glass, created a warm atmosphere, and we undressed quickly and fell asleep. It did not last – as soon as fatigue abated I woke, panic-stricken at what I had done, wondering what face-saving stratagem I could find to go back home as soon as possible. Everything I could do would take at least a year, and in the meantime I would *die* of grief, I was sure! Pari breathed gently in the next bed and I did not move lest I woke her up. I just cried myself back to sleep soundlessly.

Around eight o'clock a waiter woke us up with a tray of hot coffee and croissants. I recalled our breakfasts at home: all of us gathered round the purring samovar in Mother's room, the appetizing spread of goat cheese, butter, an assortment of home-made jams and warm flat bread, all of which I often forswore for fear of getting fat. In the years that followed I never once thought of my weight – for me as for most students the problem was finding enough food, not avoiding it! The cultivation of mind and soul came before nourishment. My meagre resources and time were devoted to books, films, plays, opera, cafés, and pretty soon flattering clothes and alluring accessories – anything but mundane, unromantic food!

'I slept like a log,' said Pari. 'Did you?'

'Yes.'

We got ready, opened the window and stepped out on to the balcony. I had seen bits of Paris in French films, or in *Shahre-Farang*, a magic-box with moving pictures inside it which an itinerant magician brought round the streets in Tehran to entertain children, and I had read descriptions of it in nineteenth-century French novels. Out of these materials I had built the Paris of my imagination. Now the real city spread before my gaze, dissolving those tenuous images. A leaden sky hung low, filtering a jaundiced light over pavements glistening with recent rain, fallen leaves whirled in the breeze, pigeons clustered around an old woman in the square below while she threw crumbs at them. On one corner a wrought-iron panel indicated an entrance to the underground: *Métro*, the very concept of which was for us synonymous with industrial development and progress.

Presently a young couple, walking arm in arm towards the Métro, stopped at the entrance and embraced: a long, passionate kiss, just as in the movies, but there in front of us, *in public*! I must have blushed, for Pari laughed at me, indicating how much more grown-up and sophisticated she was.

Imbued with progressive ideas, my group of friends had endlessly discussed the taboos that governed our lives, and we rejected them *in toto*. I was more vehement in my rebellion than my friends, perhaps because I came from a religious background and did not enjoy even such freedom as they. But all these ideas were in theory, and part of our larger political involvement – when the Revolution came all would be free, and the relationships between men and women would be harmonious and based on equality; pending which radiant future my personal conduct conformed to the traditional rules of modesty.

'Bah! Why shouldn't they kiss? Why should they hide? There's nothing wrong with it!' shrugged Pari. We went inside.

At nine o'clock Mr Raheem called for us, accompanied by a colleague of his from the embassy who was to drive Pari back to Orly airport. So we kissed goodbye tearfully and promised to write often. If only she could stay with me, I thought, we

13

would sustain each other until we got used to our new environment and eventually returned home. With her departure the last connection with the world I knew was severed. From now on everything and everybody would be new, and it would be up to me to adapt and make the best of circumstances.

In today's world of instant communication, where direct-dialling telephones connect you to the other side of the globe at the push of a button, fax-machines transmit your messages and billets-doux within minutes, while Concorde enables you to commute to America daily, it is hard to imagine the acute pain of homesickness and separation we felt. In those days it was a major production to ring another European country, let alone an Asiatic hinterland like Persia. You had to book the call the day before, then wait for hours while the operator tried to connect you, after which you spent your allocated three minutes shouting 'Hello? Hello? Can you hear me?' before being cut off and pleading with the operator to reconnect you; and the cost of this frustrating 'communication' would swallow half your monthly allowance.

As Mr Raheem's car pulled out, I looked back at our hotel, and its illuminated sign, *Hôtel Lutétia*.

'It's the name the Romans gave Paris', Mr Raheem informed me. The hotel still stands at the intersection between boulevard Raspail and the rue de Sèvres, not far from where I would eventually live.

'*Nothing* is written,' my father used to say, refuting the old Persian belief that a person's destiny is 'written' by an angel on his or her forehead at birth, that nothing can ever change it, and that all human effort at countering Fate is futile. 'We write our own destinies as we go along, within limits,' he would say. 'We choose who we are and what we do, otherwise there would be no merit in being good and no sin in being bad.' 'The limits' are circumstance and the Grace of God, the perimeters of human freedom are the Higher Design of the Creator. I agreed. I thought I could assume responsibility for the freedom

I craved, whatever the price. Yet I was no female Rastignac. On the contrary I had no personal ambitions, only adolescent ideals, and as we drove off to his '*A nous deux, Paris*' I echoed my forlorn '*A nous deux, Liberté*!'

Years later I went to Paris for a television show, arranged by my record company, and I was put up at the Hôtel Lutétia. Although the façade, with its balconies, wrought-iron railings and decorative awnings had not changed, inside the hall and reception rooms were refurbished and seemed more cheerful. The tea-room overlooking the boulevard buzzed with guests having afternoon tea, and new bars and restaurants had been added. My suite had been made welcoming with flowers, a fruit basket and chilled champagne. It was a happy occasion: my new record was being released, press and radio appearances had been arranged, and I was treated with affection by everyone. Yet alone in my room I remembered that night of arrival in Paris, and a wave of melancholy washed over me, leaving me limp with nostalgia. Then I opened the window and stepped out on to the balcony. It was spring and a pale blue sky streaked with candy-floss clouds arched high above the city; a soft luminosity poured down in gold ribbons through the branches in the square; pigeons gathered around the benches to be fed by elderly benefactors . . . and all the buildings, periodically cleaned by a wealthy city, looked much less sombre and threatening.

Twenty years had passed, a kind of home had been found and a life had been lived, *tant bien que mal*. Yet I remembered every detail of that first encounter with Paris as if it had been only the day before. The great talent all human beings share is for forgetting: 'grief and joy pass equally, as fast as a bird on the wing' goes the proverb. Yet nothing is lost, only stored away. The lucky and the wise draw on the storage judiciously, while the rest of us muddle through. So here I was, at seventeen still a lost teenager full of hopes and forebodings.

4
Hôtel Sophia

Pity them, my children, they are far
from home and no one knows them
MEISTER ECKHARD

Mr Raheem's apartment was on the fourth floor of a building
in the Champ-de-Mars – so called on account of the military
parades that took place there in the eighteenth century. From
his drawing-room window you could glimpse the Eiffel Tower
in the distance, tapering up to the clouds, while his dining-
room overlooked the street and the luminous sign of Hôtel
Sophia, a two-star establishment where a room had been
reserved for me.

As we drove there on that first day Mr Raheem explained
that the area covered a square mile between the Seine by the
Eiffel Tower and l'Ecole Militaire – the military academy which
had been built by Louis XV on the advice of his beloved
mistress, Madame de Pompadour, for the martial education of
noblemen. Among its past alumni had been Napoleon, who
was buried nearby in the Invalides. We made a little detour
along the embankment to see it: a dark monument at the end
of a long, wide esplanade, its cupola like a Byzantine crown set
upon a brooding brow pondering history's treachery. I once saw
a group of English tourists walking on the esplanade towards it
and heard a little boy ask his father: 'What's that building,
Daddy?' 'It's the tomb of the Unknown soldier,' he replied.
You could almost hear Napoleon spin!

Hôtel Sophia was very modest compared with the grand

16

Lutétia: it had only sixteen rooms, and a small hall where the owner/manager sat behind a desk and monitored the *va-et-vient*. He rose to greet us, and exchanged pleasantries with Mr Raheem, then gave us the key to No. 15. We took the lift to the fourth floor and climbed a further flight of stairs to the top, where the old *chambres de bonne* had been converted to less pricey accommodation. My room was largish, the ceiling slanting down to a window that opened on to a profusion of jagged roofs and chimneys. My eyes, used to the dazzling mountain sun of Persia, had difficulty adjusting to the subdued light that came obliquely through the aperture and lay on the bed in a wide strip. The rest of the furniture consisted of a lamp on a bedside table and a huge chest of drawers topped with a mirror.

Mr Raheem left me to settle down, and later join him and his daughter Myriam for lunch at their home. I opened my suitcase reluctantly; unpacking meant staying, when all I wished was to go straight back to the airport and fly home. I had taken few clothes – were they not coals to Newcastle? My mother had started giving me a clothes allowance when I was fourteen, so that I could 'learn to manage'. But I had spent it all on books and records and going to cafés with my friends. For special parties I borrowed my sister's dresses, as soon I reached her size. Apart from basic clothes I had brought with me a miniature bound volume of Hafiz's *Ghazals* (sonnets) and a small framed photograph of a nineteenth-century painting by a Romantic artist, which a friend had given me and which I had hung above my bed at home. It was a landscape depicting a stormy nightfall – trees bent by the gale, a stream rushing under an arched bridge, a thatched cottage whose windows glowed from the lamplight within. A solitary woman in a long hooded cape with a basket on her arm was struggling along a path towards its shelter. I had woven endless stories around the woman and had got attached to the picture as a result. As it had a thin, flat frame around its glass, and weighed nothing, I had taken it with me to remind me of home, and now I leaned it against the wall on top of the chest of drawers.

17

'I am not going to stay!' I decided, to boost my morale and be able to put on a cheerful countenance at Mr Raheem's. 'I'm going to learn French as quickly as I can and go home.' I later learnt that all foreign students, indeed even French ones from the provinces, experienced the same feeling on arrival. Yet at the end no one ever left Paris willingly. The city became a state of mind which you carried with you for the rest of your life: you interiorized your displacement, your deracination. Real exile begins when you no longer pine for 'home', when it has been lost forever, buried in the recesses of the psyche, and the only home you have is Memory.

I sat down and wrote a long letter to my sister, which I hoped she would read to my parents and the rest of our household as well. I told of our flight and arrival, the little I had glimpsed of Paris, pretending that I was perfectly content. 'A sad heart spreads sorrow on the whole assembly'. 'Never complain, or you'll lose people's esteem', etc . . . These oft-repeated sayings, of which Aunt Ashraf (our household sage) had an inexhaustible font, were so inculcated in me that I did not dare to say how miserable I was, lest I upset my family.

At midday I went down, handed my key to the manager, who looked at me with assessing eyes, and went to Mr Raheem's flat across the street. Myriam opened the door and welcomed me warmly. Inside, the soberly furnished apartment was made agreeably cheerful, with lamps and vases of roses and chrysanthemums everywhere. The open-plan drawing-room/dining-room ran the width of the building, with windows on both sides affording maximum light. The familiar smell of Persian cuisine – saffron rice, meat and vegetable stew pervaded the air and made me reel with homesickness.

Mr Raheem was in his late forties, slim, of medium height and cheerful countenance. He had a round face and full cheeks, and a moustache drooped over his lips hiding his mouth so completely that unless he smiled you didn't see where his speech came from. But he smiled often, which lit up his blackcurrant eyes. He was not particularly good-looking, but humour and charm together with elegant clothes and gallant manners made him attractive.

His family belonged to that section of society which Cardinal Richelieu called clerical aristocracy – the high-ranking mullahs whose power and influence in Persia had remained unchallenged for two centuries and whose progressive elements had played a key role in the success of the Constitutional Revolution of 1905–6. When Reza Shah came to power in 1925, he had subdued the clergy and forced them to render unto Caesar . . . or perish. Divested of power, they had lost their prestige. Their sons discarded their traditional costume of cloak-and-turban in favour of Western suits and trilby and, instead of going to the theological colleges where their fathers had been educated, went to Western universities whence they returned to run the country and its new institutions.

Mr Raheem's father was the chief mullah of a southern province and a landowner. It was an old custom of his family that, as far as possible, they should intermarry, quoting the old saying: 'Cousins' wedlock is forged in Heaven.' In fact the custom had less to do with heavenly intervention than with property preservation: Islamic laws of inheritance do not recognize the right of primogeniture, and land divided between numerous children is apt to get fragmented, so dynastic intermarriages kept everything in the family. Alas, such inbreeding had taken its toll in Mr Raheem's family, and after several generations of intermarriage some of their children were born 'odd', with either physical or mild mental deficiencies. One or two ended up in psychiatric hospitals, and several were, shall we say . . . unprepossessing.

At nineteen Mr Raheem had been forced to marry a first cousin five years his senior. She lived in another town and he had never seen her, but he took his female relatives' word for her attractiveness. On their wedding night, when he was ushered into the nuptial room and left alone with his bride, he had lifted her veil gently, hoping to be thunderstruck by her beauty. Instead he was confronted with a *looloo* – a gorgon! He had gasped and dropped the veil, then sat down to ponder the situation. The idea that this misshapen, pock-marked, hairy woman would be his companion for life made him sick. What is more, he soon realized that she was not quite right in the head. Nevertheless to save his honour he had overcome his revulsion and performed his duty. The result, nine months later, was Myriam.

The protagonist of such a scenario was usually the bride: she was the one who discovered her husband to be older than her father, ugly or half-witted, light years away from the Prince Charming of her dreams. Occasionally it did happen to men, but while women had no escape routes and had to live with their fate for the rest of their lives, men had several. Soon after his wedding Mr Raheem left his home town for the university in Tehran, leaving his wife in the care of his parents, and he never returned. Upon graduation he entered the Foreign Service and was immediately posted abroad. Every time he returned to Persia he paid a lightning visit to his parental home to see his daughter, but never again did he look at his wife. The effect on her of his total rejection was that she became even more 'moonstruck'. When Mr Raheem's parents died, his sister had inherited his wife, like an awkward piece of furniture that can neither be used nor discarded. I remember her: she came to our house once or twice with Mr Raheem's sister who was a friend of my mother's. She seemed dazed and seldom talked. When she did, what she said was unconnected with the conversation, and occasionally she laughed at inappropriate moments, as if in her own world. She bore her fate like a stain.

Alas, Myriam, too, was far from being an oil painting, despite the benefit of such modern aids as make-up, dieting, flattering clothes . . . In a society where beauty is prized above all a woman's other attributes, possessing none was a major handicap. Nor was she endowed with other qualities that might compensate for its absence, such as charm, talent, humour. And she too was a bit dotty; she had had difficulty learning at school and only a succession of private tutors had managed to get her through the Certificate, after which her father had given up on her academic prospects. Nevertheless it was hoped that some ambitious young man might marry her to acquire her family's prestige and backing. But that did not happen. Instead she became the Albatross to her father's Ancient Mariner, as he sailed around the world from one diplomatic post to another, and gaffed her way along as his hostess and companion.

Why had Mr Raheem never remarried? For after many years he had finally divorced his wife, 'to set her free'. ('What step-mother would put up with *her*?' he would ask his intimate friends, meaning Myriam.) Rumour had it that he took foreign mistresses, but no one had actually seen any with him. He ended up ambassador in an eastern European country, and just before the Revolution of 1979, he died suddenly of a heart-attack. Myriam discovered a tidy little trust in Switzerland which enabled her to live in modest comfort anywhere she wished. I recently heard that she lives in California within the large Persian émigré community, that she has mellowed, and that she is tolerated and looked after by her friends. Not altogether an unhappy ending, considering how much worse things could have been.

After lunch Mr Raheem had to go back to the embassy, and he left me in the care of his daughter. 'Myriam will take you for a walk and show you a few places.' It was a cold grey November afternoon, and we walked briskly to keep warm, towards the Eiffel Tower. It rose beside the river like a giant's watch tower dwarfing the lesser buildings around. Through its latticed intricacy a lift slid up diagonally, laden with tourists.

'To the second floor only, due to fog,' informed a placard beside the box-office. 'I'll take you up another day,' said Myriam. 'It's not worth queuing to climb half way.' As it happens during my years in Paris I sometimes went past the Eiffel Tower or walked underneath it, but it did not occur to me to queue, buy a ticket and go up – it was something tourists did, not we Parisians! Years later I took my small sons to Paris for a few days and they wanted to go to the top of the Eiffel Tower. It was mid-April and a shimmering honey-coloured veil lay over the city. Famous landmarks punctuated the urban sprawl to the far horizon. I picked out the approximate location of Hôtel Sophia, Mr Raheem's apartment, and the few other places where I had lived – dots on the map of Memory.

That first afternoon Myriam led me beyond the Eiffel Tower along the embankment, then over the bridge to the Place de la Concorde and the Obélisque in the middle. My gaze travelled unimpeded over the immensity of the square along the Champs-Elysées to the Arc de Triomphe on the one side, and the Tuileries on the other, all places about which I had read in books or seen in postcards. The inaccessible '*ailleurs*' I had so long craved was here, but already receding out of focus, moving elsewhere. What remained was History carved in stones, framed in vistas, murmuring in fountains.

'Come on, I want to show you the shops.' Myriam pulled me out of my reverie, less interested in History than Fashion. Her destination was a department store near the Madeleine which we reached after a further five minutes' walk. There were no department stores in Persia in those days, and no ready-made clothes – you bought cloth and had it made up by a dressmaker. It was only in the boom years of the 60s and 70s that entrepreneurs saw the commercial potential of department stores and created a few, while society women opened boutiques and sold Western designers clothes to each other.

Through a revolving door we entered a wonderland where all my senses were assailed: lights dazzled, perfumes dizzied, jewellery flashed, mannequins beckoned from pedestals. Sometimes friends of my mother's, married to diplomats, returned from Europe, had come to visit us wearing beautiful outfits, and I used to think that being in Paris guaranteed access to similar treasures. Now I realized that their prices put them out of reach as surely as if they had been on the moon. But my mother had given me a little money 'for myself', and as I could not afford anything substantial I thought I would buy some scent – a forbidden fruit at home. Once a friend had brought Mother a bottle of 'Soir de Paris', whose soft, elusive fragrance held the promise of untold romance to me, and it had remained in my olfactory memory. She never used it herself, but gave it to a maid as a wedding present. She considered European scents 'impure', as they contained alcohol, and instead used essence of rose, traditionally produced in a rose-growing region in Persia. Now I asked for a small bottle of 'Soir de Paris' and was told that it had gone out of fashion and been long discontinued. After trying several others I settled for something with a similar smell. I had just enough money left to buy a red beret, which would also have been considered too 'fetching' and forbidden by my mother.

On our way back we stopped at a café on the boulevard for tea and pastries. Myriam talked non-stop, discoursing on fashion, the season's colours and the famous couturiers, dropping names like a stripteaser her garments. Except for Dior, which vaguely rang a bell, I had heard of none of them. She went on to say how popular she was with the Embassy women, and how they sought her company and advice on matters of taste and entertainment. Soaring higher and higher into a realm of fantasy where only a gullible teenager could follow her, she alluded to her scores of suitors, each one of whom sounded a cross between Einstein and Clark Gable. 'But I always turn them down! How can I leave my poor Papa on his own?'

I was bewildered. Brought up in a society where a girl's desirability was measured solely by her looks, I could not understand how she could be in such demand. An enormous dowry could sometimes influence the eye of the beholder, but I knew Mr Raheem was not rich. The traditional canons of beauty as sung by poets and depicted in miniatures were challenged by modern variations conveyed through Western movies and magazines, but there was no gainsaying certain criteria. Myriam was short and overweight, and her face had none of the harmonies and proportions usually associated with beauty. Make-up only drew attention to her unrefined features – pudgy face, small eyes, large nose and uneven teeth – while fitted clothes emphasized the areas of excessive flesh on her figure. Besides, pushing thirty, she was considered by Persian standards to have 'passed it'. I rebelled, and rejected vehemently all such notions: they had to go, and the Revolution would see to it, I was sure. After it women would be equal to men and appreciated for the beauty of their souls and minds, just as we were told they were in the Soviet Union. But perhaps things were already different in France also, if what Myriam said was true?

Then one evening an incident occurred which made me understand Myriam better, and at the same time it was something of an initiation.

5
Jamshid's Cup

Whatever the Beloved pours in our cup we will drink,
Be it the Wine of Paradise or the cheapest draught
HAFIZ OF SHIRAZ

Dressed in a dark suit and redolent of eau-de-cologne, Mr Raheem left for an official, all-male dinner party, leaving Myriam and me to have a snack on our own. She seemed agitated as she fussed about her father by the door, brushing his collar, adjusting his scarf, holding his coat, to his visible irritation. Perhaps she was wondering whether the 'diplomatic' soirée from which she was excluded was not a subterfuge for an encounter with his mythical mistress? For who knew, French women were seductive and cunning, and they could manoeuvre any man into marriage, in which case what would happen to *her*?

'Daddy hates these invitations without me, but what can he do? It's part of the job,' Myriam told me, as she served us up the remains for supper. But instead of the usual mineral water she now brought out a bottle of red wine: 'You drink this, and you'll soon forget about Persia and everything else!'

Brought up in a Muslim household, I had never seen, let alone tasted, wine – even our Western visitors knew better than to expect any. Instead, they were served delicately flavoured sherbets – home-made fruit and flower essences diluted in water. The very word alcohol was avoided – people referred to it as 'medicine'. 'Poor Fatimah! Her husband drinks medicine!' they would commiserate.

The Muslim interdict against alcohol is based on two Qur-anic verses (Surats II and V, verses 216 and 92). Yet time and again the Quran promises unlimited wine to the Righteous in Paradise – thus transforming it into a sacred beverage.

'How is it that wine is allowed by Judaism, and is part of the Christian Sacrament, but is "an abomination" and pro-hibited in Islam, if all three religions come from the same divine source?' I once asked an Islamic scholar. 'The wine of the Eucharist is supposed to be a foretaste of the one you will be given in Paradise. It is not a licence for self-indulgence,' was his reply.

Perhaps it is this sacred, paradisiac nature of wine that has made it a symbol of Divine Ecstasy for Muslim mystics, the Sufis. Persian poetry brims with references to wine: from Omar Khayyam to Hafiz, through myriad lesser names, poets have sung the praise of wine in odes, sonnets, paeans. Wine is the heavenly beverage that opens the doors of Perception, eases the difficulties of Love, abates the pain of Separation from the Beloved and assuages the longing for Unity. While the hyp-ocritical mullah preaches the fear of God in the mosque, the Sufi poet gets drunk on the wine of Love in the tavern. And as the mullah accumulates riches by being sober, the Sufi pawns his tattered garments for a cup of wine. Wine becomes a meta-phor for the perennial divide between the Churchman and the Mystic, the one trading in Power and the other in Love:

> Last night the Angels knocked on the Tavern door,
> Kneaded Adam's Clay and turned it into a cup . . .

In Persian mythology the inventor of wine is Jamshid, the philosopher-king, the second link in that chain of kingship that connects the country's history with its pre-history. Jamshid had a special cup in which he could see the future. It enabled him to win battles and administer justice. Mystic poets refer to Jamshid's Cup being filled with the drink that confers Inner Vision, and to the king himself as the ideal ruler.

Such poetry was endlessly quoted, recited and chanted in our house. But we were told that the wine in question stood for Divine Intoxication, that Love referred to the Love-of-God, and that it could not be otherwise, since the poets were all devout Muslims. Rumi, the greatest of mystic poets and patron-saint of the Sufis and Dervishes, had summed it up in a poem: 'We do not need to drink wine to be drunk with Divine Love.' So in practice strict religious observance precluded the consumption of alcohol.

We progressive young were sceptical about such interpretations: we regarded religiosity and its interdicts as impediments to development and liberalism and we rejected it. How could the poet describe the effects of wine in such precise, tactile details if he had not tried it at least *once*! How could he give such accurate, loving description of his Beloved if he had never loved a woman!

So here was my chance to try wine for the first time, and experience all those delights I had read about! I accepted the cup Myriam offered me and took a sip. So repelled was I by the taste and smell that I spluttered it out into my handkerchief, and made a terrible face, at which Myriam bust out laughing: 'What a baby you are! Everybody dislikes the taste the first time, but persevere and you'll love the effect. Hold your nose and gulp it down quickly, like medicine. I did. Unaccustomed to alcohol, I only needed two cups to be completely inebriated! The room began to rotate alarmingly. I was at the centre of a vortex being pulled down deeper and deeper. Contours blurred, lights flashed, Myriam's voice came from the bottom of a well. I wanted to get up and run away, but . . . *oops*! Touch a glass lightly and it breaks! And I'm glued to my seat, head throbbing, stomach churning, gullet burning. What to do? Is this the basis of all those odes, paeans, sonnets? They can keep their ecstasy, divine or otherwise! Am I looking like Hafiz's Beloved, 'Hair undone, lips parted in laughter, drunk with Love/ She came and woke me up in the middle of the night' . . . ? I very much doubted it. A furtive glance at the looking-glass on the wall opposite disillusioned me on that score. My face undulated out of shape in all directions as if in a fairground distorting mirror.

Meanwhile I had just enough strength to refuse any further refills, hoping that the effect would soon wear off. Unlike me, Myriam went on laughing and drinking everybody's health until the bottle was empty, whereupon she disappeared for a moment and came back with another one.

'You can't live in France and not drink wine!' she pronounced. 'Daddy buys the best wines through the embassy, but I never drink. Tonight is different – I wanted to celebrate your arrival and initiate you. I bet you don't even know how to dance the cha-cha-cha!'

I didn't. She put on a record, took a jacket for a partner and began to demonstrate. I only knew how to tango and waltz, and Myriam's solo contortions seemed bizarre. She went on feverishly gyrating, explaining, demonstrating her proficiency to the naive Oriental fresh from the sticks. Then suddenly she collapsed on the sofa beside me, exhausted, and became maudlin. Tears rushed down her face, streaking it with mascara, like rivulets over peaty ground. She sobbed and bawled out unsolicited confessions of despair: that she would never find a husband, that she would go from one foreign country to another, a glorified housekeeper for her father, and that she would never be loved.

Oh dear! My eyes welled up with tears of sympathy, but what could I do? All my life I had watched women suffer around me. Told separately, their stories would fill volumes. The veil had been abolished in 1936, and I was born into a freer society, as a result of which I was sitting in an elegant Parisian drawing-room, dead drunk! Within a generation a sizeable percentage of Persia's doctors, teachers, lawyers were women. But they were still second-class citizens by law and oppressed by centuries of customs. It was the late Shah's legal reforms of 1966 that finally gave women some equality of status with men, the right to vote and be elected to parliament, to have some say in matters of divorce and children's custody.

28

But it is easier to promulgate a few laws than to change the collective psyche of a people, as was demonstrated by 1979 when women poured out in the streets in black veils!

Not that men were immune to suffering, for in an unbalanced society everybody is victimized and deserves the same sympathy. But it seemed to me that women surpassed men in the intensity of their emotions and the depth of their despair, and that they had fewer compensations or alternatives. They often paid for their freedom, such as it was, with renunciation and sacrifice. Many around me were spinsters, divorcées, abandoned. Others were hounded and ostracized for alleged sexual transgressions, including one or two of our teachers. Now after a life spent in a freer and juster society, my experience has not altered that adolescent impression. Women still pay a high price for their relative freedom, only with different currencies.

I held Myriam's hand and offered such consolation as I could, based on my rebellion and pride. She should leave, go back to Persia and work as an interpreter, secretary, anything rather than this misery, I suggested. She allowed herself to be soothed, then suddenly she got angry and turned against me: 'It's all right for you to talk! Look at yourself! And look at me! If I had half your assets . . . ' I had never thought of myself as possessing any assets, although I was anxious to acquire some, and I was cowed by her outburst. I can't recall how I got home. I was sick all night and woke up with a blinding headache.

Thinking of the previous evening I worried lest Myriam should feel ashamed, regretting her emotional outburst and aggression. Not a bit of it – she had clean forgotten the incident, or pretended to. But she seemed cooler, less effusive, as people often are when they have taken off their masks or given away their secrets. As for me, I tried wine once more, and later whisky and vodka, on the insistence of friends. The result was always the same. Clearly I had an allergy to alcohol. I decided that I did not like either the taste or the effect. It was just as well, for had I liked it, who knows to what excesses it would

29

have led me. Perhaps the poets did mean Divine Intoxication after all.

6

A Room in the Latin Quarter

La grande ville est le reflet de ce gouffre: la liberté humaine
J.-P. SARTRE

The most difficult problem confronting a student arriving in Paris in the 50s was to find somewhere to live. There was such a shortage of accommodation that unless you were born in an apartment, or extremely rich, finding one was tantamount to a miracle. All the students who poured into Paris from overseas or the provinces had to compete for the same very limited number of rented rooms.

There were many reasons for this housing crisis, the main one being that nobody for years had tried to solve it. First there was the war and the occupation, a period in which everything came to a standstill. Then hardly had the country recovered from these traumas than the war with Indochina broke out. It ended with France's defeat at the Battle of Dien Bien Phu on 7 May 1954, and the loss of her South-East Asian colonies. But before a sigh of relief could be breathed, Algeria rose up in arms for independence. Soon the conflict escalated into a war, sapping France's resources and dividing its public opinion, until at the end of the decade came Algerian independence.

So although the economic foundation of a new, prosperous France were being laid in the 50s, it was not until the return of Charles de Gaulle to power in 1958, and the advent of the Fifth Republic, that things began to get better.

Meanwhile where was I to live? Parisian students stayed put

31

with their families. Those who came from the provinces relied on the hospitality of relatives and friends, or their help in securing a place through personal contacts. Foreign students depended on luck and their finances.

If money was no object, you could rent a furnished studio at an exorbitant price, or a room in a private apartment in the residential areas of the Right Bank. Many an upper-class widow whose children had grown up let a room in her large, usually gloomy apartment as much for the extra income as for company. But apart from the price, lack of privacy was a disadvantage and, besides, nobody wanted to live on the Right Bank, away from the university and libraries, the bookshops and cafés and friends.

For someone with limited financial resources the most agreeable possibility was a room at the Cité Universitaire, a campus at one of the old gates of Paris – the Porte d'Orléans. Although a little far from the Latin Quarter, it was linked to it by direct underground. The Cité had been created to provide decent accommodation for overseas students, and various countries had bought plots of land and built 'Houses' there, giving priority to their own nationals. (The Swiss House was one of Le Corbusier's famous buildings, and everyone's favourite, but it was almost impossible to get into.)

For Persian students it was doubly hard to find accommodation at the Cité, as Persia had not yet build a House there. Nonetheless, several who became my friends lived in various Houses, as I did myself, much later.

The Cité had its own canteen, a theatre/concert hall, practice studios for music students, and between the buildings lawns and gardens where in warm weather you could lie or sit in the sun. Its only inconvenience, apart from the extreme difficulty of getting a room, was that male and female students were segregated, either in separate buildings or in two different parts of the same Houses. Some Houses were for male students exclusively, who could receive guests in their rooms, but no one was allowed to stay the night.

As far as possible most students preferred a room in the Latin Quarter, or in nearby Saint-Germain-des-Prés. There was a Students' Lodgings Bureau near the Sorbonne. I once went there with a friend who was looking for a room. It was a dingy little office at the top of a tall building. If someone was coming down the steep rickety stairs as you were going up, you had to flatten yourself against the wall to let him pass, so narrow was the staircase. You then joined the queue on the landing and waited, sometimes for hours, until it was your turn to enter the office. Inside, the tiny office had just enough room for a desk, a chair and a counter – more a barrier. It was lit by a single bulb hanging from the ceiling. A harassed, short-tempered middle-aged woman, her face drawn by fatigue like a piece of parchment, gave you a form to fill in, explaining your requirements. After examining it wearily, she handed you a bunch of cards with names, addresses and telephone numbers of potential landladies. I never met anyone who had found a satisfactory home through the Bureau.

Indeed by the time you had rushed to the nearest cafés and rung the numbers you had copied, invariably anything remotely interesting had been taken, and you had to start all over again – the rickety stairs, the queue, the office, the woman, this time even more bad-tempered. In the unlikely event that a room was still vacant and you took it, you would soon find out that there was a catch: the landlady would turn out to be '*toquée*', as they said, twirling a finger at their temples to indicate madness, a religious maniac, or in one case I knew, a sexual predator. Of course there were hundreds of students who had angelic landladies, but invariably they had found their rooms through friends and stayed put till the end of their studies, after which they passed it on to a good friend. You only heard about the unlucky ones. One girl I knew did find a room through the Students' Lodgings Bureau in the opulent apartment of a general's widow. It was large, light, and attractively furnished. She could not believe her luck. But a few days later she was thrown out by *Madame la Générale* for wearing black velvet trousers, which she considered the height of perversion: 'I know your type!' she had screamed 'Perverts! That's what you are! *Débauchées!*' And she dismissed her without further ceremony. Another young man was chased round his bed in the middle of the night by a sex-crazed landlady in a red satin négligée whom he had taken for an angel of piety and kindness.

In desperation many students lived in the small hotels that let rooms on a monthly basis. But do not allow the word hotel to give you the illusion of light, warmth and comfort. These establishments were usually run-down, dirty, dark, flea- and bedbug-infested dives whose tiny rooms were fitted with a gas ring for rudimentary cooking, a wash-basin, a wardrobe and a bookshelf. Today, when even the cheapest hotels in Paris have been renovated and refurbished with all mod cons, it is hard to imagine how sordid and uncomfortable they were in those days.

I only knew one Persian student who lived in one of these hotels. Madame Tabai was a very attractive, twice-divorced high-school teacher in her late thirties, who had left Persia two years earlier to study for a History Ph.D. at the Sorbonne. Rumour had it that she had been fired from her school following a scandal. Modelling herself on George Sand, she had expressed Feminist ideas and acted 'freely' – she had 'made men fall in love with her', and enthralled her pupils by preaching the gospel of equality between the sexes. Some parents had complained to the head mistress about her nefarious influence upon their daughters, and Madame Tabai had been asked to leave. So here she was, finishing her thesis and getting ready to go back to Teheran where she hoped to find an administrative job at the Ministry of Education. She had been to our house several times, with her aunt, a friend of my mother's, and had captivated me too.

Madame Tabai had everything a role-model needed: beauty, brains and progressive ideas. I admired her for her 'bad reputation', for daring to practise what she preached, and for preaching what she probably did not dare to practise. So after

I had been in Paris for a couple of months, I went to see her one dark wintry afternoon. A dank smell compounded of stale cooking-oil, coarse tobacco, sour wine, garlic and damp hit my nose upon entering the front door. A few steps inside the entrance led to a landing whence a narrow staircase spiralled up towards dark regions, covered with an ancient moquette so worn as to have become part of the wood beneath it. The reception desk was a semi-circular counter protruding from a wall. The chair behind it was empty, but from a half-open door of a room the disembodied voice of a female polecat snarled:

'What is it?'

'Madame Tabai, please?'

'Third floor left. Number five.'

I climbed the stairs, but just before the first landing the light went out and the whole place plunged into darkness. As I fumbled on the wall for the time-switch, it came back, someone, somewhere having pressed the button. It went out again on the third floor landing, but a dim light came through a small window overlooking a courtyard, and enabled me to find the switch. The light went on and I saw a young man approach along the corridor. Smiling with relief I asked him where room number five was.

'It's here on the left, mademoiselle. Allow me to show you.'

He motioned me to follow him along the cavernous corridor, but before I could proceed he grabbed me tight and tried to kiss me. I pushed him back vigorously, horrified and ready to scream, but he immediately let go of me and nonchalantly went down the stairs, sneering: '*Tant pis pour toi!* – too bad for you.'

'What's the matter?' asked Madame Tabai upon opening her door. 'You are as white as a sheet.' I recounted the incident. She smiled: 'You must have smiled at him – he probably took it for consent. Have you not noticed that the French don't smile, except when they know you, or wish to be charming?'

I remembered Mrs Tabai's remark when, in the 1960s, President de Gaulle launched his 'smiles campaign' to make Parisians behave more agreeably towards foreign tourists.

Inside, her room was small and packed with two years' living: boxes and suitcases piled up to the ceiling, a mirrored wardrobe bulged with clothes, books spilled all over surfaces. We sat on a double-bed squeezed up against the wall, to talk over a cup of tea.

'After the privations of the war and the humiliation of defeat the French have become somewhat cynical, and who can blame them? They are out to get what they can while they can out of life, before another catastrophe takes everything away from them again. They are right: if you allow life to get at you, it will drag even the morsel of bread out of your throat! We Persians are masochists. We wallow in self-sacrifice and self-denial and sorrow. You would do well to forget all that and enjoy life. If only I had come here at your age!'

That day as I left her I pondered what she had said. Although out of respect I had not contradicted her, I did not agree with her. I was a revolutionary, I thought, and irreproachable personal conduct was essential for our ideas to be effective. If we practised sexual freedom while we preached it, in a society where until recently adulteresses were stoned to death and non-virgin brides were killed with impunity, it would be construed as licence. In such circumstances self-denial was a worthwhile price to pay.

I later learnt that her hotel was luxurious compared with many others in which foreign, or indeed some French workers, lived.

By contrast the ideal lodging was the rare and elusive *chambre de bonne*, or maid's room – that garret beneath the roof that epitomised *la vie de bohème* and afforded maximum freedom. The service staircase that gave access to it might be steep and bare, but at least it was hidden from the habitually ill-tempered, nosy and censorious concierge. And what are six flights of stairs when you are twenty, and your head and heart are on fire? You could decorate it and make it cosy with bright curtains and posters. Then you could sit up at night, read, write, listen to music, or have friends around and solve all the world's problems.

I experienced all this much later. But at the time there was such a housing shortage that maid's rooms were often occupied by couples, even entire families. Once I visited a young author whose first play, starring France's most cherished actor, Gérard Philipe, had made him famous overnight. Yet even he lived with his wife and their baby in such an attic. Every inch of space had been ingeniously utilized, but you could see how difficult it was to both live and work in such squeezed conditions. Eventually his powerful publishers found him a small apartment, but by then his living conditions had broken his marriage, and he went off with a famous actress who – guess what – had a large and sumptuous apartment! I never saw him again, but I remembered my visit when I read Camus's remark: 'Fifteen pounds a month, factory work, and Tristan has nothing more to say to Isolde!'

The least sought after lodging for girl students was a *foyer*, or hostel, usually an ex-convent sponsored by a philanthropic foundation to provide housing for 'girl students from good families', upon whom they imposed strict rules. Though not unduly expensive, it was hard for foreign students to get into them as French students had priority. But by chance Madame Tabai had met the *directrice* of one of these establishments, and she offered to introduce me: 'I doubt there are any vacancies, but it's worth a try' she said, when Mr Raheem appealed for her help in finding me a room.

'You thought you would live on *l'amour et l'eau fraîche*, did you? – love and cold water.' Mr Raheem let a note of sarcasm tinge his remark, exasperated at having been landed with my problems.

The following day I went with Mr Raheem and Madame Tabai to see Madame Giroux, the directrice of the Benedictines' Foyer for Young Ladies. It was in a short lateral street off rue Saint-Jacques, one of the main arteries of the Latin Quarter. As it happened there had been a last-minute cancellation, and although there was a long waiting-list and French girls had priority, Madame Giroux offered me the room, seeing how young and evidently frightened I was, I thought. But then I realized that she had a soft spot for attractive men and that Mr Raheem's charm had done the trick.

'She can move in the day after tomorrow,' she said, turning to me with a reassuring smile which I grasped like a straw in a rough sea.

Sighs of relief all round. I had spent all my money on my hotel bill, and now I was left with nothing but my meagre monthly allowance, which would not have covered more than another week's stay at Hôtel Sophia. And so it was that I moved into the Benedictines' Foyer, where I was to live for nearly three formative years.

The day was dark, cold, and wet; a fine rain ran silently down the little dormer window of my room as I packed my suitcase. After I put in my clothes I went to pick up my little landscape, tripped, hit the chest of drawers on which it stood and caused it to shake. The picture fell behind it and shattered into smithereens. The chest was much too heavy for me to shift, the shards of glass too many to collect, and I decided to leave it. After all I would surely find the original in a museum, discover who the artist was, and be able to buy a larger coloured reproduction. All the same, I felt a sharp pain, as if the shattered glass echoed a breakage within me. Finally I put in my tiny volume of Hafiz.

In every Persian house, however humble, two books can always be found: the Holy Quran and the *Divan* of Hafiz, the best-loved of Persia's classical poets. His mystical fervour and tender lyricism touch a deep chord in the national psyche, making him as representative as Shakespeare in England, Dante in Italy or Goethe in Germany. His verses are quoted even by unlettered peasants and tribesmen to clinch arguments, convey wisdom, enliven conversation, express affection. His *Divan* – book of sonnets – is used for foretelling the future. You close your eyes, make a wish, and say: 'O Hafiz of Shiraz, you who know the secret of every heart, tell me if . . . ' Opening the book at random, you will find your answer in the sonnet on the right-hand page. Young people play this game to find out if their desires will be fulfilled. Now as I was putting it in my suitcase I closed my eyes and opened it at random. The poem's opening lines were:

> The lost Joseph will return to Canaan, don't grieve,
> The abode of owls will become a rose-garden once more,
> don't grieve,
> The sad heart will be joyful . . . the worried mind
> peaceful again, don't grieve . . .

I cheered up. Not that I believed in vaticination – it was a game – but the poet's soothing compassion was something I would never lose, and never have.

7

The Benedictines

Nulle part on est aussi étranger qu'en France

JULIA KRISTEVA

Rue des Bénédictines, named after a Benedictine convent that had flourished there in the nineteenth century, was a short road off rue Saint-Jacques, in the heart of the Latin Quarter, and some eight hundred yards from the Seine. The Foyer des Bénédictines was a five-storey red-brick building covering half its length, that had been built in the 1920s on the foundations of the old convent, to provide accommodation for 'gentlewomen' who came to Paris in search of work and wished to live in a protective environment. It now belonged to a philanthropic society, which explained its reasonable price.

A plaque in the middle of the façade above the front door said that the great Victor Hugo had lived at the convent in 1809–13, aged seven to eleven. And indeed, his aficionados can quote a reference to it in one of his autobiographical poems. This connection was the Foyer's only claim to glory, the present lack-lustre establishment having little else to boast about.

The original thick oak front door, discoloured and weather-beaten, its heavy knocker and handle blackened by age, was still there, and opened onto an entrance where a few stone steps led to a landing with the office on one side and a waiting room on the other. A glass-panelled door between the two rooms led into the building, so that no one could enter without detection.

The office had a large desk in the middle, where one of

Madame Giroux's several part-time assistant-receptionists sat and monitored the comings and goings. At the back of the office were a small table and chair where the receptionist had her lunch at noon while continuing to keep watch.

Facing the desk on the wall were the fifty or so pigeon-holes that held the girls' keys, letters and telephone messages. For a long time I looked at it anxiously each time I came in, hoping to find a letter from home.

As the girls were not allowed to receive visitors in their rooms, they had to be called downstairs and meet callers in the waiting-room, which was more like a prison visiting-room, with just a few wooden chairs and no carpets or ornaments. Being in full view of the receptionist it afforded no privacy and discouraged lingering. The receptionist would stand at the bottom of the stairs and ring a bell – once, twice, three times, depending which floor she was calling. Upon hearing it we would listen for her voice to hiss out the room number, and if it was ours we would run down the stairs.

But if we had more than one visitor or telephone call per day, she would grumble in no uncertain terms: 'I have other things to do, *mademoiselle,* besides answering the phone for you!' In fact the receptionists had absolutely nothing to do, for the little administration that was required to run the place was done by Madame Giroux herself. They just sat and read their newspapers, or knitted. They were all women of a 'certain age', living on their widow's pension, who supplemented their income with a few hours extra 'work' per week. The only exception was the middle-aged Mademoiselle Mori, who was a full-time clerk during the day and in the evenings, between 7 and 12, became our night-receptionist in exchange for her tiny box-room on the top floor, where she had lived for no one knew how many years.

Beyond the landing a wide staircase with a wrought-iron banister spiralled up in a grand sweep. My room was number 6, one of eight rooms strung along the corridor of the first floor. It was fairly large, or seemed so, being minimally furnished: a

41

single iron bed, a table, two chairs, a clothes-rack beneath a bookshelf. Its only luxury was a large wash basin with constant hot water. There were no curtains on the long window overlooking the street, only iron shutters. You had to close these for dressing or undressing, otherwise you could be seen from the building opposite. A single light hung low from the ceiling, capped by a cone-shaped colourless shade, and a pipe ran along the window a foot above the floor to provide central heating in winter.

'You can decorate your room any way you wish,' said Madame Giroux when she took me to my room, and by way of example proceeded to show me a couple on the next floors, like an estate agent presenting a show-case apartment.

'How pretty!' I exclaimed, genuinely impressed by their owners' ingenuity – red and white chequered curtains and table-cloths, posters on the walls, ornaments and vases . . . I thought I would never do the same, not only for lack of know-how, but because anything that suggested settling down increased my anxiety and my longing to return home. And so I set myself a pattern for all my abodes – that they were only temporary, and I always lived as if I could raise anchor and set sail at a moment's notice. Books and records were mostly borrowed and returned after use, clothes were few and idiosyncratically outside the tide of fashion so as to last, rooms were rented and left in due course.

Perhaps this attitude had to do with my background, for the population of Persia until recent times consisted largely of nomadic tribes. Also something in the monastic bareness of a room appealed to me – even though I shared the Romantic yearning for 'Les riches plafonds, Les miroirs profonds, La splendeur orientale, Tout y parlerait, à l'âme en secret . . .'

The self-exile's bid for freedom is inseparable from his/her nostalgia for Home. The dichotomy lasts through life, however submerged in the unconscious. Even now, when I have found some sort of Home, I marvel at my friends who are deeply rooted in their own soil and ancestry and family: how secure

42

they must feel! But do they? I wonder. At any rate I never did anything to that room, though in due course the bookshelf was filled with dictionaries, poetry, books autographed by writers I had met . . . Only many years later, when I found myself alone with two small children, did I make a home that would be comfortable for them and welcoming to their friends and mine. For myself I would have been content to live from a suitcase – or rather my guitar-case – and sing my way round the world: if not a movable feast at least a moving '*ailleurs*'.

Amazingly for an edifice built as late as the 1920s and 30s, the Foyer did not have a single bathroom. If you wanted a bath you went to the Municipal Baths half a mile down the road, paid 100 francs (one New Franc), and were given for about twenty minutes an exiguous cubicle with a shower and a dressing area. I did not mind this, as I was used to going to the *Hammam* (public baths) in Persia*. So I would wake up at dawn, walk down the street, have a shower and come back in time to go to lectures. Most girls in the Foyer made do with their wash-basins, filling and emptying it several times using shampoos and flannels – what in England is called 'a tart's bath'! Having been brought up in a Muslim household where ritual cleansing was an essential part of religious observance, which meant running water or a deep pool, not small quantities of liquid, it took me a long time to accept this method. But in France bathrooms were still a luxury with which only apartments in wealthy residential areas and hotels were equipped.

'Yet Parisian women always look as if they have just emerged from their baths, always fresh and fragrant and well-groomed,' Madame Tabai commented, when I expressed amazement at the lack of bathrooms in the Foyer. 'At my hotel there are only three bathrooms, and you have to book a long time ahead. When in Rome . . . '

* See: *The Blinfold Horse: Memories of a Persian Childhood* (Minerva)

Left alone in my new room, I unpacked my suitcase and pushed it under the bed. Tomorrow I would start my French course and perhaps meet some of the students in the Foyer to whom Madame Giroux had suggested introducing me. Meanwhile I sat near the hot water pipe by the window to keep warm and watch the spectacle in the street. This would become my favourite spot – warm in winter and cool in summer, when the window was open.

Being a short, cross street, rue des Bénédictines did not have much traffic, but there were some regular features. Once a week the rag-and-bone man came, pushing his overloaded wheelbarrow while shouting incomprehensible words. No one ever sold to or bought anything from him, nor did he seem particularly interested: he was like a clockwork toy, wound up to go through the motions and stopping when the spring ran down. Less regularly we had visits from the Street-Singer, a large inebriated woman accompanied by a tiny man who held her arm when they walked, and who stepped aside to become her audience while she sang, looking at her in rapt silence. You could hear her nanny-goat tremolo and rolling Rs as soon as she turned into the street – shades of Edith Piaf, whose songs she sang, and on whose legendary popularity as a street-singer she relied for sympathy and generosity. When she reached the middle of the road underneath my window, she would stop and bellow: *'Quand il me prrrrend dans ses brrrras, qu'il me parrrrle tout bas, je vois la vie en ro-o-o-ose'*. When the song was over, she would shout 'thank you, ladies and gentlemen, thank you'. Windows would open and coins would start showering down, not very many, but enough for the singer's companion to rush around picking them up and putting them in a beret. Then he would take the Diva's arm and move on as she started another song, her tremolo fading as she disappeared round the corner.

Opposite the Foyer was a small, well-stocked grocery owned by a young couple who lived in a tiny flat behind it. They were from a village near Orléans and the first members of their respective families to leave the land for 'a better life' in the city.

She had retained a milk-maid's complexion, a frank smile, and wore thick glasses that made her eyes look like two tiny beetles. He was stocky, with dark brilliantined hair and a short moustache, and looked more like a mafioso than a country lad. They both worked in the shop, she serving, he shifting stock and arranging shelves, six days a week from early morning till eight in the evening, closing only on Mondays. They seemed to have no life outside their shop, for even on their days off you could see light through the cracks of the door and hear footsteps and voices as they replenished the shelves, cleaned and put things in order. In August when the whole of Paris closed down for summer holidays, the Grocers went back to their village for two weeks and returned visibly healthier and happier. When a year later they produced a baby boy, he was propped up in a cot with a few toys, apparently quite happy, responding to clients' greetings and terms of endearment with beatific smiles. The girls from the Foyer bought their small needs at the grocery, not much, since we had our main meals at students' canteens and anything extra at cafés.

On the corner of the street was our local café – dark, drab and frequented mostly by workmen, as students and younger people preferred the larger,more cheerful and brightly lit cafés on the boulevards. Its middle-aged owner was surly and taciturn, and wore a permanent scowl. His plump blonde wife, who ran the place with him, was shrilly garrulous, and together they made up a kind of Punch-and-Judy show without the blows. They opened early in the morning, when their first clients stopped at the counter for a quick espresso, or a glass of *fine*, on their way to work, and stayed open till after midnight. They could not have had more than five hours' sleep a night, six nights a week, and unlike the Grocers they did not have the energy of youth. No wonder he was bad-tempered and she so shrill. Who wouldn't be?

I hardly ever went into the café, except occasionally to make a telephone call, to pay for which you bought a special token at the counter. But I bought fruit and cheese at the grocery and in due course became friendly with the owners, especially through their baby. They told me that they worked so hard because they wanted to save enough money to buy the lease on a café. How long would that take? And wasn't running a café, with its interminable hours, even harder work? Ah! but it was more profitable and less trouble, no stock-taking or shifting of goods or deciding on different brands . . .

Today when every shopkeeper in France is decently housed, works short hours, owns a car and goes for *le camping* at *les weekends*, it is difficult to believe how ruthless life was then for the majority of ordinary people. Some said it was worse than under the Occupation, and there was a kind of tacit civil war between various political groups with contradictory ideas as to how best these and other of the country's problems should be tackled. Meanwhile everybody complained: *La vie est dure!* – life is hard – was the litany. At the same time the Plans Monnet and Marshall were laying the foundation of a sound, mixed economy which would bear fruit later.

One day years later I was in Paris and walking down the boulevard Montparnasse, not far from rue des Bénédictines. I saw a well-lit animated café on the corner of a street, its semi-circular terrace teeming with tourists, and went in to make a telephone call. And there, behind the counter were the Grocer and his wife! They were serving clients with the same speedy efficiency and impassive good-humour I remembered, looking like actors made up to appear older between two scenes, indicating the passage of time. He had grey temples and deeper wrinkles, she was plumper and had dyed her hair a shade lighter than her original mousy colour. They recognized me as one of the girls from the Foyer and offered me a cup of coffee at the counter. She even stopped for a few minutes to talk to me, while he went on working and occasionally smiling in my direction.

When had they left the grocery shop? After five years they had accumulated enough money to put down a deposit for the café. They had renovated it with formica surfaces and glass panels and stainless steel cutlery and neon lights. They had worked hard and long hours, and finally made it a successful concern. So now they could afford two waiters, and a maid to keep the apartment upstairs clean and cook their meals. They had a Citroën and went *pour le camping* at weekends with their son, now fourteen and a pupil at the local *lycée*. No, they had not wanted any more children – at first because they worked too hard and had no time, and then it was too late. But surely the boy would take over from them in due course, I thought. As if reading my mind she said: 'He likes the country. His dream is to buy a small farm somewhere near Orléans and raise cattle. Isn't it funny – we killed ourselves to get away from the land and make a go of it in Paris, and now he wants to go back! But what can you do? These days children follow their own heads!'

I thanked her for the coffee and left. As I was going out I heard a woman's voice singing through the juke-box:

> Is this the way men live?
> And their dreams follow them from afar . . .

When you turned the corner of our relatively quiet street the scene changed: rue Saint-Jacques, one of the long arteries of the Latin Quarter which climbed uphill from the embankment towards Montparnasse, was particularly busy at our level. Crowds of students hurried along the narrow pavements to and from the Sorbonne some five hundred yards away, cars rushed by hooting and braking to avoid unwary pedestrians spilling over on to the cobblestoned road, bicycles weaved their way through the traffic.

In the middle of the block was Saint Benedict's church, a modest eighteenth-century edifice, its façade blackened by time, which on Sundays rang its bells and opened its heavy doors to receive a varied crowd of worshippers: middle-aged couples with their children dressed in their Sunday best, clutching their missals in their gloved hands, elderly women in old-fashioned hats holding the arms of their equally ancient husbands, a few

47

students. During the week the front door of the church was closed and you only saw one or two 'regulars' go in at odd times of the day through the little side entrance, sallow-skinned, doleful-eyed, inward-looking lone pilgrims, mostly women, in need of prayer or confession. A smell of incense and wax pervaded the cold air. Light filtered through stained-glass rosettes between the arches, relieving the obscurity, while a few elongated candles burned quietly beneath a statue of the Virgin in a niche creating a pool of moonlight around her feet. Saint Benedict's contained no famous works of art, but it had paintings of the Stations of the Cross along the left wall and ornamental candlesticks and vessels displayed on a table under the Crucifix.

It was the first church I had visited, and I was awe-stricken. How different from the bareness of our local mosque at home! Even the grand mosques of Isfahan and Shiraz, with their sumptuously coloured tiles and architectural harmony, were empty inside, save for the rough mats on the floor – nothing must distract from the concentration on prayer. Here images and ornaments created an atmosphere conducive to spiritual communion. Two different approaches to the same goal. I often stopped on my way home for a few minutes of quiet reflection.

One of Paris's best high-schools for the deaf-and-dumb was in this area, in a little side street by the church. At the end of the day they poured out into rue Saint-Jacques and walked in groups, talking excitedly in sign language, laughing and shrieking. Judging by their expression they were quite happy, and watching them you felt as though you had lost your hearing, or that a sound-barrier separated you from them.

But it was the row of small shops, tightly packed on both sides of the street that formed the background to the kaleidoscopic human formations, and provided for the daily needs of the district's population. Opposite the church was the newsagent's: a dark, cavernous corridor of a shop at the end of which sat the owner, always dressed in black, her head covered in a muddy-green scarf, her eyes fixed to the entrance. Outside,

48

various dailies were folded and stuck in pigeon-holes on a board; you took one out and went in to pay. Youngsters sometimes tried to pinch one, just to see if the crone hidden at the end of her dark lair would notice. She always did, even if she was occupied with another transaction, and shrieked like a wounded seal, which sent the miscreant bolting down the road. She sold stationery and sweets as well, but unlike most other shopkeepers remained resolutely taciturn and sour, as if keeping shop was her punishment for existence.

Next to the newsagent's was a butcher's, with a life-size head of a horse stuck above its door and the words *Boucherie Chevaline* written beneath it. At first I did not know what it meant, and wondered why the sides of animal hung from hooks inside were so much bigger than I had ever seen. I was told that it sold horse-meat, which was much cheaper than more delicate varieties such as beef or lamb. Horse-meat butchers have mostly disappeared as people's standard of living has improved, but at the time the shop had a thriving business, and I was told that when tenderized horse-meat could be delicious, if somewhat more pungent than beef. Once I was given a horse-meat steak by a friend, an impecunious poet and able cook who served it with a well-seasoned sauce that camouflaged any unfamiliar taste it might have. To a hungry teenage palate it was delicious.

A few yards to the left of the church was a small, cheap restaurant with the lofty name of The Garden of Gourmets, where you could have the dish-of-the-day, usually a chop or steak with fried potatoes, for a little more than the student's canteen price. At the beginning of the month we sometimes indulged in this luxury. It was a simple square room with a few tables for two or four people, covered with blue-and-white check table-cloths on which a new sheet of paper was spread for each set of clients. The walls were bare and there was no ornament, not even a poster or two, to introduce a note of gaiety. Near the door was a small semi-circular counter and behind it a trap-door that opened on to the kitchenette. Orders

49

were shouted by the owner through this hole and plates of food emerged from it a few minutes later.

The Garden of Gourmets was run by the owner and the waitress. He usually sat on a stool behind the counter, took the orders from the waitress, wrote the bills, collected the money, while she served at tables. When the place was unusually crowded he sometimes left his superior position and helped with serving. He was a large, flabby man of about fifty, bald but for few wisps of mousy hair smoothed back from his forehead. He limped so severely that his entire body bent a foot down to the right every time he took a step, and you thought he was keeling over, but he straightened up again, took another step and dipped once more, like a boat on a choppy sea. It was assumed that he had been wounded in the war, like so many cripples one saw in those days, with missing limbs, bullet wounds, scarred faces. The waitress was equally large and shapeless, but young. Her physical resemblance to the owner made us believe that she was his daughter. Perhaps the cook, whose hands we saw pushing the dishes through the trap-door was her mother? Small restaurants and bistros were usually run by families whose various members shared the tasks. But when sometime later a baby appeared on the scene (without noticeable difference in the waitress's girth, I might add) we realized that she was the wife, and that her resemblance to the owner was caused by osmosis. But why had she married a man old enough to be her father and a cripple? In Persia such odd couplings happened because women had no say in their fates, but this was the West, our Mecca of freedom and equality. 'A husband, a job, a baby, enough to eat and somewhere to live, none of which she might have if she had refused him.' Madame Tabai commented. 'And who knows, he might make up for his age by other things . . .'

We had a chemist's, with the green cross that was the sign of its trade protruding from its façade, two bakeries, a haberdashery, a millinery . . . Passing by the bakeries in early morning

50

or late afternoon you caught a whiff of freshly baked bread wafting into the street like a blessing, while the windows displayed an irresistible array of pastries and cakes.

Apart from these permanent shops, once a week, on Wednesdays, we had a street market along the stretch of the road between the church and the rue des Bénédictines where the pavement widened into a crescent. At dawn trestles were erected and covered with fruit, vegetables, dairy produce, poultry, delicatessen, fish . . . The rich display was as colourful as appetizing, the air filled with aromas of fresh herbs and sea-food. By eight o'clock the street was seething with shoppers and pandemonium reigned, the noise reaching us at the Foyer through open windows. Soon queues formed in front of stalls where salesmen and women acted their routines, calling the ladies and gentlemen to taste and buy their goods, weighing and counting aloud, exchanging pleasantries with clients. The men stood behind the trestles beneath the makeshift awnings, while the women moved about in front, taking orders, handing out packets and pocketing the money.

The Queen of the Market was a Madame Marie, the cheese-and-poultry seller and the only stall-holder to be known by name. She and her husband held the largest stall, outside the horse-meat shop. She was short, round, cross-eyed and middle-aged, while her husband was tiny, wiry, youthful, and sported a 1920s matinée-idol thin mustachio. She wore a shapeless flowery dress in summer, a heavy beige overcoat in winter, and a wide grey apron with a capacious central pocket always. Her dark hair, shot through with silver threads, was held back in an attempted bun from which most of it escaped. She never stopped talking, luring clients with her shrill exhortations and the praise of her products, taking orders, relaying them to her husband, handing out the packets and putting the money in her apron-pocket. By contrast he never opened his mouth, only occasionally whistled a fragment from some popular tune. She kept one hand in her front pocket to keep it warm and protect her money.

51

Like Royalty briefed by aides Madame Marie seemed to know her clients by name and exchanged a few words with each of them about their families, illnesses and preoccupations, always ready with a quick repartee or a risqué joke:

'I'm warming my hand on my hottest spot!', she would say aloud, moving her hand inside her front pocket, cackling like a goose choking on a chestnut, and displaying a row of crooked yellow teeth. Her husband would sketch a lopsided smile, as if he heard the joke for the first time.

Madame Marie liked students and young people, and sometimes gave them a little extra cheese. Occasionally I bought a goat cheese from her, trying not to provoke an obscenity, but in vain: '*Tiens*! The little Persian girl! 'ere, a little Brie for your smile. Pity you are a girl – you don't 'ave that teeny weeny extra bit men 'ave! Otherwise I'd take you 'ome and seduce you!' Blushes all over while everybody within earshot laughed, and Madame Marie cackled.

One day the market disappeared. We learnt that it had found a better location on the boulevard Raspail, where it is held to this day. Years later I was in Paris and happened to be passing by. I looked at the stall-holders, trying to recognize the faces I remembered. One or two seemed vaguely familiar, though much older, but no Madame Marie – she had died the year before.

There were small cafés along the rue Saint-Jacques, but we preferred the well-lit, large café's on the boulevard Saint-Michel, near the Sorbonne. At first I hardly dared to leave my room, except to go to courses, but gradually as I made friends and became bolder I preferred to work in libraries and cafés. It took me a long time to venture further afield, to Saint-Germain-des-Prés, only a few hundred yards, which in later years became my haunt. Today the cafés along the Boul' Mich' have been converted to *le fast food* – hamburger-joints and self-services. But every time I am in Paris I still go to the same cafés on the boulevard Saint-Germain, and spend the day working, seeing friends, making telephone calls, as if the intervening years had been a dream, until the time comes to return home.

But what about life inside the Foyer?

8

The Hearth and the Heart

> To know how to remain alone for a year
> in a poor room teaches a man more than . . .
> forty years of 'Parisian life'
> ALBERT CAMUS

To us students in our teens and early twenties Madame Giroux seemed quite old, although she was around fifty and still very attractive. She had an apple-blossom complexion enhanced with a touch of rouge on high cheekbones, and harmonious features. Her hair, dyed to its original chestnut brown, framed her oval face and was held back by small combs and *barrettes* which never varied. Her figure was 'matronly' – middle-aged spread checked by corsets and sober clothes, arms and legs still shapely and slim. With the students she was dignified, even politely cold, but when a man other than a dishevelled student appeared on the horizon, such as Mr Raheem, she melted into a pool of feminine charm: a girlish smile displaying a set of even white teeth, green-grey eyes wistfully narrowed into a soulful expression: '*Monsieur*? You wish?

Madame Giroux was not often in the office/reception, preferring to do her work in her apartment, on the ground-floor behind the stairs. We did not dare knock on her front door, however urgent the matter, but instead left a request for an interview with the receptionist and in due course were summoned. As she had the power to expel us at a moment's notice, we were afraid of her and on the whole never broke the rules.

Madame Giroux was a widow. She had been 'blissfully happy' with her husband, an army officer who had died just after the war. She had never worked while he was alive, but after his death she had taken this job, not from necessity but to placate loneliness, as she had no children. She liked 'the girls' whom she found bright and usually 'serious'. She did not seem to have many friends either, for she seldom went out in the evenings and hardly ever received anyone in her apartment. But she had one friend who called on her regularly, twice a week. Often they sat at the back of the office and chatted over a cup of coffee or a glass of white wine. If you entered the reception to pick up your key while the Major was there, you could see her laughing while he talked, leaning forward to impart a secret. At such moments she ceased to be the stern Madame Directrice, and you saw the pretty teenage girl who had turned the head of a young officer thirty years before.

The Major had lost a leg at the start of the war – 'You should've seen those German Panzers! *O la la*! – and his wife at the end of it; his two sons had married and left home, and now he lived alone, not far from the Foyer, and came to visit his old regimental friend's widow.

All this I learnt from Madame Monique, the daily cleaner. She believed that there was 'an understanding' between the two of them, and that they did more than indulge in remembrance of her late husband. We did not believe her, as the Major was bulky, flabby, bald, and a cripple to boot – how could she fancy him? 'For some women any man is better than none,' Madame Monique would answer with a contemptuous snort. I remained incredulous, for it was impossible for the Major to enter Madame Giroux's apartment or emerge from it without being seen, and the picture of a crippled bear with an artificial leg climbing through a narrow window was too awkward to be contemplated. But Madame Monique maintained that they found a way: 'People always do.'

The Major had replaced his missing limb with an artificial contraption that ended in a round metal disk. As he entered the Foyer you could hear the contrapuntal thuds of his walking stick and artificial leg on the stone entrance, followed by his stentorian salutations: '*Bonjour, madame! How are you today?*' he would boom at the receptionist, who would rush to alert Madame Giroux.

One night I went to bed with a cold and woke up with a temperature. A weak bulb was left on each floor after blackout in case we needed to use the lavatories at the end of the corridor. I heard the familiar rhythmic sound that announced the Major's presence coming from the floor below. At first I thought it was happening in my feverish head, but as I listened it became unmistakable. Thud, thud, thud . . . receding in the courtyard behind the building and disappearing into the night . . .

'The heart finds a way to the heart,' goes the Persian saying.

Madame Monique was in charge of keeping the stairs and corridors, the office and waiting-room clean, while the girls were responsible for their own rooms. She arrived at eight o'clock, started downstairs and worked her way to the top, which she reached some time in the afternoon, and she left around four. She used old-fashioned tools – a bucket, cloths, brushes and dusters, crouching on all fours. Around noon she stopped, sat on the stairs and consumed her sandwich and coffee which she brought with her. One or two girls asked her to help them for an hour a week to keep their rooms tidy and clean, which she did, more to oblige than for the extra cash it provided. Indeed she showed utter contempt for money and always took it with an expression of haughty disgust, as though it soiled her hand. I too asked her to help me once a week, and she accepted. On Thursdays she knocked on my door at three, or let herself in with my key if I was out, whirled round with her duster and broom, and left. But if I was in she talked non-stop while working, and sometimes sat down for a while afterwards to rest and chat. When once day by chance I told her that I had joined the Communist Youth at the *lycée* in Persia, my stock rose, she relaxed her diffidence and began to talk about her life.

56

Madame Monique came from the Eastern Pyrenees and her voice had the resonance and cadences of her lofty mountains – loud and heavily accented. She rolled her Rs like cart-wheels over gravel, with dramatic variations. During the Spanish Civil War she had helped Republican refugees across the frontier hills and learnt some Catalan. Many of her friends were Spanish exiles, and she cursed Franco and 'all the Fascists in France who supported him' for their none-too-easy plight.

She had married young and moved up to Paris with her husband in search of work. He had found a job in a factory where he stayed for the rest of his life, while she did cleaning. They had remained devoted until his death, at the end of the war, of a heart-attack. They had joined the Communist Party in their youth and were unwavering in their faith. During the war they were among the first Communists to join the Resistance, early on in 1942, and several times had nearly been caught by the Gestapo.

Madame Monique was still a card-carrying member and harboured a soft spot for the Party Leader, Maurice Thorez: 'A miner, son of a miner, grandson of a miner, no bourrrrgeois he!' She spat out the epithet with all the disgust and hatred she could muster. She had toed the Party line through all its twists and turns – the Hitler–Stalin pact, the show trials, the purges, etc . . . Any threat to her staunch belief was brushed aside as 'lies, lies, lies!' American and bourgeois machinations. When the Khrushchev report to the 20th Congress of the Soviet Party leaked in 1956, she treated it as yet another diabolical fabrication: 'Comrade Khrushchev is one of the architects of the Soviet miracle, how could he say things like that? Why didn't he say anything while Stalin was alive?' There was no point telling her he would have been shot, like the others – she would not have believed you. When Soviet tanks crushed the Hungarian uprising in 1956 and killed thousands of workers, she believed it was a 'coup monté' by counter-revolutionaries on the payroll of America. All her own and her husband's emotional and religious capital was invested in the Party, so how could she give it up? That would render their lives meaningless. Madame Monique sustained her faith by reading *L'Humanité*, the organ of the Party, every day, from cover to cover, swallowing its content hook, line and sinker, like a devout Muslim saying his daily prayers or a Christian going to Mass every Sunday. In her I understood the meaning of 'blind faith', and would encounter it in the years to come in many ideologically committed people.

The only time Madame Monique showed any weakness was when she recounted her husband's death. Then the hard, angry mask that had become part of her melted away, her eyes filled with tears and a wan smile glided over her lips like the shadow of a cloud over the plain. He had died suddenly at daybreak as he got up to leave for work, leaving her for ever with the night. She had spent all she had and bought a ten-year lease on a grave for him at the Père Lachaise Cemetery. Since then every Sunday without fail she went 'to visit him', taking a bunch of flowers. I imagined her clearing up dead leaves, silently communicating with him, willing him into some sort of life.

'Why, Madame Monique, do you go to his grave? He won't know, and since you are an atheist and don't believe in the survival of the soul, nor in an after-life, there is no one to communicate with, except in memory, which you can do in your own room?'

'I do it for me. I talk to him, I feel better for it.'

'What will happen when the lease runs out?'

'If I'm still around I'll renew it for another ten years, otherwise that's that!'

Perhaps another widow will buy it then, I thought, bury her husband and go to his grave on Sundays, taking a bunch of daffodils or violets . . . 'The heart has its reasons which Reason does not know'.

Madame Giroux's part-time assistants who sat in the office during the day were innocuous enough, but the night receptionist, Mademoiselle Mori, was 'a case' – *Ah! C'est un cas!*' Madame

Giroux used to say, rolling her eyes to heaven. She had lived in the Foyer for as long as anyone remembered, on the top floor where the rooms were divided by thin partitions into what they called 'boxes', using the English word. No one had ever succeeded in befriending her – she responded to smiles and greetings with a blank expression, as though someone else had been addressed. As she worked all day in an office and became our receptionist in the evenings and on Sundays, she only went to her room to sleep. Sometimes strange noises emanated from her box in the middle of the night, which her neighbours attributed to nightmares, and often she snored loudly, which kept them awake. As the partitions went up from the floor to a foot below the ceiling, a couple of inquisitive girls had once climbed on chairs and tables and each other's shoulders like circus acrobats to have a peep inside her room. They found it packed with years of accumulation: cardboard boxes, tatty clothes, disparate objects – a cross between a bric-à-brac flea-market stand and a tramp's hovel. And there she lived out her existence as if in expiation for a terrible sin.

Mademoiselle Mori was of medium height, thin and shapeless, without any female protuberances on her body. Her hair, short, grey and wiry, stuck out on her scalp and gave her the allure of a hedgehog, an impression increased by her diffidence. Her eyes were bird-tiny and expressionless, her complexion the colour of whey. As the night receptionist she was in charge of switching off the lights and locking up at midnight sharp. At five minutes to twelve she lit a candle, stuck it in a cracked saucer, and as soon as the clock of the nearby military hospital of Val-de-Grâce struck midnight she switched off the electricity at the main and locked the front door. By the time the twelfth stroke resounded in the slumbering district she was half-way up the stairs. Sometimes she waited behind the door, inserted the key into the lock, and turned it decisively upon sensing the clock's will to chime, so that her gesture coincided with the first stroke. That single, long iron key, similar to those castle-keys illustrated in fairy-tales, gave her enormous power over us, for if we were so much as ten seconds late, we found ourselves locked out for the night.

Once I put forward the idea of purloining the key, taking an impression of it and having a copy made. But it proved impossible to penetrate her room and find it, and anyway my friends decided that I had seen too many gangster movies! A midnight curfew may not seem too unreasonable, except when you consider that nearly all shows – theatres, operas, concerts, even political meetings – ended around midnight. As the underground ran until one o'clock in the morning there was no difficulty in getting home, but even leaving at 11.30 and running all the way from the station to the Foyer was risky. Countless last acts, encores, finales, were thus missed by us for fear of being stranded in the street.

Having failed to meet the curfew, you could sit in cafés till two or three, which was usually their closing time, then walk till five or six when others opened, but it was dangerous for girls on their own to roam the streets. There were some all-night cafés, usually near mainline stations, but they were not respectable haunts in the small hours, and a single girl (or even two or three) was bound to be harassed. We were constantly warned against the 'recruiting agents' of the White Slave Trade, their methods of persuasion and coercion, their uncanny stratagems, the police's connivance with them. Harrowing stories circulated about girls who disappeared suddenly, having been put to sleep by an anaesthetic needle in a cinema or an empty bus, and then abducted. By the time they regained consciousness they were on their way to some brothel in Africa for legionnaires! None of it was of course true, but it scared the daylights out of us and we avoided risky circumstances and sinister men who invariably approached us with offers of 'modelling' and 'film contracts'. It was better to miss the show than take the risk.

As my room was above the entrance, I often heard girls banging on the door and pleading with Mademoiselle Mori to please open it and let them in, since she was still there, and they could hear her. Ruthlessly she would click the key, turn round and slowly walk up the stairs, candle in hand, like a ghost carrying out a pre-ordained task. One night hearing a girl bang the door and calling out supplications, I came out to the landing and confronted Mademoiselle Mori, begging her to let me go down and open the door to her. She looked at me impassively, and kept climbing like a somnambulist. I perceived the shadow of a malignant rictus on her thin dry lips, and I wanted to hit her and prise the key from her, but I was glued to the ground. I went back into my room, leaned out of the window and discussed ways of hoisting the girl up to my room, but it was impossible without a long ladder. Eventually we decided that the only solution was for her to take the last Métro back to her friends' house, where she had spent the evening, embarrassing as it was to wake them up.

Several times Madame Giroux was approached with petitions to extend the curfew by one hour, but she was adamant: the Foyer was not a hotel, she wished us to know, but a respectable home for 'jeunes filles de bonnes familles'. In fact she did not wish to pay for the extra time, nor was Mademoiselle Mori willing to accept the new arrangement.

Since the war sexual mores had changed a great deal in France, to the chagrin of the older generation, who did their best to stem the approaching tide of what is now referred to as 'the permissive Sixties'. At first limited to artists and intellectuals in la vie de bohème, where it had always existed, the relaxation was now spreading, as a sort of undertow. Yet the majority of people lived by the old customs and restrictions based on religious precepts, and most young people still refrained from pre-marital sex. Even the Communists who denounced 'bourgeois marriage' as 'legal prostitution' frowned upon 'looseness' and advocated monogamous commitment. The supreme exemplars were the General Secretary of the Party, Maurice Thorez and his 'companion' as she was officially called, who had lived together for years and had several children, without having gone through legal and 'bourgeois ceremonies' – social defiance combined with puritanism. The fact that some notable communist intellectuals and fellow-travellers led such promiscuous lives as to make Casanova and Mata Hari seem positively chaste was not known by the rank and file, who only saw their outwardly monogamously happy marriages.

For Madame Giroux, as for most people, girls were still either 'serious' or 'light' – *légère*, and she did not approve of the latter. But the strict rules designed to protect the girls' virtues produced the opposite effect and contributed to their 'downfall'. Many a Foyer student lost her virginity by being a few seconds late. Her boyfriend offered her hospitality for the night at his place, which was often no more than a tiny room with a single bed, and the inevitable happened. Sometimes the circumstances were engineered by the young couple themselves: running back at midnight and reaching the door a few minutes before midnight they lingered over the parting kiss within a few yards of the door. You saw them flattened against the wall and in doorways as you hurried past, and you were reminded of Prévert's song:

> Children in love
> kissing on their feet
> Against the gates of the night . . .

They would hear the key turn in the lock, unwind themselves, and rush . . . Quick! Quick! Too late – Mademoiselle Mori's steps thudded away in the entrance like the ticking of fate's clock. *Et voilà!*

Sometimes the result was more far-reaching. My next door neighbour, a science student from Toulouse, began to put on weight, a rare achievement given the meagreness of canteen food. It soon transpired that she was pregnant. Madame Giroux rose to the occasion with unusual broadmindedness and called her into her apartment, discussed the matter with her before contacting her parents. The incident ended respectably in marriage. But this was not always the outcome: back-street abortionists carried out a thriving business, and the better-off made short trips to abortion clinics in Switzerland. A couple of years later a wealthy married woman and a Communist fellow-traveller befriended me, and I noticed that she hopped on airplanes to Geneva as often as I took the Métro. I assumed that she had a dear old relative or friend she wished to visit, and one day asked her how her trip had gone and how her friend was. She opened her heart and told me that her marriage had ceased to 'function' a couple of year after her wedding, that she and her husband were still good friends and had a son they both adored, but that she was too young to give up sex, hence a succession of lovers, unwanted pregnancies, and the trips to Switzerland.

Most girls at the Foyer went through their student years without dramatic incidents, got engaged, married, and moved on. But before I made these friends I had to get a long-term visa.

9
Cards of Identity

Comment peut-on être Persan?
MONTESQUIEU (*Lettres Persanes*)

A foreign student was given a short visa upon arrival in France. To obtain a year's residency and an identity card you had to apply in person at the police headquarters and present your university matriculation documents. The process had to be repeated every year until you completed your studies and returned home. Photographs were required for the various cards students had to carry, and a photographer near the university produced them in a day.

'*Ah! Comment peut-on être Persan?*' exclaimed the tiny photographer when I told him I was Persian, smiling at his own erudition. Indeed whenever I was asked about my nationality, the reaction was the same quote from Montesquieu's satirical novel *Lettres Persanes*. Published in 1721, it exposed the iniquities of French society through the letters of Persian travellers, and marked the beginning of 'Orientalism' and the influence of Persian culture – from Goethe's *Oriental Divan*, inspired by the German translation of Hafiz's Sonnets, to Mozart's *The Magic Flute* in which the character of Sarastro is supposed to be based on Zoroaster, right down to Nietzsche's *Thus Spake Zarathustra* and a host of lesser works, all of which evinced this idealized Persia of the Imagination. Yet prejudice and misunderstanding persisted: after quoting Montesquieu, people often asked me

64

how many wives my father had, or whether he regularly beat my mother as Muslim men were supposed to do!

The following morning I set off for the police headquarters with Mr Raheem's French secretary, who had kindly offered to accompany me in case I needed help. A policeman at the gate guided us to the residency department: a long smoke-filled hall similar to a provincial railway station's waiting-room, and dank with the odour of stale tobacco and human sweat. It was very crowded and the only seats were a few wooden benches against the walls, tightly occupied by elderly applicants. Three long queues stretched from the corridor to desks at the far end of the room. We joined one queue. The crowd was made up of various races and nationalities – black, brown, yellow, North-Africans, Asians. Few looked like students – they were mostly immigrant workers. I noticed that European and American nationals were directed to a separate office, opposite ours, where there was no queue. They entered and emerged within a few minutes, much as today at London Airport U.K. and E.C. citizens are guided to special exits. The difference was further marked by the subtle change in attitude of the policeman in the corridor as he guided people to the appropriate office – imperceptibly more courteous towards the Western group, while registering indifference or boredom with the rest. We Persians waited with 'the others', non-Europeans, members of the Third World, although the phrase was not yet in common usage the way it is today.

The Third World was born in April 1955 at the Bandung Conference, which was attended by the leaders of twenty-nine Afro-Asian countries, including such stars as Nehru, Tito, Chou En-lai, Nasser . . . The world-wide repercussions of this gathering marked the entry of the Third World into the international political arena as a force to be reckoned with. Some eighteen months later a French writer, A. Sauvy, published an article in *Le Monde* under the title of 'The Third World, Underdevelopment and Development', in which he defined the expression he

65

himself had coined two years before: 'For at last this Third World, ignored, exploited, despised as was the *Tiers Etat* [before the French Revolution], wants to be something.' This time the phrase stuck.

It would not have occurred to me to place Persia in such a category – where she certainly belongs today – because like the Russian intelligentsia of the nineteenth century our Persian counterpart had been Liberal and turned towards the West. At school we were inculcated with a sense of pride in the 'six-thousand-year history' of an empire that had stretched from the Indus to the Mediterranean and produced the first human right's charter, the postal service, great poetry and art, etc . . . But we, the post-war generation, imbued with internationalist ideals, and seeing the under-developed state of our country, were sceptical about such claims and mocked the grandiloquence of our teachers.

Evidently History, which according to Nietzsche was invented by the Persians, had left us behind, and we wanted to catch up with it fast. Meanwhile here I was, standing in the Third-World queue, and no amount of indignation, of waving miniatures and rugs and mystic sonnets would make the slightest difference!

Reflecting years later upon those days, I realized that when people of the Third World move to the First or Second World, not only do they become *déracinés* but also *déclassés* – their roots are pulled up, and their social status is downgraded as well. In the 1970s I travelled with the Bakhtiari nomadic tribes of Southern Persia on their spring migration. I was the guest of a tribal chief, a tall, handsome, intelligent man who commanded a sub-division of thirty thousand people. Unlike the majority of tribesmen he was wealthy, possessing large flocks of sheep and goats, and while his people spoke only their own dialect, he knew Persian and was literate. In the mountains he wore the tribal costume – a long tunic over baggy trousers and a felt hat – sported a whip and rode stylishly upon his magnificent black stallion. He was treated with awed respect by his people, on whose behalf he negotiated with government officials in the towns, and whenever we stopped *en route* he sat in his tent and held an audience, listening to the tribesfolk's complaints, counselling, arbitrating, dispensing largess.

When we reached Isfahan after the arduous six weeks' journey, he was to hand me back safe and sound to the governor of the city, as I had been entrusted to his care. For the visit to the governor's house he changed from his tribal costume into civilian clothes: a cheap black suit bought in the bazaar, and no hat. These simple changes produced a metamorphosis, like an image dissolving into another on a cinema screen: his stature shrank, his regal demeanour became humble, and his attitude servile. In his mountains and his tribal clothes surrounded by his people he was a prince, but here he was just a rough, primitive 'mountain man', to be treated like an underling.

I finally reached the desk, presented my papers and was issued with an identity card. '*Comment peut-on être Persan?*' smiled the official as he handed it to me. Recently I found that French identity card in an old box and detached the tiny photograph from it to show my sons. 'You do look different!' they said. True: it is the picture of a young, rather sad, dreamy girl who bears no resemblance to me at all – a different identity!

The Alliance

The force that through the green fuse drives the flower
Drives my green age
DYLAN THOMAS

I did not speak any French when I arrived in Paris. At second-ary school in Persia pupils could choose English or French as a foreign language, and before the war the majority opted for French – the language of the Court and of diplomacy. *'La culture est française,'* they said. Culture was French, and to be educated presupposed knowledge of French language and literature.

After the war the situation changed. Nearly every high-school pupil chose English, considered easier and more useful, and French classes shrank in size to half-a-dozen eccentrics. I had started learning English before I reached the *lycée*, perhaps in the hope of understanding American movies. My teacher was Mrs Souratgar, an Englishwoman married to a poet friend of my father's, who taught at the university. She gave me one lesson a week free of charge, and the rest of the time I poured over books and dictionaries on my own. But I had no oppor-tunity to practise speaking, except during my lesson, so that in the end while I could read with relish Shakespeare and Dickens, I was unable to ask for a cup of coffee or understand a word of what Hedy Lamarr and Robert Taylor said to each other before they embraced.

As for French, I always wanted to go to France, and thought I would learn it once I got there, in no time at all! This illusion was among the first to be shattered upon my arrival in Paris.

68

I discovered that merely by breathing the air of a country one does not learn its language, and that this has to be learnt like everything else, painstakingly, although it helps to hear it spoken all around and to have others with whom to converse. Nor did I find myself one of those natural linguists who just pick up a new tongue the way children do. I could only learn by understanding the grammatical rules – of how the language is put together.

I started this task upon arrival, giving myself six months: the sooner I mastered French, the quicker I could return home with some 'baggage'. So Mr Raheem enrolled me at the Alliance Française, a language school for foreign students sponsored by the Ministry of Culture, similar to the British Council. I had to report three weeks later and sit for a test to determine in which class I should be put. Meanwhile I bought an English–French teach-yourself manual, which I proceeded to study. During the two weeks I lived at Hôtel Sophia I worked at it constantly, thereby keeping homesickness at bay, and learned the whole book by heart. A young mind learns quickly, and my previous study of another foreign language had made mine flexible enough for a second one to be easier. By the time I went for my test at the Alliance I was able to jump the preliminary classes and start a proper language course. Soon I had grasped the rudiments fast enough to have no difficulty communicating with people.

Today it seems to me that I have always spoken French like a native, without a foreign accent. Looking back on those first months, perceived vaguely through a shifting cloud of remembered bewilderment and grief, I can hardly recall any time when I did not somehow understand French or was unable to speak it. Yet my reason tells me that this came about actually from dogged hard work over a long period.

Exiles who leave their countries in mid-life following political and social upheavals are less lucky than young students, because their minds are cluttered with worries, their time consumed with earning a living. This was first brought home to me when I went to visit Madame Tabai in her new studio-flat, two converted maid's rooms in Montparnasse. She had borrowed it from a friend who had gone abroad, and was delighted to leave her mingy hotel for the last few months of her stay in Paris and write her thesis in peace.

Her next door neighbour was Madame Lublia, a Russian widow in her seventies who had left Russia after the 1917 Revolution. Her husband had been a White officer whose regiment was decimated by the Reds. For a while he had roamed the country, concealing his identity, then escaped to Berlin where he had met and married Lublia. Eventually in 1923 they had come to Paris where a kind émigré friend had found them a maid's room at the top of this tall narrow building. It was meant to be temporary accommodation, but here she was over thirty years later. Her husband had died, her only son had married a Frenchwoman and moved to the Provinces, and she seldom saw him.

Madame Lublia did not speak French, except for a few words which were never connected by any particles that might turn them into sentences, but she surmounted her inarticulacy by warmth: half of the two dozen French words she knew were terms of endearments which she used prodigally to anyone in her proximity – everybody was *Colombe, Lapin, Petit Chou*. She was all alone in the world: 'At my age everybody dead.' She looked much older than her age, with rheumy eyes, blotched skin and bent back, and she was so lonely that as soon as she heard steps on the stairs she would open her door and put her head out with a huge smile. You had to have a heart of stone not to stop and exchange a few words with her. She hardly ever went out – her entire world was contained in that little dark room, stuffed with a life's disused accessories.

Madame Tabai was kind to her and knew exactly how to handle her. She sometimes invited her to her own spacious and warmly furnished flat and offered her a cup of Russian tea – weak, with a slice of lemon – and let her rattle on incomprehensibly in her mixture of Russian and French. As soon as she had finished her cup of tea, Madame Tabai would gently lead her to the door and kiss her goodbye. Even after the door was shut Madame Lublia would carry on talking, in the hope that Madame Tabai would be tempted to let her in and listen further.

Once or twice she was there when I went to visit Madame Tabai, and proceeded to tell me her life story, regardless of the fact that our hostess had heard it many times before. She said she was 'waiting for these terrible Bolsheviks to go away' so that she could go back to Moscow. Like Chekhov's Three Sisters she had spent her life pining for her home town, convinced that bolshevism would burn itself out, like a virulent fever, and that Russia would recover from her nightmarish infection.

Poor Madame Lublia! She died in that little room a few years later. Now that the Bolsheviks have almost disappeared she must be smiling from her celestial abode – every exile's Moscow home, where all longings for return are finally consummated.

The Alliance Française was on boulevard Raspail, and I could walk to it in twenty minutes by taking a short-cut through the Luxembourg Gardens. Every morning I set off at 8.30, entered the garden by the main door on the boulevard, walked down the wide central alley, then took a diagonal route along the chestnut avenues and emerged near my destination. Sometimes on the way back I would change my itinerary to explore various parts of the park, walk past the Children's Corner and its merry-go-round, the English Garden, linger by the pond or sit awhile by the Médicis Fountain. I had seen postcards of the Luxembourg Gardens in Persia, old ones in which the women had long dresses, large hats and parasols, and the men frock coats, top-hats and canes – and new ones sent by friends. I had glimpsed them in French movies, and I had read about them in novels. I visualized Cosette, in *Les Misérables*, sitting on a bench, Gavroche skipping along merrily, his *képi* rakishly tilted back, poets like Victor Hugo, Vigny, Verlaine, Musset sauntering along the shaded paths with their Muses, real or invisible. I imagined their ghosts forever haunting the darker corners, the breeze whispering their poems, their statues coming to life at night to roam among the moonlit flowerbeds and lawns.

I remembered all this as I walked that first cloudy November morning. The gardens were empty, except for a few students hurrying towards various Faculties in the area. Here and there an early-rising park attendant half-heartedly swept the last decaying leaves and shovelled them into his wheelbarrow. The trees were already denuded, their branches charcoal drawings against the milky sky. In the months that followed I walked through the gardens daily and witnessed their changes, reflecting each season and Nature's cycle of death and resurrection. Soon the first snows covered the ground and turned the naked branches into crystalline coral sprays; later it melted away, unveiling the snowdrops and crocuses on the ground and the buds on the trees. Then one day suddenly it was summer and ablaze with flowers. 'I'll be back home in time to go to the country,' I thought.

Later I visited other parks, both in Paris and around it. Many, like Versailles, are far grander and more beautiful, but whenever I am in Paris it is to the Luxembourg Gardens that I am drawn by some invisible melancholy thread of memory.

Madame Ballard was considered one of the best teachers at the Alliance, a vocational pedagogue who knew instinctively how to engage the interest of each student. After a few days she called me *la Petite Rêveuse* and brought me poems to read. They were short and simple at first, longer and more complex as we went along, and she spoke about them and the circumstances in which they were written in such a way as would have enthralled the least poetically inclined student, and which made vocabulary and grammar far pleasanter to learn. Before long I was hooked, and learnt many by heart, as I had done with Persian poems. This delighted Madame Ballard, who later con-

72

fessed that she wrote poetry herself and had even published some in various obscure periodicals. But she never showed me any, though I expressed genuine interest in seeing them.

Madame Ballard was in her early fifties. She had short grey hair, blue eyes and a pale complexion. In class she wore reading glasses perched on the tip of her nose, which made her look older and more earnest. Her only concession to *coquetterie* was a bright red lipstick, like an accidental brush-stroke on a tawny canvas. She always seemed harassed and in a hurry. She arrived one minute late, laden with books, and left promptly when the class was over, having glanced at her watch several times towards the end. While other teachers lingered in the hall, talked and joked with their students, even went with them to the local cafés, Madame Ballard bolted before you could issue an invitation. Sometimes I walked with her to the tube station nearby, and once or twice we did stop at the corner café for a cup of coffee and that is how I learned something of her life.

She had married young, a fellow teacher, and produced a son and a daughter. The latter was now also a teacher at a *lycée*, but her son had been killed in a car crash a few years earlier, at the age of twenty. His loss had plunged her husband into a deep depression from which he had never recovered. He had given up work and stopped going out of the house. Nowadays he was slightly better, took in some translating from German, read a great deal and wrote a little, but still . . . Now Madame Ballard earned their living, without any resentment, supplementing her salary from the Alliance by giving private lessons – hence her air of harassment and rush.

In the highly politicized climate of France in those days conversations nearly always veered towards politics, and everyone was passionate in his or her convictions. Madame Ballard was a Socialist and a fervent anti-Communist. She believed that the French Communist Party was Stalinist and subservient to the Soviet Union. My head was still full of the simple books I had read in Persia when I joined the Communist Youth organization at the *lycée* a couple of years earlier. These contained all the answers, I was told. The Soviet Union was the pioneer socialist country and the natural ally of all oppressed peoples against Imperialism, so what was wrong with going along with it?

Madame Ballard argued forcefully – about the terror, show-trials, deportations, mass murders . . . The whole history of Russia after 1917. I only knew and believed the official version. She said I should read Arthur Koestler's *Darkness at Noon*.

If you are a teenager, reasonably bright and blatantly innocent, people naturally try to win you over to their side. Communists, Socialists, Catholics, Anarchists, all the friends I made in those early days found in my eager mind fertile ground in which to sow their ideological seeds. But as it happened I was not easily swayed, and my spiritual and mental evolution followed an independent course. So at the time I thought Madame Ballard was a victim of anti-Soviet propaganda, while she believed I was brainwashed and would soon find out the truth.

All that academic year I worked and read. Nothing is more satisfying for a teacher than a keen pupil, and Madame Ballard took a warm interest in me, and made sure that I did not go astray before I had learnt the highways and byways of the best of French poetry and prose. She tried to inculcate in me the French *sens critique* to balance my enthusiastic and passionate responses. She cut all superlatives out of essays with sarcasm: 'Orientals go in for flights of fancy. It may be fine in poetry, but when you are analysing a text you need to reason.'

By the summer I had made several good friends and was less acutely lonely. My eldest brother invited me to Germany for a holiday and persuaded me to follow my original plan of going to university to read Classical Arabic and Persian as a prelude to Islamic philosophy. I duly presented my documents at the Sorbonne and enrolled. Meanwhile I loved music, singing, theatre, cinema, all of which I had been deprived of at home and could now pursue in my Parisian freedom.

One day coming out of class I found a small crowd surround-

74

ing a young woman sitting at a table in the middle of the hall. She had leaflets and posters and cards, and was explaining about *La Jeunesse Musicale*, an organization founded by Pierre Boulez in 1950 to popularize contemporary music and generally enhance the musical life of Paris. For a small annual subscription you became a member of the *Jeunesse* and could buy tickets for concerts, operas and ballets at reduced prices. There were student concessions at theatres too, and generally even the most impecunious students could have a full cultural life if they wished. By then I had made some friends, French, Persians and assorted nationalities, without whom I could not have taken advantage of such artistic manna, as I was too timid to go to shows on my own – I only went for long solitary walks, visited art-galleries and the Louvre, learning the topography of the Left Bank until I knew it in detail, like the lines of a familiar face. But now, feeling bolder, I took out membership.

'You are born French, but you become Parisian.' I never learnt who said this, but it is true. All foreign students soon became Parisians and navigated the turbulent waves of the great city to their advantage.

Life on the Left Bank was conducive to friendship. You met fellow students of all nationalities, talked, exchanged notes and books, and if you liked each other you became friends. Relationships were spontaneous, based on mutual sympathy, uncontaminated with social or professional considerations, as is the case later in life. Although nothing could heal the rupture in my soul caused by leaving Persia, nor assuage the deep loneliness of youth, at least I no longer had to be alone all the time as I had been at first.

Once or twice after I had left I went to the Alliance to see Madame Ballard. She was pleased, but as ever had no time to linger: 'My husband is waiting.' Eventually we lost touch, but I have never forgotten her, nor the gratitude I feel for the concord she forged between me and her language, which has endured through the years and brought me much reward.

Jamila and Michelle

Give all thou canst; high Heaven rejects the lore
Of nicely calculated less or more
WORDSWORTH

One winter evening I walked home through the Luxembourg
Gardens. It was almost deserted – no lovers in the darkened
alleys, no elderly couples on benches, no children in the play-
ground, the merry-go-round abandoned, its snow-covered
horses frozen in mid leap. A sharp snow-breeze stung the face
like relentless salvos of needles, soundless and deadly. Snow
had fallen through the day and now lay thick on the ground,
trees and statues, glowing in the oneiric stillness.

By the time I reached the Foyer I was frozen, and, despondent at not finding any letters from home, I decided to forgo a
hot meal at the students' canteen nearby and make do with
biscuits and tea in my room. I choked over the first gulp,
overwhelmed by a combination of cold, hunger, and loneliness,
and dissolved into a torrent of tears. I lay on my bed muffling
my sobs in the pillow – not an infrequent occurrence, I might
add, that first winter.

A knock on the door. Who could it be, since we were not
allowed visitors in our rooms? Madame Giroux! I thought, and
quickly wiped my eyes. It was Jamila, a Jordanian girl Madame
Giroux had told me about, and the only other foreign girl at
the Foyer.

'What's the matter? You're homesick!' she said, and
embraced me warmly. 'It'll soon pass. I felt the same at first,

76

but wait another six months and you'll be worried about having to go back one day. You know what our societies are like, especially for women, that's why you ran away, not to go to university which you could have done just as well at home, as I could. I have another two years left and I'm already dreading my return – to interdicts and coercion and gossip and marriage and all that . . . '

We talked over tea and biscuits till late. She was a moderate Arab nationalist in favour of Arab unity, and I an international-ist, Persia being a non-Arab country with an Indo-European language. But we agreed on Westernization, and independence for Algeria. Soon we became firm friends and arranged to go and see a new production of Racine's *Bérénice* at the Comédie Française together.

Jamila means beautiful in Arabic, and although it seldom matches the reality, it is a common name. This Jamila's name was apposite: black curly hair cut short framed her face, and she had large greenish-brown eyes, an opaline complexion, and a dimply smile revealing a perfect set of teeth. Though her father was an Arab, her mother was of Circassian origin – Circassian women were famous for their beauty, and had been favoured by the Ottoman sultans and their viziers for their harems. Their union had produced the exotically attractive Jamila.

Next evening we met and went early to queue under the arches that surround the building of the Comédie Française. We waited for over an hour, shivering in our duffle-coats, as the queue, already substantial before we arrived, lengthened behind us. We were thin, and I remember feeling painfully cold for years, as teenage vanity prevented me from wearing appropriate clothes which would be too bulky and unprepos-sessing. Soon the box-office opened and the queue began to move until it was our turn to show our student cards and ask for our tickets: two in the Gods, at 100 francs (One New Franc) each.

We climbed the narrow stone stairs at the back, up and up

77

as if indeed heading for heaven. The seats were not numbered and if you were late you could end up behind a pillar, unable to see the stage, but we were among the first and found seats in the first row, with a perfect view of the stage. Bending down over the parapet we watched the theatre fill up and the atmosphere charge with excitement. Finally the auditorium lights went out, three knocks announced the start of the play, and in the hush that followed the curtain rose, revealing an antechamber – the neutral ground in which the Racinian tragedy unfolds towards its inexorable dénouement.

Theatre in its Western form came to Persia after the Second World War. At school I had acted in plays staged by our teachers, usually edifying tales tracing the evolution of a school-girl from naughtiness to virtue, a role in which for some reason I was always cast. The best professional theatre was founded by a Persian director who had been educated and performed in Berlin before the war, then idealistically returned home to start something new. He put on plays from the European repertoire and one day my elder brother took me to see his production of Shaw's *Mrs Warren's Profession*. I was enthralled, and would have joined the company there and then, but there was no question of acting professionally for a girl of my back-ground – it was as if the daughter of an Archbishop or an Earl had expressed the desire to 'go on the boards' in Victorian England. Indeed I was forbidden to act even in school plays when I 'grew up' at thirteen. Others took the roles I was offered, and I watched them play with admiration and sadness, feeling bitter revolt at the bigotry that deprived me of an innocent pleasure.

Now here I was watching a magnificent play, in a sumptuous temple of the gods. The actors had impeccable diction and enunciated the verses, among the most beautiful in all French poetry, 'trippingly on the tongue', as Hamlet enjoined the Play-ers to do. I was moved particularly by the parting scene between Berenice and her lover, Emperor Titus, for although

78

I had not yet experienced erotic love, I was suffering real sorrow from the loss of my home and family. Also Persia's long history being woven with cataclysmic tragedies whose wounds had become part of the sensibilities of her people, I felt acutely 'the majestic sadness which is the essence of tragedy', as Racine wrote about his play. It was love at first sight, for both the theatre and Racine, and for life.

During the interval we ventured downstairs to the stalls bar, sparkling with Parisian elegance, to have a look. Jamila was wearing trousers, still frowned upon outside Bohemian circles, which caused two hundred pairs of eyes to swivel round and unleash laser beams of disapproval which chased us back to the Gods. We had to miss the end of the play and the curtain calls to get home in time for the midnight curfew, running all the way to the Foyer. We lingered in my room by candle-light and discussed the play and its central theme – the *raison d'etat* which thwarts the lovers.

'I would have died of grief,' I said.

'It is to Racine's credit that he doesn't make her commit suicide, and not only because historically it would have been wrong,' Jamila commented. 'It is only in "station-novels" that people die from love.'

Revolt is proportionate to the tyranny that provokes it. Like me Jamila came from an Islamic country and had experienced the oppression of women at close quarters, if not at first hand. Of course we were told that this had nothing whatever to do with Islam itself, which had been a liberating and progressive force, but with power and politics, yet there it was. Great advance had been made in both our countries in recent decades, but hundred of years of fossilized customs and taboos were buried deep in our national psyches and would not disappear overnight just with legislation. We rejected every restriction and were more 'free thinking' on the subject of sexual freedom than many of our French contemporaries. Jamila had once declared her disapproval of the cult of virginity and was as a result ostracized by a number of her compatriots, male and female. At the same time she had many admirers, in particular an Arab aristocrat who courted her with gentleness and patience. He was not a matinée idol, far from it, and Jamila did not fancy him, but they were friends. 'Nice men don't drop you because you refuse them sexually,' was her opinion. Instead she fell in love with an Austrian scientist, in Paris for a year on a research project, who was straight out of a Hollywood movie: tall, athletic, with blond wavy hair and gentle blue eyes. His only imperfection was a missing leg – he had been called up at the tail end of the war and immediately had had his leg blown off above the knee. He used one crutch only, and walked quite nimbly.

Pity can be a strong ingredient in love, and Jamila loved him all the more for his misfortune: her eyes melted with tenderness as she watched him grip his crutch and tighten his muscles to move.

'He has a perfect body, you know,' she confided. And he must have been the tenderest of lovers, for Jamila's initiation into erotic love was as happy as her marriage later. I connived with her by taking her key on the nights that she 'slept out'. As her pigeon-hole was above mine I could pick up both keys in one movement under the vigilant eye of Mademoiselle Mori.

When at the end of his year her lover had to return home, Jamila was disconsolate. 'I can't marry you – I'm a cripple,' he told her. Was it an excuse? Or genuine self-abnegation? Jamila believed the latter. She used to come to my room late at night and weep talking about it: 'You see, there is also the religious difference. I don't care two hoots, but he is a devout Catholic, and he knows my parents would have a fit and never agree to a Christian marriage.' The day he left Paris Jamila accompanied him to the station and came back straight to my room, eyes swollen, hair dishevelled, and lay on my bed like an injured bird, palpitating with sobs: 'I'll never get over it . . . I'll never love anyone else . . .'

Years later, in the late 60s when travelling to Persia, I had a two-hour stop in Beirut airport, and I wrote to Jamila to meet me for a drink at the terminal. She had married her long-time Arab suitor, who had stood by her while she lived through the loss of the Austrian Adonis. He was a diplomat and now they were *en poste* in Lebanon.

We sat at the bar and talked, as if only a week had gone by since our last meeting, instead of years. They seemed harmonious and loving. 'Next time you must stay with us and see the country, it is paradise!' I promised. I have not seen them since – they moved around the world and we lost touch. Now I look at pictures of Beirut on the television, their paradise transformed into a hopeless hell.

That first night after we had seen *Bérénice* she told me 'Only in station-novels do people die from love . . . ' In tragedy as in real life something worse happens – you go on living and suffering until your soul becomes a throbbing wound, and gradually it gets covered with ashes: 'You don't forget anything/You just get used to it,' ran the refrain of a current popular song.

'There is a nice girl you ought to meet,' Madame Giroux told me one day. 'She lives in No. 12, down the corridor from you and I've told her about you.' Nothing happened for a long time, as somehow we did not coincide in the office reception when Madame Giroux was there to introduce us. But one afternoon as I was picking up my mail when a girl rushed in and took the No. 12 key. 'You must be Michelle,' I said, and introduced myself, whereupon she invited me for a cup of Nescafé in her room. Decorated with posters and photographs, her room was extremely tidy, with everything in its place – books on the shelf, clothes concealed behind a blue curtain, a little Chinese rug at the foot of the bed. She kept a loaf of wholemeal bread in a tin, biscuits in a jam jar and butter on the windowsill to keep cool, while I only bought things that could be consumed instantly when I was hungry, and kept my room unadorned, like a nun's cell, relieving its austerity with flowers from time to time, temporary visitor as I was.

Michelle had red hair tied up in a ponytail, blue eyes and a freckled complexion. She was vivacious and enthusiastic, and blushed easily. She had been born and raised in Saigon where her father had been a colonial administrator. He had retired before Indochina's war of independence had begun, and had bought a farm in the Pyrenees where he now lived with Michelle's mother. Her older sister had married an Army officer in Saigon and the couple were now stationed in Germany. Her mother, knowing that Michelle's chances of finding a suitable husband in the idyllic valleys of the Pyrenees were remote, had dispatched her to Paris, ostensibly to study English, a language she already spoke perfectly.

Michelle's colonial background meant that she was more cosmopolitan and open than most girls in the Foyer, who on the whole belonged to the provincial bourgeoisie. Unlike me she was unrebellious and conservative, and like her mother, to whom she was devoted, a devout Catholic. She spent all her spare time in activities relating to the Circle of Catholic Students. The priests who ran the Centre were of the highest quality – intellectually brilliant, many of them Jesuits, and physically attractive, charming and open-minded. One of them, Father Lustiger (whom I never met because he had moved on before my time) is now Cardinal Lustiger, Archbishop of Paris and France's supreme prelate. Recently, browsing in a bookshop, I came upon his book, *Le Choix de Dieu*, in which he describes his conversion to Catholicism during the war, when his mother perished in Auschwitz, and his subsequent career, including his work with the students at the Sorbonne.

Although from opposite poles of the political spectrum, Michelle and I became close friends, perhaps because I too came from a religious background, and although I had repudiated its dogmatic and temporal aspects, I had not lost interest in the mystical side which had inspired Persia's greatest poetry and art. Whatever the reason, Michelle thought that sooner or later materialistic philosophy would leave me dissatisfied and that I would find my way back to a spiritual path, and she generously wished to share her convictions with me. Meanwhile we avoided discussing politics for fear of coming to verbal blows. Instead she introduced me to Christian mystics – Saint Francis of Assisi, Saint John of the Cross, Saint Theresa of Avila – while I shared with her my limited knowledge of Sufi philosophy and literature. Her favourite 'saint' was Saint Exupéry, whose *Little Prince* she presented to me for my birthday: 'He was an agnostic, but he converted to Christianity after watching Muslims pray in the desert in Morocco – which shows God's ways of touching people with Grace are mysterious,' she said. In her dedication she put a quote from Tertullian after my name: *Anima naturaliter Christiana.* I still have the book, but it took me half a lifetime to appreciate fully her faith in me.

Michelle had a small record-player she had brought with her but never used due to Foyer prohibition. I borrowed it, together with her few records, and since there were no electric points in the rooms, I took the bulb off the light that hung from the ceiling to a few inches above my desk, and plugged the record-player in to it. 'Don't blame me if you get caught and expelled!' she warned.

In the evenings I played records and worked by candle-light, which I preferred because I fancied it was more poetic and scholarly, and had the thrill of clandestinity. In Persia I had only listened to Romantic composers, and Michelle's little collection introduced me to Bach, Couperin, Rameau, Corelli . . . I hid the machine and records under my bed whenever I was out, in the unlikely event that Madame Giroux might decide to inspect my room in my absence. I had many months of pleasure undetected, then one evening I was working by candle-light and softly playing my records when there was a knock on the door. Thinking it was Michelle or Jamila I said: 'Come in.'

Madame Giroux! A little gasp as I rose. She calmly walked to the desk, unplugged the record-player, gathered the records and took everything away without uttering a word. That was that . . . but my notice of expulsion never came. Eighteen months later, when Michelle was leaving the Foyer, she reclaimed her gramophone. 'Ah! It was yours?' exclaimed Madame Giroux and handed it back to her without comment.

Michelle spent most of her free time at the Centre Richelieu and was one of its pillars, but her entire life was focused on just one thing: finding a husband. Naturally charitable and energetic, she set up all sorts of activities to help other students, and to proselytize – assisting African students, finding homes for the homeless . . . until eventually her efforts bore fruit, and she was introduced by her Confessor to a young man in the throes of preparing his *Agrégation* of Classics, and they hit it off. The *'Agrég'* was the most difficult exam and the candidates worked constantly. As a result Michelle did not see much of her fiancé, but she was happy. A year or so later they married, and he became a Classics master at a provincial *lycée*. She wrote to me periodically and sent me printed cards announcing the births of her numerous children. After the fourth I lost track of her. I sometimes thought of going to her parents' house near Perpignan where I once spent idyllic summer holidays, and enquiring. But would it still be there, or would it have vanished – like the enchanted castle of a fairy-tale?

Michelle used to persuade me to go with her to meetings at the Centre Richelieu, and she introduced me to several priests with whom I became friendly. There was a small chapel in the basement of the Centre, and a hidden side staircase led to it, away from the noise and bustle of the street and the entrance hall. Once or twice I left Michelle to deal with her tasks and retired to the chapel. It was tiny, with just a few benches and a make-shift altar against the wall consisting of a long table covered in maroon velvet, two large candlesticks, and a crucifix suspended above it. There were no windows and the only light emanated from the two altar-candles and a few lesser ones in a corner. A faint smell of incense pervaded the air, and in the dim light you could detect the silhouettes of two or three people deep in prayer. The silence was almost palpable, like a physical barrier keeping at bay the harsh noises of human strife above.

For some reason I was reminded of my father's study and my heart contracted; I sat down at the back and in a moment the turmoil within me gave way to peace. I lost track of time and when I emerged everyone had left (Michelle having thought that I had got bored and escaped) except one priest, Father Jean-Claude, a Jesuit, and we sat down to a long theological discussion.

He evinced no condescension or impatience towards a teenager ignorant of everything except her own rebellious doubts and rejections – my only redeeming feature must have been that eager for knowledge, I was good at listening.

'Just because they are disciplined with their vow of chastity doesn't mean that they are not susceptible to women,' said Michelle later, when I told her about our discussion. 'He probably liked you for your *beaux yeux*!' Or perhaps he thought that the eyes belied the half-baked dialectical-materialist formulae I had mouthed with apparent conviction. At any rate I went back to the Centre from time to time and quietly sat in the chapel for a few moments of reflection. I left France in 1960 and settled in England, but I went to Paris periodically, and one day walking down the boulevard Saint-Michel I went to the Centre Richelieu to enquire after one or two of the priests I had known. The place had disappeared, and there was now a bookshop where it stood. I went in and asked what had happened to it, but the assistants were young and knew nothing about it; they informed me that there was a Circle of Catholic Students round the corner, in the Rue de la Sorbonne.

Today, a quarter of a century later, I went there again and asked after Father Jean-Claude. The priest who was about to celebrate the midday Mass wore blue jeans and a pullover instead of the cassocks I remembered, the chapel at the back could be cut off with a flimsy curtain, and the place looked more like a students' union headquarters. But one young girl turned out to be the daughter of a contemporary, and she looked so much like her mother that for a moment I felt I was a time traveller returning to the past. She told me that Father

85

Jean-Claude had died last year, and that the others had moved to duties in different parts of the country.

Once in New York I was taken by a friend to a similar chapel, in Greenwich Village. It was always full of young people. I remembered the Centre Richelieu, and how the spiritual life of a city is often hidden from the apparent passions and pursuits of material life, but it no less preserves and sustains the community.

12

The Cell

Rien n'est plus dangereux qu'une idée,
quand on n'a qu'une idée

ALAIN

I met Jeannette, a second-year medical student, through Madame Monique, the Foyer's cleaner. She was the only other communist girl in the Foyer which was otherwise 'full of bourrrgeoises'. One day there was a knock on my door and in walked Jeannette: 'Madame Monique says that you're a comrade; if you like I can take you to our cell meeting at the Sorbonne tomorrow lunchtime.' We arranged to meet outside the university gate the next day.

Though she wore no make-up or any other adornments, Jeanette was a pretty girl, with delicate features, oat-coloured skin, and dark eyes. Her hair was pulled back into a thick long black plait, which lay on the collar of her white duffle-coat like a big silk tassle. But her looks were not what you noticed when you met her, rather she impressed with her intelligence and earnestness. We soon became friends, although she was not cosy and had no time for 'individualistic' relationships. She believed that human intercourse was valid only if based on a common purpose and the collective pursuit of social change.

Hers was not a shoulder you could weep on, nor were her ears attuned to adolescent soul-searching. Yet as time went by I realized that though not demonstrative she was kind, steadfast and affectionate.

All the students I knew worked hard, their various exams

87

being in effect obstacles to be eliminated, but 'medics' even more so, and their training was strewn with various extra *concours* – competitions. So Jeanette had little spare time, and all of it was spent on the Party. Seldom could we sit and talk over a cup of coffee, whether at home or in a café, and when we did we always discussed politics, she toeing the Party line, and I varying, and sometimes totally dissenting.

One day, coming back from a meeting, I asked about her family, and she told me that mother was French and her father Moroccan-Jewish. When the Germans had occupied Paris her mother had taken little Jeanette to stay with friends in the country where her father was supposed to join them after winding up his business. He did not think there was any hurry – after all he was a Frenchman – and at first the Germans behaved themselves towards the population. But when the Gestapo began rounding up French Jews, he was arrested – betrayed by a neighbour Jeanette's mother believed – and deported. He never came back, and her mother never remarried.

Until a year ago she had lived with her mother in a flat in the Gobelins district, one of the areas on the outskirts of the Latin Quarter into which the student population overflowed. But then her mother had moved to Clermont-Ferrand, to look after her aged grandmother, and Jeanette had taken a room in the Foyer.

After that conversation I understood her diffidence better, and we became closer – I was an outsider too. She had become a Communist as a result of the war, and I had been drawn to the Left because it was easy for a teenager from a privileged background to be won by a doctrine that preached justice, equality and prosperity for all, in a society where differences of wealth and status were vast and blatantly displayed: coming back from school at noon I would walk past workmen on building sites sitting in the shade of a wall eating their lunch – usually bread and cheese, with a melon or cucumber or grapes. They would call out the traditional hospitality greeting: 'Be my guest, help yourself,' to which I would answer 'Thank you, enjoy it,' feeling guilty at the discrepancy between their modest fare and the relatively sumptuous meal that awaited me at home. Even less fortunate were the beggars, especially women with babies, and in the country the poor peasants.

That first day I went with Jeanette to a small room in a university annexe containing no more than half-a-dozen people. Although there was a large contingent of Communists among the students, not everybody had the time for militancy. Some appeared from time to time, and there were always new faces. The secretary who conducted the meeting was Suzannah, an Egyptian-Jewish émigrée from Alexandria, plump, made-up and well-dressed. She was warm and welcoming when she recognized a fellow Middle-Easterner. 'How can you be a Persian?' someone quoted as Jeanette introduced me, everyone smiled, and I was put at ease. There were a few others, one of whom, Jean-Paul, a Law Ph.D student, was a regular and became a friend whom I went on seeing long after we both gave up the Party.

There was one boy that first day whom I can still see: Claude. He was tall and thin, with dark, intense eyes and black shiny hair. He sat at the back and said nothing while we argued. Clearly he had been there before, for Suzannah asked him if he had made up his mind to join the Party. 'No. I'm still searching,' he replied laconically. He left at the end without a word, and one day ceased to appear. No one seemed to miss him. A few years later I bumped into Suzannah on the Boul' Mich' and asked after everybody. 'And Claude, what happened to him?' 'Oh! The Mute! He became a monk; he is living in a monastery somewhere.'

I remembered him saying: 'I'm still searching,' and was reminded of Pascal's words: 'You would not have looked for me if you had not already found me.' Clearly he had, lucky fellow!

The French Communist Party followed the Soviet line, trying by all sorts of ideological acrobatics to justify Soviet policies and sell them to its members. The Khrushchev Report was at first deemed a CIA forgery, then accepted as genuine, but played down as just an example of how the Cult of Personality had led to 'a few mistakes'. The Hungarian uprising was denounced as a Counter-Revolution by Fascist elements which had been crushed by the Hungarian people, to whom the Soviet tanks had given a friendly helping hand.

'But they *look* like workers and peasants to me,' I said to Jeanette. 'Anyway why kill them?'

'Revolutions are not children's picnics! You can't help a few people getting killed if you want to save millions. You know something? I sometimes think you are not a Communist, but an Anarchist – you remind me of some nineteenth-century Russian Anarchists. I'll give you a book on them.'

The Party's attitude towards the Algerian war of independence was ambivalent too. The uprising had begun in 1954 and by 1955 it was obvious that it was not going to be crushed – indeed it had escalated into a war. I argued that instead of sticking to generalities and pious formulae about 'oppressed peoples' and 'the right of peoples to freedom', etc, the Party should come out squarely on the side of Algerian independence and tell Communist soldiers and recruits to desert *en masse*, and that this would develop into a national movement and force the hand of the government to negotiate. But the Party was afraid of losing popularity with the voters, the majority of whom still believed in 'French Algeria'. By 1956–7, however, it became clear that the war could not be won, and news of atrocities and tortures perpetrated by the French Army began to leak out, turning the tide of opinion. The Party, like all other Leftist groups, finally came out in favour of total independence for Algeria – not for the *beaux yeux* of the Algerians, but for fear of losing its supporters.

We all had our copies of *l'Humanité*, the organ of the Party. We were enjoined to read it every day without fail, to keep abreast of events and know the Party's views – reading other dailies contaminated the mind and undermined the faith. It was like being recommended to say so many Pater Nosters or Hail Marys each day by a priest. In addition we were asked to comment on the leader, and assigned certain tasks. Mine was once a week to sell *l'Humanité* outside the gate of the university early in the morning. Every Wednesday I stood there, shivering and stamping to keep my feet from aching with cold, blowing on my numb hands, a batch of newspapers clutched to my chest, hollering: *'Demandez, lisez l'Humanité! Lisez l'Humanité!'* Sometimes I volunteered to work on Saturdays too, as many comrades left for their homes in the suburbs or in the provinces at the weekend.

There was a middle-aged accordion player who busked on the other corner of the street. He played popular tunes and favourite 'Standards' – by Charles Trénet, Edith Piaf, Yves Montand. Passers-by dropped coins into his upturned beret on the ground and he thanked them without interrupting his playing. Sometimes we talked about his songs, many of which I knew and sang. He told me that he had started life as a factory-worker and learnt to play the accordion in his spare time: 'I thought I could join a band, play at balls and in cabarets, and have a good time while making a living. But by the time I had reached professional standards, the guitar had become fashionable, and nobody wanted an accordion player. *'Bah oui, mademoiselle*, times change!' he concluded philosophically. Did he earn enough from busking? 'So-so,' he said, and gave me a tobacco-stained, crooked smile – he had decided I was on his side. I did not tell him that I sang and was taking up the guitar to accompany myself.

Meanwhile various French governments came and went in quick succession. Even Mendès-France, a social-democrat and one of the most intelligent politicians in the country, who had successfully negotiated the end of French involvement in Indo-china, did not last: the Fourth Republic, risen from the ashes of the Third and of the Vichy regime of Marshal Pétain during the war, was simply unmanageable. It was not until the advent of the Fifth Republic under de Gaulle that France at last became governable and began to prosper.

There were endless rallies and marches and fêtes, some of which Jeanette and I went to. We listened to speeches by Party bigwigs and famous intellectuals, and sang the 'Internationale'. After a few months of these meetings I asked Suzannah if I could have my Party card. The following week she said that since I was a foreign national, I could not officially be a member of the French Party, though I could go on working with them. Alternatively I could join the Iranian Students' Organization. By then I had made several friends among Iranian students, one or two of whom were Tudeh (Communist) members, and so I joined their 'clandestine' cell. There were only about five of us, and we met in the house of Shahini, an old Communist married to a Frenchwoman who had lived in France for twenty years and whose ideas about what was going on in Persia were, to say the least, out of date.

We kept it all up for a while, but gradually my friends went back to Persia, where they pursued their various professions. Some became heads of institutions, others architects and engineers, yet others prominent academics. Now they are nearly all back, exiles once more. I see them whenever I am in Paris. We have had such different lives, yet there are powerful bonds between us.

But what happened to Jeanette?

Around the time of our first meeting she got engaged to a fellow medical student, but none of us saw much of him, nor indeed did she, as he was a few years older than her and was in the throes of preparing his Housemanship – a very difficult competition which did not allow him any free time. They met whenever they could, and she fitted in with his plans: 'We're not a bourgeois couple who have to be together all the time to the exclusion of anybody else, just to mooch around,' she would say scornfully. In the holidays, when he went away to stay with his family, they wrote to each other periodically: 'Only idle middle-class people write daily. We write whenever we feel like it or have something to say,' she told me. I must have looked doubtful, for she went on: 'You're not bourgeoise because you're not European. Orientals being a hundred years behind are stuck in Romanticism. Read Freud.' She always ended up our argument by recommending a book or an author that would enlighten me! 'We are lovers, and that is enough of a commitment.' It was agreed that when he had finished his training they would get married: 'Not because we need a piece of paper to ratify our feelings and allow us to sleep together, but because in our society marriage makes life easier for children, and because his parents are keen on it.'

Meanwhile on Saturday nights Jeanette 'slept out' – that was her weekly ration. Her fiancé was a Communist voter, but never came to meetings or rallies for lack of time. One Saturday evening he came to collect her and I met him by chance. Jeanette introduced me as 'The Odalisque' and I left them after a few minutes, disappointed at his ordinariness – Jeanette was anything but that. Yet I was amazed to notice that in his presence she changed: the seemingly strong, cool-headed, purposeful militant metamorphosed into a kittenish, carefree, affectionate girl, a young *amoureuse*. I liked it, and the next day teased her about it and we laughed.

I saw less of Jeanette when I ceased going to cell meetings, while her workload became heavier with hospital duties. Then I left the Foyer and went to live at the Cité Universitaire, while Jeanette found a room near the hospital to which she was assigned. One day just before the start of the summer holidays I came across her in the Luxembourg. We were both on our way to other engagements, but we sat down in the shade by the Fontaine de Médicis for a quick chat.

She was pale and much thinner: 'Night duty takes its toll,' she said. 'Sometimes you can't go to bed at all.' I asked after her fiancé – by now they should be married. 'Oh, he dropped me as soon as he qualified. He went off with another girl.'

Had she been very upset? Why had she not rung me? 'What

could you have done? A man who breaks his pledge is not worth having. The girl he married is a bourgeoise, pretty in a banal way, and if that's his choice I wouldn't want him.'

She said her astonishment and sorrow had soon given way to anger, and eventually to contempt. I would never see her crying her eyes sore, as Jamila had done, but then their predicaments were different – fate and circumstance in Jamila's case, betrayal in Jeanette's. We promised to get in touch, both knowing that it would not be easy.

Time passed. One day near rue des Bénédictines I met Madame Monique and asked after Jeanette. '*Ah! Ma pauvre amie!* Don't you know what happened to her?' I confessed I did not, and that we had lost touch. 'Well, her worthless lover just dropped her like a soiled sock as soon as he finished his studies. Little Jeanette took it very well, it seemed, but then six months later they found her dead in her bed. Apparently she had been on night duty and then gone home to sleep for a while, and she had swallowed enough pills to put a horse to eternal sleep!' Madame Monique had heard about it from some Party activist. 'Of course being in a hospital she had access to sleeping pills,' she concluded, as if the difficulty of obtaining them would have made a difference.

Poor Jeanette! She had spent her short life denying or controlling her feelings, but in the end they had got the better of her. They always do, don't they?

13

Learning to Learn

A little learning is a dang'rous thing;
Drink deep, or taste not the Pierian spring
ALEXANDER POPE

'For the past two hundred years France has been governed by people who know how to pass exams!' This remark was made by an old friend whose son had just failed the entrance competition to the Foreign Service. Yet he himself was an example of the system he decried: he came from a modest background and was educated entirely on scholarships. Later he became a diplomat and was French Ambassador in an Islamic country where he died in an accident a few years ago.

The French education system as it had evolved since the Revolution was both democratic and élitist: in principle any Frenchman, regardless of class, could progress to become part of the cultural and ruling élite through education, if he was sufficiently gifted and hard-working. As there was no university entrance examination, the Baccalaureat being considered sufficient, more and more students poured into universities each year, only to fail their exams at the end and fall by the wayside. Many left after a term or two, discouraged by the workload and conditions. One such drop-out was Françoise Sagan, who left to write *Bonjour Tristesse*, the novel that launched her at eighteen in 1954, and added a word to the language – *Saganisme*, which indicates the mild hedonism of the gilded youth of those days.

The volcanic eruption which became known as 'The Students

Revolt' and later 'The Events of 68' had begun with deep rumblings a decade or more earlier. May 1968 led to major reforms and the splintering of the Sorbonne into several branches spread over Paris and its suburbs under the collective name of The University of Paris. What was formerly called the Sorbonne is now Paris Four, which does not have the same ring or reverberate with a thousand years of history, but it probably offers the students more humane conditions.

Over the centuries other universities had been created in France and had acquired good reputations, but in the 1950s the prestige of the Sorbonne remained unimpaired. From the early twelfth century, when students flocked to hear Abélard's lectures on philosophy and theology, to the present, France's great men of science and letters had studied and taught there; their statues and pictures decorated its spaces (in the cobbled central courtyard the busts of Victor Hugo and Louis Pasteur symbolized the two branches of knowledge), their spirits haunted its corridors and halls, their books enriched the shelves of its library. In Abélard's days students and teachers all spoke Latin – which gave the surrounding area its name, the Latin Quarter – though today our common language was French, wherever we came from.

As soon as my French was good enough and the barrier of language was removed, I matriculated at the Sorbonne and began attending lectures. Unless you arrived early you could not find a seat. You stood at the back and on the sides, trying to take notes as best you could. I remember once arriving as the lecture began: Professor A . . . , a tiny, elderly man with a white goatee and a bow-tie, sat at the podium far, far away and read his paper, quite out of hearing of all but the front row. That was typical.

Then there were smaller 'practical work' classes for your chosen subject, and in these you did get to know your teachers a bit better, and were given essays to write, reading lists, advice – but even there a personal master–student relationship was missing. You had to be self-motivated, work hard, and pass your exams at the end of the year. That was all.

'All learning is self-learning,' my father had said to me. 'The teacher is only a guide. What you learn at university is *how* to learn by yourself.' He taught philosophy at the University of Teheran, the first Western-style university in Persia (and modelled on the Sorbonne). But he himself had been educated in the *Madrassah*, in the traditional system similar to that of Medieval Colleges of Europe, whereby you attached yourself to a Master until you had learnt his subject thoroughly, and then moved on. That tradition no longer worked in these more crowded times, but he knew it to be the best, and so he always was available for any student who was eager to learn more. I remember several who came to our house early in the morning or in the evening for discussion or personal tuition, or simply to be with him.

My eldest brother Nassir was a young diplomat posted in Germany. He had an account with a Left-Bank bookshop, and to enhance my meagre allowance he suggested that I buy my academic books at his expense – poetry and novels and other unrelated books were excluded! The first three books I bought were *The Philosophical Dictionary*, Descartes' *Discours de l'Méthode*, and Bergson's *Evolution Créatrice* – the latter because I had read about him in Persia. His spiritual philosophy, critical of the Positivism prevailing in his time, advocated intuition in philosophical investigation, influenced contemporary writers such as Proust, and became fashionable before the war. It eventually reached Persia and articles appeared about it in literary magazines. I was attracted to his ideas, though I barely understood them, being only fifteen and not having the necessary baggage. But his personality captivated me. He had converted to Christianity from Judaism before the war started but had not advertised the fact – it was a personal matter and clearly the result of years of reflection. When Paris was occupied, as France's greatest living philosopher and Nobel-Prizewinner, he was given a tacit dispensation from persecution. By then he was

97

old, ill and dying, but when French Jews were ordered to wear the yellow star and register with the police, he dragged himself out of bed, put on his star and went to the local police station to present himself. He died soon after, in 1941, sparing the occupying authorities further shame. I thought that was how my father would have behaved, and loved Bergson for it. Like many great men his intellectual rigour was tempered with lightness of spirit: on his eightieth birthday he said 'I'm not four times twenty, but twenty times four!'

Night after night I poured over my *Philosophical Dictionary* and my other books. What seemed obscure or unintelligible I attributed to my ignorance and stupidity, and I persisted. I recall how I suffered over certain passages of Sartre's *Being and Nothingness*, unable to make head or tail of them. My confidence was further shaken by the fact that other sections were clear and easy to comprehend, as were the same ideas expressed in his plays, essays, pamphlets. Recently I returned to that book, and reading it again in the light of experience realized that I was not entirely to blame, that certain sentences and paragraphs are indeed cloudy to the point of meaninglessness (perhaps written under the influence of drugs). I then understood why Heidegger, whose philosophy had been a powerful influence on Sartre's development, had described the book as 'muck' – not that *he* was a model of clarity!

My first essay was on Descartes' *Discours*. I read and re-read it carefully, but instead of demonstrating my understanding of it, I expounded my own 'philosophy'! Not surprisingly I came a cropper! 'We are not interested in *your* views, mademoiselle, but in Monsieur Descartes' was my professor's icy reaction. Quite right! I learnt my lesson: the trick was to show what you knew, by reading around the subject and putting in appropriate quotations. Afterwards you could 'philosophize' to your heart's delight in cafés with your friends.

To study Islamic philosophy it was essential to know Classical Arabic and Persian. Traditionally philosophers in the Islamic world had written their treatises mostly in Arabic, much as European thinkers had used Latin for their writings. Arabic was considered the Sacred Language, God having spoken it to reveal the Holy Quran. More profanely, one could say that Islam was Arabo-centric in its temporal and political manifestations, the language being the cohesive substance binding together otherwise disparate ethnic elements. From North Africa to the Euphrates, wherever the Arabs went their language was adopted by the conquered peoples – the task being made easy by the fact that the language is rich, eloquent, malleable, and capable of expansion.

Persia was the exception: when the Arabs conquered the country in 661 they tried as usual to impose their language on the population, but met with strong resistance and lost the contest. Nevertheless their alphabet was adopted, and adapted to Persian, and a good deal of Arabic vocabulary, altered often beyond recognition, entered the language.

At the *lycée* in Persia, Arabic was a compulsory subject, as Latin and Greek used to be in the West. But it was badly taught and unpopular. The pupils hated it: it had to do with religion, prohibitions, and backwardness, whereas we believed, in Rimbaud's words, *'Il faut être absolument moderne,'* which meant Westernized. But I liked it and worked at it, wishing to know the origin of the words that had entered Persian, their development and ramifications.

The Classical Arabic and Persian courses at the School of Oriental Languages of the Sorbonne were held in rue de Lille, in the heart of Saint-Germain-des-Prés, and were full of students who wanted to pursue diplomatic or academic careers. Classes were small and we had real contact with our teachers and lecturers. The atmosphere was cosmopolitan, as many of the teachers were natives of the countries whose languages they taught: Chinese, Russian, Eastern Europeans, Hebrew and Arabic speakers.

Our Arabic teacher was Professor Perrin, a clever, attractive army officer who had lived and worked in North Africa and knew not only Classical Arabic but many regional dialects. He had dropped the army in favour of Academe, but kept the forceful, no-nonsense method and taut physique of a desert-hardened soldier. He did not suffer fools easily, and teased students whose work was sloppy or unclear: 'You may be learning Middle-Eastern languages, but we do not tolerate Middle-Eastern *à-peu-près* – approximation, vagueness. Precision, clarity, that's what is needed,' he would say if a translation was not perfect, or if he detected any trace of mental laziness in an essay.

I found Arabic fiendishly difficult. Indeed French students had less trouble with its guttural sounds than I did, but it was logical and you could play it like a game: given a two or three-consonants root, you could build up endless words expressing a variety of concepts if you knew the rules.

Persian was taught by Professor Lalay, who knew the language and literature deeply, spoke it like a native, and was the author of the best Persian grammar in French. He was quiet and unassuming, but impressed us with his understanding of Persia and its heritage, and was kind and generous to his few Persian students, giving them advice and help. Persians are always awed and flattered by the interest such 'Orientalists' show in their culture. We take it for granted that we should know Western languages perfectly and do not expect to be similarly honoured with the title of 'Occidentalists'! While I can recite hundreds of verses in English and French, my jaw still always drops in admiration and gratitude if a European knows a couple of Khayyám's Quatrains! So I liked and revered Professor Lalay.

But more than our teachers the works of two eminent Orientalists had a long-term influence on my development. They became my Masters in the traditional sense – they continue to inspire and guide long after their deaths. Indeed the events of the last decade have given their works and personalities an extra relevance.

First was Louis Massignon – one of France's greatest Arabists and Islamic scholars, who translated and wrote a number of books and commentaries, most of which are still in print. He was a Roman Catholic, who in his youth had thought of becoming a monk, and whose deeply spiritual nature combined a formidable intellect with simple piety. Perhaps his greatest contribution was to be the first Western scholar to discover the legendary Muslim mystic Hallaj, and bring him to the attention of the public. Hallaj was born in 857 in Persia, but taught in Arabic. He led the wandering life of a true seeker-after-truth, and preached the doctrine of unity with the divine. Some high-ranking courtiers and administrators of the Abbasid Khalif adopted him as their spiritual guide, but he fell foul of their official mullahs who feared he would undermine their authority, when he stated that nothing should impede the soul's pilgrimage towards the Divine Friend, that no third person was needed. 'I am Truth,' he said, referring to his total identification with The One. But as Truth – *Haq* – also used to indicate God, they accused him of heresy, condemned him, and in 922 had him stoned and burnt to death.

As usual in history, removing the man did not annihilate his ideas: the seed was planted, and he had cracked the carapace of rigid orthodoxy, revealing the esoteric, mystical dimension of Islam, which over the centuries grew and produced the exalted philosophy and poetry we know. In Islam, as in Christianity, Judaism, and other great religions, it is the esoteric, spiritual, that sustains the exoteric, temporal edifice of faith and preserves it in times of trouble and decline, just as the hidden spring feeds and replenishes the pond which would otherwise become stagnant and putrid. When churches become darkened by corruption, intolerance and laxity, the flame turns inward and smoulders until the black storm has passed. Yesterday the Inquisition, today Fundamentalism, East and West – they come and go like plagues, while Love endures and redeems.

Legends and stories grew around Hallaj, his life and martyrdom, and were handed down the centuries by Sufis. One related to his execution in Baghdad. You could imagine the scene: Grand Mullahs in the front row supervising the operations, surrounded by a mass of townspeople whipped up into a frenzy of zeal, then the victim being dragged to the centre of the square and tied to a pole, the shower of stones . . . To protect themselves from accusations of heresy many of Hallaj's followers and indeed religious dignitaries who knew him to be innocent were forced to attend the proceedings and throw a stone. The story goes that Hallaj looked up, acknowledged them with a smile of acquiescence, and withstood the blows. But when Shebli, his beloved disciple and friend, came forward and threw a rose at him, he broke down and wept.

Massignon had discovered Hallaj in 1907 – or perhaps Hallaj discovered him – and it had changed his life. Subsequently he wrote his major study, *The Passion of Hallaj*. Of all early Muslim mystics Hallaj is the most Christ-like, and Massignon had the idea of getting the Vatican to canonize him, as an ecumenical gesture, making him the first Muslim saint of the Christian calendar, and compensate centuries of suspicion and misunderstanding between the two great traditions. But it did not happen, and recent events have destroyed all the bridges that holy men like Massignon were beginning to build. I last saw him at our finals, and recall his gentle smile and quiet voice, while all the other examiners looked suitably serious and forbidding. But men such as he are beacons along the dark road of life – they go on burning and shedding light through their works, and through memory.

The second Master whose books I read but did not meet until much later was Henri Corbin. He was a very rare phenomenon – a philosopher and thinker who was also an Orientalist. He had started life as a straightforward academic philosopher and philologist. As a young graduate he discovered Heidegger, and he was the first to translate his work into French, starting with *What is Metaphysics?* published in the 1930s. He visited the then little-known German philosopher, impressed him, and they became friends. But he also studied European Medieval philosophy and theology, and learnt Arabic and Persian. Then through Massignon, whose lectures he attended, he discovered the works of Sohravardi, the Muslim philosopher-mystic and founder of the School of Illumination. The discovery was for him like the revelation on the road to Damascus, and from then on his professional life was devoted to Islamic philosophy, studying, illuminating and presenting his chosen subject, and becoming its greatest exponent in the West.

Sohravardi was born in 1155 in Persia, but taught and wrote both in Persian and Arabic. He forged an original philosophy by combining Islam with Zoroastrian elements and Neo-Platonism. He believed that to arrive at wisdom – *Sophia Perennis* – both intuition and reason were to be used, and that one without the other would lead to error. Needless to say he was accused of heresy and martyred in Aleppo, in 1191.

Corbin wrote over twenty books of incomparable scholarship and depth. He also translated several seminal philosophical treatises by Islamic philosophers. He believed that European philosophy after Descartes had become too drily rationalistic and no longer satisfied the spirit. His book on Sohravardi, *L'Archange Empourpré*, had a profound influence on all of us who read it, though at the time it was above my head and probably still is. But the mystic soul finds echoes, however dimly perceived, of its own aspirations in the works of those who have achieved higher stations. My father was considered the last great traditional philosopher of Sohravardi's School – there are of course younger disciples both in the West and in the East, trained in modern universities – and so I was doubly drawn to it.

I did not meet Henri Corbin in my student years, although he knew my father, and in later years became a friend of my brothers', their friendship being that of Master-and-Disciple. In the 70s I went to Persia one early summer, and by chance Henri Corbin was in town too. My eldest brother gave a luncheon in his honour for a few of his friends and admirers. The small gathering was at the Ministry of Foreign Affairs Club, in the foothills of the mountains near Teheran. My brother and I arrived early, and inspected our table set in a quiet spot in the shade of an old plane-tree, it was a perfect day, the air moist with recent showers and fragrant with the smell of saturated earth and grass and jasmine, the heat tempered with a breeze from the snow-capped mountains around, the sky an azure vision of a clement world. Soon the others arrived, one of them accompanied by the guest of honour: a middle-aged Frenchman, with a warm, welcoming smile and courteous manners. I was introduced and placed beside him at the table. He had the genuine modesty of great men, and was delighted that I had read his books and admired them.

I told him that his translation of Heidegger's *What is Metaphysics?* was one of the first books of philosophy I had read years earlier, and that although he clearly had done his best to render it less obscure than the original, I had found it still nearly incomprehensible even on a second, recent reading: '*En effet!*' he smiled, with an expression of connivance. Talking about Sartre he said: 'The French took to him because they couldn't understand Heidegger; and also because, being a creative writer, he produced works of art that expressed his philosophy better than any treatise – and put it within reach of non-professionals.'

Corbin was a Protestant mystic, a very rare kind of Frenchman, and he spoke most movingly about what he called 'the genius of Persia', which had produced the great philosophers and poets, who had almost invented Love, and had certainly given it its highest expression in poetry for generations to come. Then, speaking with admiration of my adopted country, he told me about the English mystics, such as Julian of Norwich, and that whole esoteric tradition which has gone into decline in the Anglo-Saxon world since the Reformation. We also spoke about politics and the state of the world generally. He was aware of, and preoccupied with, the fundamental problems: population, the despoliation of Nature, the ever-widening divide between haves and have-nots and its consequences . . . I remember him concluding: 'They say about a sick man that his condition is serious but not hopeless; one can say about the world that its state is hopeless, but luckily it is not serious!'

I meant to write down everything he had said, but somehow was drawn into the whirlwind of an all-too-brief stay. I never saw him again, as he died not long after. When such men die life itself seems diminished, as if a candle has gone out that illumined one corner of our dark world. But while the reputation of many of his famous contemporaries has declined, Corbin's has spread far beyond the confines of Islamic scholarship. Today artists, writers, scientists, even the *Nouveaux Philosophes*, have discovered the Orient of Light through his work at a time when the Occident appears to have conquered the whole world.

There were other teachers and lecturers, at the School of Oriental languages and the Sorbonne whom I admired, and for whom I felt affection. Their guidance and clarity of vision have sustained me in times of confusion and despair. And I made many friends, some of whom have stayed close ever since.

After the course you could go on working for a doctorate, in the language, history, or literature of your chosen country. Several of my friends did, but unlike them I did not have a career in mind. By the time my finals came I had decided not to pursue academic studies any further, but instead follow my awakening artistic interests.

Today I have all but forgotten Arabic, though doubtless it would come back with a refresher course. Language like a neglected tool gets rusty if not used, much as a limb gets weak or stiff. But if 'culture is what remains after you have forgotten everything you learnt', then nothing I had learnt was wasted. It had opened vistas into unknown regions – the poetry of the pre-Islamic Arab bards, the tales of past and present story-tellers, the vision of the Muslim mystics. And I had acquired a permanent curiosity about human beings, their ideas and emotions. What artist, however humble, can do without such sources of inspiration?

14

The Thrush and the Brush

Her voice was ever soft, gentle and low, an excellent thing
in woman
WILLIAM SHAKESPEARE

One of the students who befriended me at the School of Oriental
Languages was Julie More. She was in the last year of the
School of Political Sciences – *Sciences Po* – and had just started
to learn Chinese. She was interested in Chinese art and porcelain, and hoped to help her father, who was a dealer in that
field. As it happened she never had the chance to work. Being
beautiful and having many admirers, she was married within a
year, started a family and settled down to the life of a cultivated
bourgeoise. It suited her well, and she was happy.

Julie's parents were divorced – which was still rare in France.
On the whole a well-to-do Frenchman preferred to take a mistress and keep his family life going. He would 'visit' her at the
end of the day, on his way home from his office, between five
and seven o'clock, hence the expression *de cinq-à-sept*, which
indicated the time and the arrangement as well as being a
euphemism for extra-marital liaisons. A French friend told me
the other day that the *cinq-à-sept* had died a natural death:
nowadays in those hours French businessmen are still working
in their offices, moving stocks around the globe and making
deals through computers and faxes: 'We now divorce like everyone else, *comme tout le monde*.'

Julie lived with her father, who adored her, and her step-
mother, who got on well with her, having produced no children

of her own. Her father was a devout Catholic and rather strict: Julie's admirers were vetted carefully before she was allowed to go out with them, and she had to return home no later than half an hour after the show, whatever time that was before or shortly after midnight. She could not spend the night out, even with a girlfriend who was the reincarnation of the Virgin Mary.

Despite such parental vigilance Julie got pregnant. Fortunately her father liked the young man who presented himself as the father of the baby and requested Julie's hand. He was a tall, blond, rather charming if dull young man, who had graduated from the *Sciences Po* the year before and now worked in some ministry. His career was secure, he was serious-minded, and he loved Julie. His request was granted.

I went to their wedding. It was a small family affair at the church of Saint Mathieux, in the 16th Arrondissement, near Julie's home. In her white satin dress and antique lace veil she glowed with that soft, diffused apricot-pink that expectant women acquire after the first turbulent months of pregnancy. As she walked down the aisle on her husband's arm, smiling at the congregation, you could see her tummy curving out as in a Cranach painting, her demeanour exuding placid contentment, her eyes twinkling with amused connivance – as if to say: 'Of course only virgins marry in white!' Her father bought the young couple a two-bedroom apartment near his own home, some basic furniture and a few Chinese ornaments, and off they went on life's – with any luck – long journey.

Shortly after our first meeting Julie invited me to her home for tea. It was a large, gloomy apartment with rooms strung along a dark corridor. A grandfather clock stood sentinel in the entrance, tick-tocking nonchalantly, while Chinese vases and chests filled the rest of the space along the walls. Julie's room was at the end, overlooking the plane-trees of a church garden opposite. It was furnished simply, with everything buried beneath a thick clutter of clothes, books, papers, records, posters and souvenirs. Only the protruding panels of the bed indicated its presence, and two chairs were cleared for us to sit on.

A maid brought in some tea and a cake, and we settled down to a long chat.

She told me that she had gone to university on her father's insistence, but that what she really was passionate about was singing, that she was having lessons with a teacher who had been a famous prima donna in the 20s and early 30s and that the current piece she was learning was 'Summer Time', from Gershwin's opera *Porgy and Bess*: 'Not grand opera, but I love it and my teacher said I could do it, because it doesn't matter what you sing while you are learning, as long as it has the right range and is at the right level.' She sang it to me: her voice was not large, but it was sweet, and she sang with feeling.

I complimented her, and told her that I too loved singing and had sung all my life, as far back as I could remember, starting in nursery school, but that coming from a strict Muslim background I had never been allowed to take lessons or indeed sing in public. I had a friend at the *lycée* in Teheran, Betty, who studied operatic singing with a teacher, and she taught me everything she learnt. Now that I was free, if only I could train my voice properly! I had thought of it as soon as I had settled down in Paris, but it was financially out of my reach. I then sang Julie a Persian folk-song, a lullaby with tuneful legatos and modal embellishments.

'You must come with me tomorrow and see my teacher! I'm sure she'll come to an arrangement with you once she hears your voice!' exclaimed Julie. 'She must be rich from her past success, because she doesn't seem to care about money, and her rich students pay her very well. She lives in this area, in a grand building. So don't worry, just come with me.' I agreed, though I did not harbour much hope.

So two days later I went with Julie to meet Madame Carlotta Bussoni, the celebrated 20s' and 30s' prima donna, at the J.S. Bach School of Music, in avenue Victor Hugo.

The building had been the *hôtel particulier* – the town house – of the Marquis de D. His heirs had been unable to keep it after his death in the 20s, and had sold it to an impresario who had emigrated to America just before the war. The Germans had taken it over during the Occupation and used it as part of their high command headquarters. Afterwards it was sold once again and converted to a music school. Who owned it now, or ran it? There was a secretary on the first floor, but she was seldom there – the place seemed to run itself, and indeed there was nothing much to run: rooms were let to teachers who held their classes there instead of in their own homes. Some of the rooms were divided and soundproofed to be let as practising studios, while the large salon on the ground floor served as a small concert hall.

A wrought-iron gate led from the street to a square garden of roses and shrubs with a small pool in the middle. It had once been charming, though now everything seemed covered with a film of neglect: on a pedestal at the centre of the pool stood a Cupid with a broken arm and a chipped quiver of arrows. In the past water had sprouted from his head onto a reclining Psyche and then into the pool, but it had long ceased running, and the water in the pool was a foot lower than formerly and greeny-opaque, the water-lilies mere sparse languishing leaves. Similarly the plants seemed permanently parched, although there must have been a gardener somewhere, even if no one ever saw him, or they would have died altogether. At the end of the little garden double stairs curved grandly up to the front door.

The entrance hall was flooded with the sounds of music emerging from behind the doors of class-rooms and studios – violins sighed, cellos moaned, flutes and clarinets whistled, pianos trilled in a pleasant cacophony – it was as if a whole orchestra were tuning up before a concert. Madame Carlotta's class was first on the right: a large, bright room overlooking a side street through double windows, empty save for a grand piano and half a dozen chairs. She did not give individual lessons, as she believed that in a small group students would learn from each other as well as from her.

An aria was in progress: Madame Carlotta Bussoni was at

the piano accompanying a large, voluptuous soprano in a dark suit: la Contessa, a Frenchwoman married to an Italian count, who was one of Madame Bussoni's oldest students both in years and the length of time she had been studying. About forty, she wore *haute couture* clothes, heavy make-up, and a delicious scent produced by her furrier, as she informed us when we complimented her on it. Her main attraction, apart from her Rubensesque figure, was her mane of thick blond hair, which she coiled around her head in an elaborate criss-cross like a bird's nest. Singing was her hobby, though she hoped to sing at the Paris Opera some day, in a future whose distance she did not care to measure. I nicknamed her 'the pension' – she would provide Madame Bussoni with a regular income for as long as one could foresee.

Two men were sitting on chairs and listening attentively, their eyes fixed on the Contessa. One was a young Jewish businessman from Egypt, whose family had emigrated to France at the beginning of the 50s. He worked in his father's antiques business, but wanted to be a singer and hoped to be let off the hook if he landed a contract with an opera company. The other was a commercial traveller for a pharmaceutical firm. In his thirties, he had been studying for two years already, and very seriously: singing was for him the only way out of his drab job, and he meant to become a professional at whatever level as soon as he could. Meanwhile he juggled his times of travelling so that he could attend lessons twice a week, practised many hours every day, and already had built up a substantial repertoire for auditions.

The aria over, la Contessa sat down and Madame Bussoni greeted us with a broad smile. She was in her fifties or sixties – it was hard to say exactly how old – and dressed unlike any Frenchwoman I had ever seen: instead of the sober, elegant clothes usual in women of means, she wore flamboyant mauves, violets and other bright colours, like some exotic bird of glittering plumage. Material and design belonged to no particular period or fashion. Her hat, which she wore always, was a mauve basket with a bouquet of violets on one side, and a velvet-dotted voilette which she sometimes lifted in class, only to pull down again when the lesson was over. Her aquamarine eyes were surrounded with midnight-blue shadow, and sparkled from behind her voilette, while her straight nose seemed sculpted from thin ivory, amid a complexion of the translucency of alabaster. A few blond curls lay limply on her forehead, like brush-strokes on a painting. Only her lips betrayed her age, having lost their shape, with cherry-red lipstick running in tiny rivulets all around them.

Madame Carlotta had a permanent smile, which often blossomed into ripply laughter, revealing a set of perfect teeth – natural or false? It was impossible to tell. She was an actress dressed for an Edwardian play and waiting in the wings to go on stage – and all her silk chiffons and kid gloves and flowery hat and make-up and laughter were part of an attempt at preserving the beauty she had once undoubtedly possessed.

Her students knew that Carlotta Bussoni had been a famous and successful soprano, and had sung many of the great roles of the operatic repertoire in the major opera houses of Europe; that afterwards when she had retired, she had become a teacher in order to pass on her great experience and techniques to the younger generation; and that she lived nearby in the 16th Arrondissement. Yet an aura of mystery surrounded her: had she ever been married? No one knew, but she had a son, Jeanot, of whom she was very proud. He was a painter and she mentioned him often as being talented, sensitive, beautiful, the apple of her eye – indeed her *raison d'être*.

She had been 'discovered' by the great Italian tenor Giovanni Bonardi, who made her his protégée and launched her. Was Jeanot the child of their love? Or was he the son of the Hungarian fiddler with whom she had run off after Bonardi had abandoned her and broken her heart? At any rate Jeanot had been brought up by her alone, had done very well at school, and had joined the army at the outbreak of the war, when he was barely eighteen. He had been wounded soon after, and spent some time in hospital, where his physical wound had healed soon enough. But he had suffered shell-shock and had never quite recovered from the resultant nervous breakdown. He had regular black bouts of depression, paralysis, violent behaviour, was unable to hold a job, and made very little money from his painting.

This overall picture was put together from the crumbs of information that Carlotta Bussoni scattered, as no one had ever seen Jeanot. 'My son is an *artiste peintre*,' she would say with pride and affection, 'very talented, very refined.' Often she peppered her lessons with anecdotes from her past, of her encounters with famous singers and musicians of her day, of her important roles, always going back to 'the great Bonardi' and what he had said and done to convey a piece of professional know-how. But she was never really specific – just gave us the materials from which our imaginations could unconsciously build a picture. We saw her as Violetta dying in the arms of Armand-Bonardi, we saw her as Lucia di Lammermoor going mad with love, as Marguerite, patient and sweet, waiting for Faust, as Euridice following Orpheus out of Hades. . . We saw her in ornate dressing-rooms bedecked with bouquets at the end of each performance, pursued by swooning lovers threatening suicide for the love of her. How romantic it all had been!

That first day she asked me to sing something, and I sang a cappella an Irish song I had learnt from Betty at the *lycée*: 'The Last Rose of Summer'. She listened, and when it was finished she went to the piano and gave me some notes to sing, going higher and higher as far as I could follow. Then with a dramatic gesture she turned to Julie: 'You have brought me a present!' she said, and went on making more complimentary remarks. I thought she was being kind, or perhaps she thought I was a rich Persian princess who, like the Contessa, could be a source of income. But Julie told me that she had already informed the prima donna that I was just an impecunious student, unable to pay her full fee.

'What counts ultimately is the tone, timbre,' she said. 'It's what makes two voices in the same register different from each other. It's the finger that touches the heart-strings, the gateway to the soul. Just as with eyes – it's not their shape or colour that counts, but their look, *regard*. I like your timbre, my dear, and I'm glad to hear it. I will teach you.' It was soon agreed that I would attend her classes and pay whatever I could, whenever I could. But I had qualms of conscience, despite Julie's assurances that it was all right: 'You see she "milks" the Contessa and the Egyptian boy even the commercial travel-ler pays her the full rate. Anyway, she probably doesn't need the money – with her past career she must be well provided for.'

So twice a week I took the Métro to avenue Victor Hugo and attended Carlotta Bussoni's classes between five and seven in the afternoon: 'There are two great voices,' she explained, 'the soprano and the tenor. Nearly all the great parts in opera are written for them. At present you are a mezzo, but there is no reason why your voice shouldn't expand to acquire the extra few notes needed for a dramatic soprano. You can then sing mezzo parts as well as soprano – like Callas, who now sings Carmen as well as Violetta. It will take a year, maybe more, maybe less.'

I myself liked the contralto and the baritone, for they seemed to me deeper, darker, reaching a league or two further down into the turbulent waters of the psyche. Or perhaps because those were the voices I had heard as a child: my father praying and reciting the Quran, traditional women singers heard on the radio and at weddings, and country women at harvest-time singing, or wailing lullabies for their children:

> Go to sleep my little heart,
> The harvest of life is but sorrow . . .

I went to the music shop on the quai des Grands Augustins and bought my exercises in vocalization and the songs she had suggested: Fauré, Duparc, Ravel, to poems by Baudelaire and

Verlaine. I cut down on everything to pay at least a minimum for my lessons, and over the months my voice did naturally expand to reach the higher notes I needed. But I only really liked the lower and middle registers – I could go lower than most sopranos and had almost three octaves.

Carlotta Bussoni taught us to sing without straining the voice, to breathe properly, to phrase, to convey emotion with control – techniques that would stand me in good stead thereafter. 'You must let the voice glide over a cushion of air,' I can hear her saying, and then proceeding to demonstrate, breathing in deeply, distributing the intake of air through the long phrase, then letting it die away . . .

That was only the first stage of training, but essential. Now whenever I hear certain melodies, arias, snippets of opera, I remember them in Carlotta's classes; I see her standing up from the piano stool and singing a line – a sound curve, natural and graceful like a rainbow. She still had a lovely almost girlish lyrical soprano voice. Whatever life had done to her, it had not corrupted her vocal cords: God's gift, and well protected.

One evening before the summer holidays I went to J.S. Bach's and arrived a few minutes late. The classroom was empty, and there was no secretary, but a man walking up the stairs told me that Madame Bussoni had cancelled her class at short notice, being indisposed, and that her other students had already been and gone. As she lived nearby I thought I would buy her some flowers and fruit and pay a visit, in case she needed help – although undoubtedly she would have a maid. I discovered her address from another teacher, bought a little bunch of violets from a flower stall, some cherries from a grocer's, and walked to her building. Inside I found the concierge's lodge under a vaulted archway and asked for her apartment.

'She lives at Madame de Berry's, second on the right.'

I had imagined her home as grand, and full of the mementoes of her glorious past, so what did it mean? Surely she couldn't be a lodger in someone else's home? I climbed the stairs and rang the bell. There was no answer but the door was not locked, so I pushed it open and went in. The corridor was dark and quiet, with a fusty smell compounded of stagnant air and mothballs. A large ornate gilt mirror leaned slightly forward from the centre of the wall over a table on which stood an empty porcelain vase. To the left was the drawing-room, with Louis XVI chairs and low tables. I could hear voices emanating from behind a closed door at the end of the corridor, like two people having a heated argument. I followed the sound and knocked gently; hearing no response I pushed the door slightly and slipped in, to be confronted by a strange scene.

The room was long and cluttered with furniture, clothes, ornaments, bric-à-brac. A large, ornate bed shaped like a boat, with maroon and gold tassels hanging from the headboard, rested against the wall opposite the window. A bedside lamp with a pink shade stood on a round table beside it. Maroon velvet curtains gathered to the side draped a floor-to-ceiling window overlooking a well-like yard, whence a hazy crepuscular light cut a swathe across the floor. A huge gilt mirror over the mantelpiece reflected a section of the room; commodes and chests and chairs all covered with clothes and objects filled the rest of the space. A woman in a loose flowery dressing-gown was kneeling by the bed and sobbing: 'Stop it! . . . *Assez! Assez* . . . ' Her robe had slipped and bared a shoulder, and you could see her skeletal body, her shoulder-bone protruding through the flesh, her breasts like crumpled desiccated gourds hanging on her hollow chest. Her thin hair was stuck to her scalp, with a few yellow curls falling forward onto her forehead which she kept hitting with her knotted hands. The object of her supplication was a young man standing by a chest of drawers near the window: small, thin, with curly black hair and eyes that glinted in the penumbra like two embers – Saint John the Baptist in a primitive painting. Jeanot! I thought. The talented, refined *artiste peintre*.

'Why didn't you get rid of me like the others?' he sneered. 'Why did you allow me to come into this world? Carlotta Bussoni my arse! Charlotte Bussot, the slut of Bonardi! A failed singer! You never got beyond dingy theatres in little towns! La Scala indeed! More like the Municipal Hall in Clermont-Ferrand! I have a good mind to come and blow your cover with your precious students and let you starve! . . . '

'*Arrête!* I beg you!' she interjected. It occurred to me that I was not supposed to be there, watching this secret ceremony of recrimination and grief between mother and son. Shut up in their inferno they had not heard me tiptoe in, and perhaps I could retreat quietly . . . but too late! Something made Jeanot swivel his flaming eyes round and see me. He shot across the room like a lynx and would have knocked me over had I not stepped out of his trajectory. He bolted. I heard him run along the corridor and bang the front door. Carlotta pulled herself up and collapsed on the bed, like a battered rag doll. She saw me too, and uttered a desperate moan. I approached and sat on the edge of the bed, holding her hand, trying to calm her down: 'I came to see if you needed anything and brought you these,' and I gave her the violets, as if their simple beauty could soothe her misery. She managed a smile and a thank-you. Was there anything I could get her? She motioned to a cupboard where I found a bottle of cognac and brought it to her. She took a glass from her bedside table and I poured her a little draught which she drank.

'He is not like that normally, I swear to you. He is as gentle as a lamb, loving, funny, *Oh Dieu*! It's these attacks . . . What can I do? . . . I wish you had not heard all that . . . '

'No one will ever know, never, never! Please be completely certain,' I assured her. She kept her eyes closed, and without her usual attire she looked old and decrepit. I stayed with her for a few minutes and left, limp with pity and utterly drained. I walked back along the Seine to recover. It was a warm summer evening, with the setting sun spreading a soft light over the trees, the glimmering water, the slowly tugging barges. Everything quivered, echoing the trembling within me caused by the scene I had witnessed. I realized how cleverly Carlotta had built an edifice of past fame and fortune in our minds.

'When I was Desdemona in Milan . . . ', and we had unconsciously added 'at La Scala'. 'When I played Marguerite in
Germany . . . ', and we thought Berlin. Violetta in Angleterre
was surely at Covent Garden; Paris Opera, Vienna . . . She did
not affirm, just planted the seed in our youthful imaginations.
In reality she had been just a minor success working in second-
ary opera companies, who had ruined her chances with love
affairs, pregnancies and abortions. Her beauty had been her
undoing – men had taken her and left her. But what did all
that matter? She had a lovely voice, even now, round and sweet
like a peach, and she was a good teacher – enthusiastic, solid,
knowledgeable, kind and generous.

That day was to be our last before the summer break, and
I decided I would not go back – it would embarrass her to be
reminded that I had seen behind the veil she had elaborately
woven in order to survive. Who could blame her? And are we
not what we choose to be? Who has never had to hide weakness
and shame behind a social mask?

Julie was getting married and having a baby, the voluptuous
Contessa would continue forever, keeping her fantasies going,
with no plans to become a professional. The commercial travel-
ler would find a contract with a provincial opera company in
the South, and at last give up his hated job with the pharmaceutical firm, whatever the consequences. And the Egyptian antiquarian would give up singing altogether. I bumped into him
in London several years later, and we stopped for a cup of
coffee. He told me the rest of the story: they had all gone back
after the summer holidays but as far as he was concerned not
for long. He had finally come to the forlorn conclusion that he
did not have a voice worth sacrificing his life to, and he had
decided that it was better to be a successful antiquarian and
able to afford going to the opera often than a second-rate tenor
'pulling the Devil by his tail' all his life. He was still passionate
about the opera and in fact he was in London for the season.

What about Carlotta Bussoni? The Contessa saw her until

she died, a couple of years later, of what seemed to be a strange form of galloping cancer. I thought she died of heartbreak, kept at bay for as long as she could. No one knew what happened to Jeanot. I myself never went back to see her, although I often wanted to, because it would remind her that I shared her secret. I felt it was best to remove myself and let her forget. After all, I was only a foreign student and perhaps had gone back to my country. It was agreed that Julie would present the excuse if she asked after me.

Yet many of the songs I studied with her I still sing, though in the lower register natural for me. The last piece I did with her was Marguerite's song in Berlioz's *la Damnation de Faust*. I can still see Carlotta looking into the distance and singing: '*J'étais tant aimée! J'était tant aimée!*', her eyes moist with nostalgia, her expression that of infinite helplessness at time's tyranny; then having demonstrated the phrasing and emotion, switching off and saying: '*Alors?*' At my last lesson I sang the whole piece, and she took up the end:

Nous verrons-nous jamais dans cette vie? Folie! . . .

the question asked with longing, and the answer given with a wistful smile of resignation, the melody curving down in a deep resolution . . .

Only now, at last, am I about to record the song I sang that first day I went to her class, Thomas Moore's 'The Last Rose of Summer':

Oh soon may I follow, when friendships decay,
And from love's shining circle the gems drop away
When true hearts lie withered and fond ones are flown,
Oh we would inhabit this bleak world alone . . .

15

The Maestro and the Prima Donna

Il n'y a pas d'artiste sans qu'un malheur s'en soit mêlé
JEAN GENET

One day at the beginning of September I went to the Conservatoire de Musique, in rue Madrid, on the Right Bank, to enquire
about singing teachers, for I wanted to continue my training.
The receptionist gave me a list of the professors, and said that
all of them gave private tuition to prepare students for the
entrance *concours*. First on the list was a man who sounded very
angry when I rang him, as if I had interrupted important
business – he had more students than he could accommodate,
and would take no more even if Melba herself were resurrected
and turned up at his doorstep!

Next I rang Madame Beatrice Galet, whose list was also full,
but when I told her I was Persian, she asked me at once to go
and see her, and perhaps she could 'place' me with a colleague.
(It emerged that she had once had another Persian student
with a golden voice who had died suddenly at the age of twenty-
two).

Everything that Carlotta Bussoni was in fantasy, Beatrice
Galet was in reality. She lived in a grand building on Avenue
Foch, near the Arc de Triomphe. From her windows the view
stretched on one side as far as the Obélisque and beyond, to
where the urban sprawl dissolved into a chimerical mist, and
on the other to the green patch of the Bois de Boulogne.

I entered a cool quiet hall covered with red carpet, where a

120

wide staircase of shallow steps and shiny brass rods led to the floors above. There was one apartment on each floor, and Madame Galet's was on the third. A wrought-iron and glass lift stood by the stairs, which I took. Her maid opened the door and led me to a study next to the drawing-room, where a lesson was drawing to its close. I could hear the sound of the piano, a male voice singing, then a female voice repeating the same phrase, an exchange of words . . . and presently the maid reappeared and led me into the *salon*: a vast, sumptuous drawing-room in blue and cream, furnished with Empire pieces and a huge crystal chandelier. Lace curtains covered the panes of the long windows, framed with thick blue silk draperies that overlooked the quiet front garden. A grand piano stood on one side, strewn with music-scores and a few photographs of people in fashionable clothes, from before the war. Portraits of herself, landscapes and drawings, and a large painting of a conductor in front of an orchestra, hung on the walls.

Beatrice Galet was in her late fifties and still very attractive. Of medium height, she had clearly spread round the middle, but then she belonged to a generation when singers were supposed to have ample proportions and heavy busts. Her face was youthful and her complexion fresh, with no evident sign of time-ravage. Her chestnut-brown hair was pulled back behind her ears, and held with two *barrettes*, with a parting in the middle. She wore a single diamond on a delicate chain in the cleavage of her blue dress and a matching solitaire on her right hand. She had the proud carriage and the poise produced by life-long practice of display.

After a few words she introduced me to her accompanist, Mademoiselle Jacqueline Rolland, a young woman of about thirty, very pretty, with wavy brown hair and eyes as blue and sparkling as a mountain lake on a summer day. My nervousness was immediately assuaged by her reassuring smile.

'As I said on the telephone, I have no vacancies,' said Madame Galet. 'I only have one or two students to prepare them for the entrance competition of the Conservatoire, and if they pass I take them in my class. But let's see what you're like.'

Playing it safe, I gave her Duparc's setting of Verlaine's poem 'Le ciel est pardessus le toit', with Jacqueline accompanying. Madame Galet was less gushing in her reaction to my voice than Carlotta Bussoni, but she smiled: 'You have a good voice and a lovely timbre, but you have to learn technique and some theory.' At this Jacqueline volunteered: 'I can help her with that.'

I told them how I had always loved music, and that a music teacher at my primary school in Persia had offered to teach me free if a small violin could be procured for me, but that my parents had vigorously opposed the idea. I had learnt to read music at school, but that was all. When I left, Madame Galet said she would telephone me the next day after speaking to a colleague whom she would try to persuade to accept me. But when she did ring, it was to say that she would take me on herself, and that Jacqueline would teach me sight-reading and theory, and start me playing the piano.

Of course I would have to get a piano, either by renting a practice-studio by the hour, or hiring a small upright. But where could I put it? We were not allowed even a radio in our rooms, never mind something much noisier and more disturbing for the other inmates. And how to pay for it all? Back home I spoke with Madame Giroux, who suggested that I hire a piano with a silencer, put it in the basement, and use it only for a short while every day, so as to minimize disturbing anybody. The basement was empty except for broken chairs and tables, a few boxes, piles of old rags, discarded books, and it stretched the whole width of the building. It was ideal.

Near the canteen where we had our meals, on the boulevard Saint-Michel, there was a musical instruments shop and they let me have a little upright for a tiny monthly rent. Beatrice Galet made me pay a nominal fee for my weekly lesson, and Jacqueline suggested that we exchange lessons: I would study music with her for one hour, and then teach her English for one hour. Why she wanted to learn English became apparent only much later.

Being still a full-time student at the Sorbonne, I had to manage my timetable carefully. So every Wednesday I turned up at avenue Foch at the end of the day for a singing lesson, and on Mondays I went to Jacqueline's flat on the rue Saint-Denis for sight-reading and rudimentary piano, giving her an English lesson afterwards – my English was only just good enough to teach a beginner. But often Jacqueline simply did not have any spare time, and after giving me my hour she would say: 'I have too much work today, maybe next time.' In fact that so-called English lesson was really just an excuse so that she could teach me free without making me feel obligated.

'Since you are Persian we will start you with the aria in Handel's *Xerxes*,' Beatrice said. It was a perfect choice: melodious, wistful, simple as the best tunes always are, and it suited me in every way, for by now I was a dramatic soprano and bought scores to fit my register. I also sang songs, starting with 'easy' ones such as Schubert's 'Ave Maria' and Grieg's 'Solveg's Song' and going on to *lieder* and various arias, all in French translations.

A friendship soon developed between me and my new teachers, and sometimes I stayed on for a cup of lemon tea and a chat after the lesson. One day Beatrice took me to another room, behind the salon, where she kept her old costumes – a space dedicated to the past, to the preservation of memory. On dummies, in glass cases, spread over settees, were the mementoes of her glorious career: costumes in gold and silver lamé, in velvet and chiffon, some heavy, others diaphanous, bejewelled or unadorned, while on the walls were large photographs of her wearing them. Here she was in *Thaïs*, there in *Salome*, as Marguerite in Gounod's *Faust*, as *Manon*, and most touching as Mimi in *La Bohème* – 'All the great lyrical roles, over more than thirty years,' as Jacqueline put it. Accessories, shoes, veils, everything was arranged as if in a costume museum, and kept in perfect order by her maid, Solange. The curtains were drawn to protect everything from the sun's rays, doors and windows were proof against dust, and no central heating altered the level of warmth and moisture.

Instinctively I lowered my voice as if indeed in a sacred place, and I asked how often she visited this temple of memory: 'Oh, almost never!' she giggled nervously. It was knowing that they were there, within reach, that mattered to her, gave reality to her past life. I finally summoned the courage to ask her why she had never married? 'Ah! That's a long story!' she said as she led me back to the drawing-room and closed the door. Then one day she told me.

She came from a modest family of small traders, the youngest of her parents' three children, with two brothers much older than herself, who were now dead. Early on her beautiful voice was noticed by her mother, who encouraged her to sing, and paid for music and singing lessons. At eighteen she passed the entrance examination to the Conservatoire, where she was immediately recognized as a star pupil. Three years later she graduated, winning a first prize. Most graduates had to make their careers the hard way, auditioning for opera companies around the country, giving recitals, teaching. Some might eventually reach the great opera houses of Europe, but the one or two first prize winners each year were spared all that slog, and as a rule they were immediately offered a contract with the Paris Opera: they would start at the top of the pyramid, and barring calamity they would have a smooth passage throughout their entire working lives.

Beatrice arrived at the Paris Opera at the age of twenty-one to play Marguerite in Gounod's *Faust*. Night after night she had gone to the Opera and watched others perform, dreaming that one day she would be standing on that very stage. And now there she was, already a star, and surrounded by people eager to please her. Yet her excitement was tempered with apprehension – it was one thing being a brilliant student, another conquering the public. Her contract was for only a year, and she would have to prove herself.

The orchestra was conducted by a young composer and conductor, Denis Roussel, some seven years her senior, whose reputation had already spread in the music world. They were introduced by the director of the Opera, he bowed gently, kissed her hand, and went down to the orchestra pit. The rehearsal passed smoothly, and afterwards Beatrice was congratulated by the conductor and the director – her meteoric ascent into the operatic firmament had began, and within a few years she would be one of the handful of most famous and best loved prima donnas of the Paris Opera.

But something else happened that first day: she and her conductor fell in love passionately and irrevocably, and would remain tied to each other for the rest of their lives. When she came home at the end of that first day a huge bouquet of roses was delivered to her small apartment, with a short message of welcome, signed Denis. And the next day he invited her to lunch in a little quiet bistro near the Opera House, and began to court her assiduously.

'*Eh voilà*! Only he was already married and had two little children,' she recounted. 'So I resisted for as long as I could, although I had fallen in love with him that very first day. Watching him conduct as I sang, somehow I felt secure, as if he held me by the hand and guided me into a new world. All my life he only had to appear on the horizon for clouds of anxiety to disperse.

'Yet I did put up a resistance. But he was not a man to take no for an answer. He said he had married young because he had thought that it was the natural thing to do, that he had not known what real love was until he met me, but that now he knew and would never let go of it. So eventually I gave in.'

She became the centre of his life and his muse. Everything he wrote was dedicated to her, every score was marked with her initials. But he was also fond of his wife and adored his children, and they agreed that he would keep his family intact.

On tour they were treated as a couple by the company, and everyone in the musical world knew of their liaison. But in Paris she had to make do with his afternoon visits, whenever he could get away from teaching, composing, conducting, and family life. Whenever she gave recitals, he acted as her accompanist, playing the piano for her in order to follow her around the world, putting aside his own work:

'But years were passing, and I seemed to be always waiting for him; even when he was there I was waiting! So sometimes I rebelled and encouraged one of my other admirers. He was fiendishly jealous, and as soon as he found out that an affair might develop, he would show up, make a frightful scene, threaten the poor man and force me to break up a relationship I had barely started. He kept watch over me like a dragon, but in truth I didn't want anybody else; he was the only one for me, he occupied my heart and soul entirely. Men are different, they can have several women, but I believe that each woman loves one man only, the others are only mistakes, or desperation.'

Usually in such situations some busybody puts the information on a silver plate and presents it to the wife; surely this had happened to her? 'Whether they did or not I never knew. Certainly *she* never confronted him, nor did he ever volunteer any information to her.'

Over the years their respective careers had flourished, and now they were both professors at the Conservatoire, he of composition and she of singing, and he was also a celebrated composer, but he had retired from conducting. Occasionally I heard one of his pieces on the radio, or saw his name on posters for concerts. Jacqueline Rolland worked for him as orchestrator and copyist, and she told me that he still came and had tea with Beatrice every day after she had finished teaching, that after forty years their sexual life was over but their love was stronger than ever. I had occasionally seen a tall, elegant elderly man going up in the lift as I came down the stairs, and now I knew who he was. Beatrice told me that if one day he didn't come she knew something was wrong. She would ask Solange or Jacqueline to ring up his home and enquire, pretending that the call was about work. Invariably his wife would answer and explain that he was indisposed with a cold or some other ailment and unable to come to the telephone, but that she would give him a message. Jacqueline was sure from the way she spoke that 'she knew everything'.

I pondered their situation, wondering how I would have responded to her situation. Already my generation was rejecting such 'arrangements', wanting romantic, passionate love without any compromise. But would Beatrice and Denis's love have lasted and grown ever stronger had he left his family and married her? Or had the absence of cohabitation preserved it, like a delicate plant in a greenhouse, sheltered from the indignities of daily life? I thought I would have preferred Beatrice's position to his wife's, but who was I to judge? Now I realize that probably his children played a more important part in their equation that any of us childless observers could conceive.

'I have spent my life waiting for him!' Beatrice told me one day, with a hint of resignation in her voice.

I learnt the end of their story from Jacqueline last year: eventually when they were both in their seventies Denis Roussel's wife had died, and he had married Beatrice and moved in with her. She had decorated and furnished a room for him, with a mini-grand piano where he could work in peace. His two children, now married and with families of their own, had made a terrible fuss, fearing to lose their inheritance to this 'wicked woman' who had usurped their mother's place, and they had threatened court action. Beatrice had reassured them that, far from wishing to inherit anything from her life-long lover, she was leaving him all her considerable estate, and that should he die before her they, his children and grandchildren, would be her heirs. But only when the arrangement was made legally binding had they calmed down and accepted her existence.

And so Denis and Beatrice had a few perfectly happy years

together, until old age and illness overtook them. Then one night Beatrice died, peacefully in her sleep, presumably of a heart attack. Denis was too old and frail to bear the blow, and everyone agreed that the news should be kept from him. Solange went on looking after him, and he was told that Beatrice had gone to a spa for a while, for her arthritis.

'I used to go and visit him,' Jacqueline told me. 'He had almost lost his sight and all notion of time, and he would say "You know I've just received a letter from Beatrice, she'll be back tomorrow." Because Solange would sometimes pretend there was a letter for him from Beatrice and read it to him. Occasionally he would talk about the distant past as if it were the day before: "Beware of César Franck – he's a hypocrite!" he would say, referring to something that had happened fifty years earlier. Solange was getting very old and crippled too, so when Denis finally died, she went back to her village and eventually passed away.'

Beatrice and Denis had left all their papers, letters and scores to Jacqueline, who gave them to the Bibliothèque Nationale. So far no one has written their biographies, nor told the story of their love, around which their lives were centred. As for those sumptuous costumes and pictures, they were auctioned by their heirs, and presumably bought by younger musicians and collectors.

But what about his music? 'No one ever plays it,' Jacqueline informed me. 'It is neither atonal or the electronic sort that is fashionable today, nor really old-fashioned; so it falls between two stools and is ignored. But some of it is very good and it might come back one day.'

Whenever I hear the Verlaine/Duparc song I sang the first day I went to see Beatrice Galet, I think of her. The poem was part of *Sagesse*, the collection Verlaine wrote in prison, where he was incarcerated after shooting Rimbaud and committing several other offences. Solitude, remorse, abstinence and reflection led him back to Christianity, and like Oscar Wilde's *Ballad of Reading Gaol*, the poems reveal an extra spiritual dimension and depth born of suffering. But what was originally for me just a ruefully lovely, lyrical song, now means much more:

> Mon Dieu, mon Dieu, la vie est là,
>   Simple et tranquille.
> Cette paisible rumeur-là
>   Vient de la ville.
>
> —Qu'as-tu fait, ô toi que voilà
> Pleurant sans cesse,
> Dis, qu'as-tu fait, toi que voilà,
> De ta jeunesse?

But what happened to Jacqueline Rolland? That is another story.

16

Mothers and Daughters

. . . Paradise is under the feet of mothers
THE PROPHET MOHAMMED

Jacqueline Rolland lived with her widowed mother. They occupied a tiny flat on the top floor of an old building off the rue Saint-Marc, a street lined on both sides with small shops, and seething with a motley local crowd, that looked like a 1920s film set. A tailor sat by one window in front of his whirring sewing-machine all day, while next door the hardware-man's array of tools and utensils spilled over onto the pavement, and all along the road the butchers, bakers, launderers, all looked like actors dressed up for parts, so true were they to type.

In between the shops were the gates of buildings, usually closed. You pressed a button and the small door in the middle of the gate clicked open to let you enter into the cobble-stoned courtyard. A staircase at the far end, its stone steps hollowed in the middle by centuries of use, led to her home on the fifth floor.

She had been born in this little apartment, her parents' only daughter. Her father was a violinist who played in an orchestra and gave private lessons. He had fought in the First World War, when poison gas had damaged his lungs and heart permanently, causing the angina pectoris from which he died relatively young soon after the Liberation in 1945, leaving Jacqueline to earn a living for herself and her mother.

A gifted musician, she had won a scholarship to the Con-

130

servatoire where she had studied piano and composition. Her father's death just at the time of her finals had caused her to miss by a fraction the coveted first prize, which gave the winner a year in Rome with a grant, free to compose without financial worries, and a start in life. Instead she had won the second prize, prestigious enough but without such material advantages.

In those days musicians were not well paid in France, and she had to work hard – being Beatrice Galet's accompanist, teaching, orchestrating for famous composers – to make ends meet, and had no time for composing, which she regretted. Yet a few of her pieces were sometimes performed, notably a flute concerto which I heard and liked, and which a group of her contemporaries had recorded. But despite such disappointment she never complained. Her attitude was: life is difficult but you just get on with it. And in her kindness she gave me some of her precious time almost free, as my few English lessons in return were not worth much.

Inside, her flat was divided into three tiny connecting rooms. The sitting-room was where Jacqueline worked and taught; the upright piano – the same she had used since she had begun playing at the age of five – stood against the window overlooking the courtyard, whence sun-light filtered through the lace curtains and dappled the photographs on the walls. One of these showed a young soldier in uniform, standing at ease, his rifle leaning against his leg, his helmet pushed back, a cigarette in the corner of his mouth, and an ironic smile in his eyes. The sepia was already fading, like the memory of the corporal it enshrined – Jacqueline's father.

On the piano stood two other photographs in ornate frames. One showed an attractive American officer in uniform, sitting at a piano, his smiling face turned to the camera; the other was of the same man in casual clothes in a country lane, one hand holding his bicycle and the other around the waist of a laughing, younger-looking Jacqueline.

Towards the end of the war Jacqueline had joined the Resistance. Her job was to carry false passports and identity-cards which she usually hid among her scores and musical compositions. One day as she was about to catch the Métro to her appointment, the Gestapo invaded the station, blocked the exits and began to search the people waiting on the platforms for the trains: 'I thought I had had it,' she recounted. 'If they found the papers they would arrest and torture me to find out about the organization, and then they would shoot me. If I tried to run for it through the tunnel, they would catch me or shoot me in the back. I stayed glued to the ground. Two soldiers and an officer approached me to search my case, and I pre-empted their order and opened it, inadvertently letting fall a few sheets of music and exposing the score of Bach's cantata *Ich habe genug* (I have enough!). The officer immediately changed his attitude, bowed gently and bent down to pick up the papers, which he handed back to me and helped me close my case – he forgot to look inside! He smiled and said: 'Ach so, mademoiselle? You are a musician? So am I, I was a clarinettist in our orchestra in Hamburg.' He then asked if we could meet and play together, and I gave him my telephone number – a false one.

'Not long after that Paris was liberated. I went to the Champs-Elysées to see General de Gaulle march up to the Arc de Triomphe – you can't imagine the euphoria. Who could believe that the French would be at each others throats before the cries of *Vive la France* had died down!'

She had worked alongside the Communists in the Resistance, but had been disillusioned by them afterwards, and now she was apolitical. 'I joined the Resistance to free France from the Germans, not to put her under the Russian yoke!' I was still a fellow-traveller, and I tried to argue in favour of higher internationalist ideals, whatever the shortcomings of individual parties; but she thought I was naïve and had been deceived, and we did not discuss politics any more.

Jacqueline's mother was not a merry widow. She had married young and never worked. Now with her husband dead and her daughter out at work all day, she was bored out of her wits.

Eventually a local milliner took her on as an assistant, to relieve Jacqueline from her complaints. Sometimes when I stayed to give Jacqueline her English lesson, I saw her come in – a stout middle-aged woman of infinite indolence, exuding dissatisfaction like an odour.

Mother and daughter were clearly very close, and Jacqueline was always affectionate towards her – she embraced her when she returned from the shop, and asked solicitously how her day had been. 'So-so,' she would whine, putting as much discontent into her voice as she could muster.

Months passed. One day Jacqueline told me that she could not make our lessons on the Monday, but would I go on Sunday morning instead, when her mother would be away visiting her grandmother, and stay afterwards for a bite of lunch. I knew that this was an exceptional act of kindness on her part, because they never entertained, and I was delighted. I bought her a bunch of flowers and arrived early to fit in two hours' work before lunch. It was over coffee that she told me about the young American officer in the photographs.

About five summers previously, Denis Roussel had arranged for Jacqueline to spend two months in an artists' colony near Fontainebleau, where in exchange for cataloguing their library's musical manuscripts she lived free and had time to compose. The flute concerto as well as several short piano pieces I had heard were the result of this sojourn.

'There were two grand pianos in the reception-room which opened on to the lawn, and one afternoon when everyone was outdoors I sat and played until late. Suddenly I became aware of someone behind me, and when I finished the piece I heard applause. I turned round and saw a man standing by the door, casting a long shadow on the sunlit floor. He introduced himself as 'Howard', said how much he'd enjoyed listening to me, then sat down beside me to play. It was as if we were twins! And had played together all our lives – we could have gone on for ever.

'At last, when it became too dark to see the score, he invited me to dinner in the village bistro. Afterwards we sat on the lawn in the dark and talked half the night, and that was the beginning of our story.'

Howard had first come to Paris with the American Forces at the time of the Liberation, and had fallen in love with the city and come back several times since, with various bursaries and grants, to study with French teachers. He was a pianist and musicologist, and was now teaching at a New England University while finishing his doctorate, and composing as well. This was his sabbatical semester.

'We used to work during the day and meet at the end of the afternoon to go for a walk or a bicycle ride in the woods. We would stop for an outdoor dinner in a village square, then come back and play or talk till late.' He told her about America, describing the grand pristine Nature of his native New England, its centenarian trees, and the translucent lakes of upstate New York where his family had a summer house. He described the feast of colours in Autumn, the curvaceous hills around Lake Placid – the oldest in the world, so polished by time as to look like waves, making perfect ski slopes in winter. They held hands lay on the grass and kissed, and one day towards the end of summer he proposed to her.

He told her that he had fallen in love with her that first evening, when he had been drawn to the sound of her playing: he had immediately recognized her as the girl he had been looking for all his life, and he would always love her. He had thought about practicalities too: in America she could get a teaching post without any trouble if she wished, or he would provide and she would just compose.

But what to do with her mother? Of course she would go to America with them – there were French teachers at his university, and several French wives. Before long she would have a good life of her own, and in due course there would be grandchildren to keep her busy and happy.

For Jacqueline it was like a dream. She worked so hard that she had no time for day-dreaming; life would just bring her whatever it chose, and she would accept. She never thought that it could be a fairy-tale.

One day Howard took her to Paris and bought her a sapphire and diamond engagement ring. Then they went to see the priest who had christened her and was her Confessor, and he immediately liked the charming young American and gave their love his blessing. They even arranged the date of their wedding. Then a few days later her mother returned from the country, where she had been spending a month with her own mother, and Jacqueline told her the news: 'Oh Mother! It's so wonderful – you'll love him! He is everything I ever dreamed – handsome, kind, a wonderful musician!'

But instead of being overjoyed by her daughter's happiness, her mother had gone pale and begun to shake: 'An *American*! But you have gone out of your mind! What's wrong with French men? You don't mean to say you are contemplating marrying a foreigner and moving to *America*? And what about me? How can you be so heartless! Don't you ever think of your poor widowed mother, who has no one but you . . .' Tears, hysterics, threats of suicide . . .

Jacqueline managed to calm her down, and took the news to her fiancé. He thought that he would be able to charm her, but she refused even to meet him. When he finally insisted upon visiting her, she was odious, saying she would never consent, that they would have to get married without her blessing, and that it would kill her.

'She who had grumbled every Sunday about visiting her own mother was suddenly the perfect daughter, saying she could not possibly leave her aged mother behind! When Howard offered to take her as well, she screamed at him and locked herself in her bedroom.'

They decided that the best course of action was for Howard to go back at the end of his sabbatical, and leave Jacqueline to bring her mother round to the idea gradually: 'I had known him only eight months but I couldn't imagine being without him. Every minute of my day centred around our meetings. He

was my life – and now there would be an ocean between us . . .
After he left I felt paralysed for a while, unable to do anything.
I just cried and cried. My mother showed no sympathy, just
said I was selfish, sex-mad, ungrateful. Sometimes she would
pretend to be nice, and say that I would soon meet an attractive
Frenchman. But I told her that for me it had to be Howard or
no one. Then she would just shrug and sulk.'

Howard wrote every day, telephoned often, came to France
the next summer and spent an idyllic month with his fiancée,
hoping that her mother would relent. Instead she threw fits,
blackmailed, faked illness, used a whole emotional arsenal to
thwart them, and he went back empty-handed.

Jacqueline's hope was that her grandmother would die, and
remove her mother's chief excuse, but the old woman endured,
senile, crippled, always ill, but apparently immortal!

Then only a few months ago Howard had written to say that
he was tired of waiting, and that he was getting married to one
of his colleagues: 'She is not you – no one will ever be you –
but life must go on.'

I kept in touch with Jacqueline after I finished studying with
her. When I left France and got married, I wrote to her from
London and later visited her briefly once or twice on my trips
to Paris. Howard's photographs remained on the piano: had
she overlooked them, or did she keep them to remember their
romance? I noticed she was putting on weight, neglecting herself. But while her private life withered her career flourished,
and within a few years she was offered a post teaching composition at the Conservatoire and ended up as professor.

Last summer I was in Paris and rang her up. We arranged
to meet at the Conservatoire and have lunch. 'It is the last day
of the examinations, and Mademoiselle Rolland is examining,
but she won't be long,' the receptionist informed me. (*Mademoiselle*, so she had never married.)

Presently a door opened and Jacqueline came out, stretching
her arms in welcome. She was a little heavier, her hair lighter

and thinner – but her sapphire blue eyes were undimmed by age, still with their bitter-sweet twinkle and warm, reassuring smile. We embraced and went to a nearby bistro.

She told me that this was her very last day at the Conservatoire – she was retiring after over twenty years of teaching, with a full professor's title and pension, and the Conservatoire itself was moving to new, larger premises on the other side of Paris. She lived in the same flat off rue Saint-Denis, and had acquired a holiday home in the South of France as well, where she planned to spend most of her time and compose. Her mother was still alive, but very old, somewhat senile, 'and much nicer!' She laughed. Her life had been centred around her work, she said, and her students. She wanted to see photographs of my children, hear my songs, read what I had written: 'It had better be in French, because I have forgotten every word of English you taught me!'

Did she regret not having married Howard?

'No, not now – I wouldn't have had my career, and all the satisfaction it has given me. I would have loved children, but I think of my students as my children. Of course they come and go, but so do children! Except for me, *I* didn't go! Who knows what would have happened if I had.'

We talked about Beatrice and Denis, and I asked if any of Beatrice's students had become well-known singers, and she gave me their names. Two I had heard in various opera houses, the others, pouring out of the Conservatoire each year, had just melted away.

'Beatrice had a soft spot for you – we both did. But you were so wild! I told her she might as well expect a butterfly to think about the future or a career!'

I said that I believed everything had its price, that if you don't plan and calculate and manipulate but follow your heart, you may suffer much, but your mind is free, you take life as it comes, and sometimes it brings you unexpected gifts. Then we ordered champagne to celebrate her retirement and our reunion. I asked about Howard, and whether the photos on

137

her piano were still there: '*Toujours!*' she laughed. 'Only a real new love could take his place, and I have had none – plenty of offers, but somehow I never felt the same about anybody.'

In my photograph album there are only two photos of my music teachers. One shows Beatrice Galet in her thirties, with wavy hair parted on one side, chin lifted up, and eyes looking into the distance, smiling. The other is of Jacqueline, very young and beautiful, with longish hair, liquid eyes, and her sweet, happy smile. She was damaged, like most of us, but not entirely defeated.

17

Outsiders Inside

As for you few remaining friends
You are dearer to me every day
How short the road became
That had seemed to be so long
ANNA AKHMATOVA

Although students met and made friends with people of different nationalities in the atmosphere of the Latin Quarter, they
were naturally drawn to their own compatriots, and their closest
friendships were within their own national group. The older
and more traditional a society, the harder it is for outsiders to
become part of it. You can be accepted as an American in one
generation, but not English or French. Marriage helps – foreign
wives and husbands are graciously accepted – otherwise the
best you can hope for is to be 'adopted'.

I first noticed this through a Russian friend whose family
had emigrated to Paris after the 1917 Revolution. The French
had taken them in and introduced them into society, as a result
of which their younger members had made good marriages,
and now their children were French. But the milieu of the
original émigrés was still tightly knit together with nostalgia,
bewilderment and sorrow. Thirty years later I experienced the
same thing at first hand, when members of my own family fled
to the West after the revolution of 1979 in Iran: their lives are
more circumscribed than before, their world is enclosed, their
thoughts are fragmented, but from all this they gain a measure
of emotional security and of identity. Then there are the 'born
exiles' – those who feel ill-at-ease in their own societies and
really only flourish as outsiders, such as Henry James, Joseph

Conrad, James Joyce and Samuel Beckett, as well as many lesser mortals.

The number of Persian students in Paris was then relatively small. There was a Union of Iranian Students, whose meetings I attended once or twice. But it was full of factions, with the pro-Communists trying to take over the whole organization and the others resisting, as a result of which nothing was ever decided. But I did meet some Persian students, a few of whom became my closest friends and helped me overcome the home-sickness that at first paralysed me.

One day walking down the boulevard Saint-Michel I bumped into Madame Tabai accompanied by a friend – Hameed, a philosophy student who wore glasses and the obligatory duffle-coat, and who sported a blue-sheened velvety black goatee. He was in his last year but planned to stay on for a doctorate and an academic career when he returned home. He said he would come and see me at the Foyer, which he did a week later, bringing his best friend, Cyrus, a would-be architect. We went to a café and talked until late. I told them that I knew nobody, and they said they would introduce me to their friends. Hameed was formal and knowledgeable, and unlike most students in those days had no interest in Marxism, though unlike many he had studied it. He regarded its blend of messianism and materialism as trite, sustained only by Soviet power. Nowadays such opinions are commonplace, but in those days when even Sartre, one of our gurus, was a fellow-traveller, they amounted to the most daring iconoclasm.

We all argued passionately but good-humouredly, and it soon became apparent that hard work and seriousness had taken their toll on Hameed, and banished all traces of humour from his life. 'He is serious twenty-four hours a day!' complained Cyrus, who by contrast applied a healthy needle of irony when-ever our discussions became too inflated. The two friends were like a comedy duo, one artistic, light, funny, charming, the other intellectual, ponderous, and touchy. Yet I soon discovered that behind Cyrus's jokes lurked both sensitivity and sadness. Though he had been brought up in a non-religious family, he had longings which he tried to assuage with a quest for a spiritual path. Attracted to Christianity, for a while he even flirted with the idea of becoming a monk and retiring to a monastery. He took me to exhibitions and art-galleries and taught me about art. His spiritual home was Italy whose artistic heritage he knew well, and to which he introduced me through art books. What he designed and built in Iran in the years before the upheavals of 1979 reflected his unusual eye for beauty, his originality and inventiveness.

Among the friends I met through Hameed and Cyrus were Hormoz, another architect, Iraj, a post-graduate sociologist, and Masoud, a civil engineer. They all lived at the Cité Universitaire, in various 'Houses', and urged me to try and find a room there. But how? It was almost impossible – they had all stayed long on the waiting-list before succeeding. But being tired of the restrictive life at the Foyer, I decided to try, and meanwhile I visited them often, and I liked the campus atmosphere and the variegated cosmopolitan crowd.

Cyrus named our little group 'Snow White and the Five Dwarves', as I was the only girl. But one day I received a letter from Fifi, a close friend in Persia, saying that she was coming to Paris to study at the Music Teacher's Training College. I was overjoyed! We had become close friends in my last year at school. She was the daughter of one of my mother's best friends, and had recently returned from France, where her father, a senior diplomat, was stationed. Fifi herself had spent nearly all her life abroad, going to French schools to keep a continuity in her education, and she was now at the French lycée near my own school in Persia. Our families had been friends for three generations. Her grandfather had been a powerful mullah and a famous Sufi Master, and after his death his wife, called simply The Lady, had become the focus of their large circle of family, friends and disciples. She kept his establishment going by holding prayer sessions, Quranic recitations, commemorative services and other rituals. I remember going with my mother once or twice to these gatherings, which usually started with chants and prayers and lamentations at some Saint's martyrdom, and afterwards turned into very jolly parties – with food and soft drinks, gossip and anecdotes, everybody speaking at the same time, and much laughter, presided over by the quiet, diminutive Lady. In a society not noted for its tolerance, where any deviation from the norm was blown up and criticized, The Lady was considered a saint. Although in her seventies, she was truly beautiful: her intense, humorous eyes, her warm gentle smile, her rosy complexion, all exuded benevolence and were suffused with a light from within, which made everyone from beggars to patrician women flock to her house.

The Lady had transmitted some of her spiritual qualities to her granddaughter, in particular gentleness and compassion. Her name, of which Fifi was a diminutive, meant 'unique', and I believed she was. She played the piano, which was quite unusual for a girl of her background and clearly the effect of her being raised in the West. I used to go to their house after school, do my homework and read while she practised – Chopin, Schubert, Beethoven.

Her tales about Paris and her encouragement were instrumental in my resolve to go there, I sometimes wrote to her how homesick I was, and she, used to a wandering life, assured me that I would soon adapt to it and start enjoying my freedom.

Fifi and her older brother gave me introductions before I left to a few French and Persian friends, but I did not use them at first – the French ones because I did not speak the language, and the Persians for fear of slowing my efforts at learning and adapting. Or perhaps these reasons were just rationalizations for shyness, for the anxiety that paralysed my sociability at the beginning. Then slowly as time passed and I became accustomed to my new life and spoke French better, I did make friends, both Persian and French. To begin with they were mostly fellow students, but later included many older people, some of them well-known intellectuals and artists. A few became surrogate parents or siblings.

One of these older friends was Farhad, a film-maker and historian of cinema, and a friend of Fifi's older brothers. He had been taken to France by his diplomat father at the age of seven and sent to school. Two years later his parents had been posted elsewhere, and in order not to uproot their only son once more and disrupt his schooling, they had left him behind, in the care of a family friend. Not unnaturally he had thought himself abandoned, communications being difficult in those days. When war broke out he was even more isolated; letters never reached him and he thought he had been forgotten. In turn he relegated his family to the back of his mind, and nearly forgot his own language, which he only recovered later, when he finally returned home.

Farhad had joined the Resistance as a teenage schoolboy, but he minimized his part in Hitler's downfall. He spoke self-deprecatingly about his activities – how pusillanimous he was, how he had wet his pants at the sight of a German soldier, what a hopeless shot he had turned out to be, etc. Yet everyone knew that he had been brave and active, and had worked with the Communists, including many intellectuals and artists now prominent in the Party. He had thought himself French, but once the war was over he realized that he was not. No matter how much his friends accepted him, he was a Persian citizen, and could never have the same expectations from society as they did. An exile has no automatic rights to work, a home, a livelihood, and if he grumbles there is always the 'if-you-don't-like-it-here-go-back-to-where-you-come-from' response. Farhad did go back to Iran, but he soon returned to Paris, where he now lived in a large, well-furnished room in a widow's grand apartment in the 16th Arrondissement. Had he wanted to pursue a conventional career in the administration in Iran, it would have been easy, given his family's position, but he was an artist, and that posed many problems.

One of the most gifted members of the Persian community,

Farhad was a comic genius. He invented, impersonated, and acted a formidable variety of characters – and could provide hours of entertainment at any gathering if he wished. An American or European would have made a fortune from such talent, but he was a prince, and being an entertainer was out of the question for him. Luckily, he was also serious-minded and knowledgeable – he knew more about the cinema than anyone else in Paris, had helped set up the Cinémathèque and later wrote a history of theatre in Persia, from Zoroastrian times via the Islamic Passion Plays to the present day, which has remained the most authoritative work on the subject. He wanted to make films, which was not easy, and meanwhile he wrote scripts and led an enjoyable life with a wide circle of interesting friends, mostly from the world of French cinema. As he was part of our five- or six-strong Communist cell, we met at his house once a week for a while – until everything fell apart, either because people went back home, or when it became clear that the Hungarian uprising of 1956 had not been a 'counter-Revolution led by a small fascist band', but a genuine popular revolt crushed by Russian tanks. It took a couple of years.

Farhad introduced me to a young Persian couple, Manou and Manijeh, a writer and social historian who worked for the United Nations in Paris, and wrote numerous books on a variety of subjects in French, and his famously beautiful wife. They were popular, wealthy and hospitable, and lived in a large apartment where they entertained their numerous friends and acquaintances – film-directors, writers, journalists, politicians . . . I enjoyed their soirées whenever they invited me, and liked Manijeh – she was kind and sweet, unusually innocent despite her allure of sophistication, and she had the beauty of a Persian miniature. I told her everything, and she confided in me. Her marriage was almost dead, though she liked and respected her husband. Why did she not divorce and start again, being still under thirty and childless, I asked? There was no one else she loved, and they had a life.

Then two years later she went home for a visit and by chance re-met her childhood sweetheart. It was as if the intervening years had vanished, they fell in love all over again, left their respective partners and married. It would be wonderful to say that they lived happily ever after – if only life were like a romance-novel! But deaths and tragedies in Manijeh's family affected her sensitive soul and burned her to ashes. She became unhinged and depressive and started drinking, and spent long periods in Swiss sanatoria. Eventually she took an overdose and died. I found it hard to believe that such beauty and innocence could be destroyed. Although I had seen her in Persia once or twice on my visits, we never met after the onslaught of her illness, and perhaps that was for the best. Many years later, I saw a home-movie of those days, made by her first husband, still a good friend, in which she looked like a butterfly flashing its colours in a full-blossoming orchard, just as in a miniature – that is how I always remember her.

Not mentioning anything about her being a musician, for clearly she would need to practise several hours a day (but being much better off than me she could afford a practice studio), I sang Fifi's praises to Madame Giroux and begged her to find her a room at the Foyer. She did, but Fifi did not like the Foyer, and through her father's contacts strings were pulled and she was given a room in the Mexico House at the Cité Universitaire. Built by a South American architect, 'the Mexico', as it was called, was one of the prettiest and most luxurious Houses on the campus. Fifi's room overlooked the lawn and parterres at the back, and was large, airy, and attractively furnished. Many nights I slept on her floor, having missed the last Métro.

As I had no one to pull strings for me, I decided I would go myself and see the director of the United States House, because it was the largest and often took in students of other nationalities. He was a kindly, quiet man, and he said that there was a waiting list a mile long, but that he would see what he could do. Three months later he wrote to me that if I wanted there would be a room for me at the Cité.

In the large entrance hall of my House there was a reception desk like a hotel's, where you left your key and received your mail and messages, and on either side stairs and lifts led to the male and female parts of the building. Behind was a vast reception room which could be transformed into a lecture theatre, with a raised platform that was used as a stage for plays and concerts. We were not allowed visitors of the opposite sex in our rooms, but at least the reception room was comfortable enough to meet in, and there were pleasant grounds all around.

My room was on the sixth, top floor of the building, and overlooked the ring road around Paris. Twenty-four hours a day cars, articulated lorries, motor-cycles, heavy traffic of every sort roared past . . . It seemed that every vehicle changed gear just underneath my window, screeching, coughing and jerking until its sounds melted into the massive background boom. For the next eighteen months I never really slept properly, and I noticed the difference when in summer I left Paris for a few weeks.

As time passed, one by one my friends finished their studies and returned to Persia. At the end of the fifties I was the only one of our group left in Paris, and wondering whether to continue my *vie de bohème* for a while longer, or go back also. The situation at home in Iran had changed: vast revenues from oil had ushered in a period of extensive development and prosperity – which later created other problems that led to revolution, but that is another story. In the years following the downfall of Mossadeq in 1953, the Shah began to co-opt the communists and all those who had flirted with the Party – he granted a tacit amnesty for 'past errors of judgement'. It was a wise decision, for the Left comprised a large part of the country's educated élite, which it could ill-afford to reject – a mistake often made by repressive post-revolutionary regimes, which by destroying the previous regime's cultured classes create a desert in which nothing grows and no renewal is possible. The Shah was helped at the time by Khrushchev's denunciation of Stalin and acknowledgment of the existence of the Gulags and then by the Hungarian uprising, both of which disillusioned many Communists and fellow-travellers. So well-known Leftists entered the administration and the new industries, and reached positions of power. Over the next few years Farhad helped set up National Television and ran one of its channels; Cyrus and Hormoz built universities, hospitals, office-blocks; Iraj became a professor of sociology and wrote books; Hameed taught Western Philosophy; Masoud set up a factory; and Fifi married a young doctor and taught music.

After the 1979 Revolution, far from being rewarded for contributing to the cultural enrichment of their country, nearly all of them were blamed for being part of the *ancien régime*, and risked imprisonment, even death. Most emigrated to France, where they had been educated. Only Hameed has stayed, for never having had an administrative job, he could not be accused of political involvement. He has never married and lives a quiet scholarly life: it is better to put up with difficulties than suffer exile, so long as your life is not in danger, he believes. I often talk about him with mutual friends – the way he always missed the point of jokes, or was out of sync with them! Fifi too has stayed; her parents have died, her brothers and sisters have left, and her marriage has broken up. Staunchly she works on, training young musicians, collecting folk music in remote parts of the country, and occasionally coming to Paris to see her relatives and friends.

Whenever I am in Paris I see these old friends, either in their homes or at one of the cafés in Saint-Germain where we used to meet in the old days. Their children have grown up and left home, many marrying Europeans and melting into their new communities. A few are academics or work in international institutions, several write and publish books in French, give lectures, travel. Their circumstances are reduced and their lives are difficult. Like the Russian emigrés of old they are adrift, nostalgic, tied to the past, longing for eventual return home, hoping against hope that one day it will be possible.

18

Elysium of Illusions

> It is the task of the poet to find a solution, a unique point
> where the understanding of love is realized in truth
>
> S. KIERKEGAARD

I had an introduction to Anne, a young poet who had published her first thin volume of verse, from a friend in Persia. For a long time I did not contact her, but when at last I did find that she had been told of my presence in Paris. Warmly welcoming, she invited me the coming Saturday to her home in Gardennes, a suburb some thirty miles east of Paris.

I had hardly ventured out of the Left Bank, and going to her house was an adventure: in the crowded and confusing Saint-Lazare Station I found the right train among hundreds leaving for suburban destinations, made a forty-minute journey on it (today twenty-five minutes), and then walked for another ten minutes through drab streets and nondescript buildings before reaching her mother's little two-up-two-down house.

Anne lived in the attic with her Russian-born boyfriend Sergei and their nine-month-old son Ivan. The front door was open, and led to a small garden shaded with a couple of cherry-trees. A smiling face appeared at the attic window saying: 'Come right up!' which I did, and found myself in the middle of domesticity: Anne sitting on the floor bathing her baby, who was burbling with delight at his mother's tickling and splashing, Sergei preparing a meal of minced meat and vegetables (appetizing aromas pervaded the air) in the adjoining kitchenette, the cat miaowing and pleading with Sergei for a share of the repast, and Moussorgsky providing loud background music with 'Night on a Bare Mountain'. Now the baby claimed his evening bottle vociferously as I was welcomed and asked to sit on the bed for a few minutes while they finished.

The room had a low ceiling sloping down to windows on either side, and was furnished with a bed at the far end, a cot at its foot, a chest of drawers, a wardrobe, a couple of Moroccan pouffes, and the walls were lined from floor to ceiling with bookshelves and record-racks, with a built-in space for the record-player. Everything had been made by Sergei, who was good with his hands, and every inch of space had been utilized to provide maximum room, yet it was hard to imagine how three people could live comfortably in such a tiny space. But there they were, happy and light-hearted, free from the tension and grimness so prevalent in Paris in those days of scarcity and confusion.

Anne was tiny and vivacious, and had short wavy hair, big dark intelligent eyes. Sergei was tall, blond and very Russian: blue eyes, high Asiatic cheekbones, an innocent, mild disposition – he reminded me of Dostoevski's Prince Mishkin, and of my mother's youngest brother.

When the baby had been fed and put to bed and the food was ready, we sat at a little pull-out table in the kitchenette and consumed our meal as if it were manna from heaven. There is love-at-first-sight, and there is friendship-at-first-meeting, and such was ours. Anne, at twenty-five years old, soon became the older sister I had longed for: experienced, protective, caring, affectionate and non-judgemental. I loved my own older sister, but we were poles apart: she was 'good', conventional and docile, while I was 'naughty', rebellious and independent, and we had quite different tastes and aspirations: in the end she was the one-who-stayed, while I was the one-who-left. In Anne I found a perfect substitute; gay and defiant of conventions, she refused to marry the man she loved and by whom she had a child, believing that marriage was an obsolete 'bourgeois'

institution that curtailed freedom. In those days and in a fundamentally Catholic country, these ideas were rare indeed.

Anne's optimism and joie-de-vivre were all the more unusual
for her life having been difficult from the start. Her parents had
divorced acrimoniously when she was ten and her mother had
remarried. She and her younger sister had lived with their
mother and were prevented from seeing their father, who had
moved to another town, and they had more or less forgotten
him. At first life had been 'normal', then, dissatisfied with her
second husband, their mother had grown increasingly 'difficult',
and the more the girls asserted their individuality, the harsher
she became. Anne's sister had married a much older man and
escaped, and their mother had turned all her bitterness and
tyranny upon her older daughter.

She had already forced Anne at fifteen to give up a scholarship and leave school, take a short secretarial course and work
in an office. Later when Anne had begun to have boyfriends
her mother had gone insane with jealousy. Appalling scenes
had ensued – boyfriends had been abused and chased out of
the house – reaching a climax when Anne produced Sergei, 'a
Russian, for Christ's sake! Either you give him up or you leave
my house!' Well, at eighteen and in love, you can imagine
which option Anne took. For a while the couple lived in cheap
hotels while looking for a room, but when Anne, became visibly
pregnant and they were asked to leave their last hotel, in desperation she turned to her mother who relented and agreed to let
them have her attic.

I met Anne's mother on subsequent visits: short, plump and
hard, she had a grey moustache almost like a cat's whiskers,
and rough curly hairs on her chin – things curable today but
then simply accepted by ordinary middle-aged women as bad
luck. She did not like 'foreigners', but as time went on came to
accept me. In summer Anne and I would sit under the cherry-
trees in the little garden of a Sunday, and occasionally she
would come out and join us. Her second husband was so down-
trodden that he never appeared: you could hear him moving

about inside the house like a ghost, sometimes casting a fugitive shadow on the lawn. His wife despised him, and referred to him always as *lui* – 'him'!

She was obsessed with sex: she would chase away the neighbour's cat with a broomstick when it was on heat and pursued by a tom, lest she witness their coupling. Sometimes a blow would hit its target and you could hear the cats shrieking with pain as they bolted over the low partition wall.

Sergei's widowed mother had left Russia in the late twenties with her two small children, Sergei and his sister, and come to France where she knew some émigrés. Her daughter, a few years older than Sergei, had married an Englishman and moved to Australia, but for reasons which I never discovered Sergei's mother's papers were not quite in order, and as a result she was still officially 'stateless'. I once met her at their house: she was sad and gentle, beaten by exile, and regretted leaving Russia. Anne's mother treated her with utter contempt (once she caught her picking a couple of cherries from the tree and screamed *'voleuse'* in fury) and sometimes the Russian was roused to retaliate – after which she would disappear for weeks; until, missing her son and grandson, she would swallow her pride and drop by with bonbons and fruit for the baby. Given these relationships, it was not surprising that Anne abominated the idea of 'family' – indeed she subscribed to Oscar Wilde's dictum that 'Friends are God's apology for relatives', and cultivated her friends as a solace, among them a group of young poets some of whom became my friends too.

Sergei too had been forced to leave school early and go to work, but he had trained himself as an engineer and now was employed by an engineering firm. Both he and Anne had proceeded to educate themselves, and like many autodidacts were better read and more knowledgeable than most qualified people. Their library and record collection were awesome in range and quality, and although they both worked long hours they managed to keep abreast of important cultural events. Anne would take her baby to a local baby-minder in the morning and pick him up in the evening (in those days everybody worked from 8 a.m. to 6 p.m. with a two-hour break for lunch). Pay was bad, and people grumbled, but Anne still managed to work at her poetry, of which her first book was but a small selection. She also wrote children's stories and art reviews for literary journals of high standard and low budget, for which she was not paid, though as compensation she received invitations to openings, and sometimes I accompanied her.

One day I plucked up courage and showed Anne some of my own poems and stories. To my surprise she liked them and was encouraging. She asked me to go with her to a poetry reading at the National Committee of Writers, where I would meet others in their group of young poets. The National Committee had been started clandestinely during the war by a number of non-collaborationist authors, and its notable founder-members included Vercors, François Mauriac, and Louis Aragon – among many others. After the war it had been gradually taken over by the Communists, and those who did not agree with their cultural politics, even if broadly on the Left, were marginalized and eventually pushed out. Now it was virtually an offshoot of the French Communist Party, under the leadership of Louis Aragon and his Russian-born wife Elsa Triolet. Aragon was Editor of the weekly *Lettres Françaises*, the cultural organ of the Party, much as *L'Humanité* was its political daily, which determined the Party line and ensured against deviation. In those days Leftist artists and intellectuals clustered around two monarchs and their consorts: Aragon and Elsa Triolet ruled the Communists, Sartre and Simone de Beauvoir the fellow-travellers, each surrounded by a large and powerful court of princes, fools, and other hangers-on. Like Chanel and Dior in the fashion world, among thinkers they were the supreme arbiters of cultural *Haute Couture*. An idea, an author, even a word, was either 'in' or 'out' to them, and woe betide him or her who disagreed. Though not sent to Siberia, such a 'non-person' would be cast in the role of the 'Baddy-Rightist', isolated and vilified. Some, like Arthur Koestler, could not stand it and left the country; others of tougher fibre, such as Raymond Aron, Albert Camus, and André Breton, stayed and bore their contumely stoically, convinced that one day, even if posthumously, they would win both the political and the moral contests. It is hard to imagine today that we, the politicized young, never read Aron – because he wrote in *Figaro* which was considered the organ of the Right, and so beyond the pale. In the following decades I read some of his books – *The Opium of the Intellectuals* in particular – and his weekly articles in the *L'Express:* lucid, objective, far-sighted comments from a mind uncluttered by dogma or ideological vapouring, while the 'gurus', especially Sartre, turned out to have been wrong on so many political issues. The last photograph of Aron, taken in 1983, shortly before his death, showed him leaving the Palais de Justice, emaciated and ill: characteristically he had left his sick bed to testify to a man's innocence in a trial.

The headquarters of the National Committee of Writers was an old seigneurial town house near the Presidential Palace, in the rue de l'Elysée. There were frequent meetings open to the public, at which writers and poets read their work, made speeches, received foreign literary dignitaries, and staged celebrations. In Persia we had read about the Resistance through some of the literature it had produced, notably Vercors' famous novel *The Silence of the Sea* and Aragon's patriotic and lyrical poems. These authors had become cult figures among our intelligentsia, but the idea that one day I would go to France and meet them was fantastic to me. Now I had read Aragon's poetry in French and was even more captivated by the beauty and eloquence of his language, the fire of his passion, the intensity of his love for France and for Elsa. I had seen him far off at political rallies, and here was my chance to hear him recite his own poems and those of the dead Russian poet Miakovsky, translated by his wife, even perhaps meet him. Miakovsky was the one Russian poet we all knew and read: a wild romantic, sometimes humorous ('I am not a man/ Only a cloud in trousers', or 'Madame, your son is wonderfully ill/ His heart is ablaze!' etc . . .), he had served the Revolution, and had committed suicide – his credentials were unimpeachable. And Lily Brik, Elsa Triolet's sister, had been his companion and muse until his death, though I later learnt that he had had endless other simultaneous affairs. As for the 'Great Four': Akhmatova, Mandelstam, Pasternak, and Tsvetayeva, we never heard anything about them – they were non-people in the Soviet Union, and so not translated into either French or Persian.

The lecture hall was full of young people, mostly students, would-be authors, and apprentice poets . . . Presently a door opened and Aragon entered, accompanied by his entourage. Applause. Beside him, a small middle-aged woman with enormous blue eyes, dressed in a dark coat and a black velvet hat, surveyed the audience and smiled, before sitting down: Elsa Triolet! So this was the woman who had inspired all those heart-rending love poems, the dedicatee of *Elsa's Eyes*, the worshipped muse! The couple's courtiers settled down in the front rows, while the great poet climbed the podium. Slim, handsome, elegantly dressed in a dark blue suit, his grey hair smoothed back from a high brow, his expressive eyes flashing blue, he began to read . . . I can't recall all that he read, but I remember the clear, beautiful diction, the dramatic inflections, the passionate crescendos that ushered in our thunderous applause.

The last poem he read was Miakovsky's 'My Soviet Passport', which ends with a resounding affirmation of pride at being in possession of such a document, pride transmitted and amplified by Aragon's own commitment to everything it represented.

After the reading we stayed on, spilling into the room next door, where the poet, his wife and friends stood in a cluster. Soon a human screen of courtiers formed around them, like today's 'groupies' surrounding a pop-star. It was not easy to penetrate, but I thought that this was my chance to draw attention to censorship in Persia, since the demise of the Party in 1953 and the clampdown on Left-wing activism. Holding the same ideals, surely we were all equals, big and small countries alike? And solidly united in our struggle for the Revolution and the Universal Republic of Virtue that would follow it?

'I am sorry to trouble you, I know you have no time . . . ' I began to say once I had managed to reach the poet.

'I always have time for pretty girls!' he said and smiled.

What had my prettiness or otherwise had to do with it? And how was I supposed to respond to the compliment? Not wishing to allow any diversion or trivialization I just went on, pouring out information about intellectual life in Iran, mentioning writers who had translated and propagated his work, and how some of them had been arrested, but later released. He did not seem remotely interested, and soon his attention was drawn away by one of his protégés, a prolific journalist and writer.

Afterwards I voiced my disappointment to Anne, but she was more worldly-wise than I: 'These people have so much to deal with that individual problems leave them cold,' she said. But nothing ever left *me* cold: I felt passionately for oppressed people everywhere. I made friends with Spanish exiles, South American and North African students; I heard about poverty and injustice in their countries, and I took it all to heart. I shared their rebellion – the size or importance of the country did not matter. I thought 'That is what we are all about.' Reading my thought, Anne added: 'One should never meet people one admires – they are nearly always disappointing in the flesh.' Not always, as I would find out later, but at the time I felt I would do well to follow her advice.

I went to several other readings and lectures at the Committee, but the next occasion I strongly recall was a reception for the Soviet writer Ilya Ehrenburg, his country's cultural ambassador-at-large to the Peace Movement congresses and international writers' meetings, and the only Soviet writer with a diplomatic passport. Ehrenburg had close links with French Communist writers, especially the Aragons, and wrote numerous blockbusters in the Socialist-Realist style decreed by Zhedanov (Stalin's formidable Minister of Culture), which contained just enough criticism of stupid bureaucrats and 'bad Communists' to sound plausible, and which always lavished praise on Stalin – 'the defender of life, warmth, and peace', 'the beloved father of the people'. Although they had been translated into French and Persian, I had not read them – even then sometimes life seemed too short! After the famous Khrushchev Report and the slackening of Soviet censorship, Ehrenburg produced *The Thaw*, a novel about the passing of the ice-age that had gripped Russia under Stalin, and which had caused devastation on a scale we would not appreciate until many years later. Its title became a symbol of Khrushchev's era, but even in this book he was reassuring: all was now well in the best of all possible worlds, just as he had assured us previously; and he was safely on the new bandwagon.

I had read *The Thaw* and I was bewildered – it alluded to a world of which I, like many young recruits to Communism, was ignorant. To be sure, some of Miakovsky's poems flayed at the monolithic and crushing bureaucracy – but surely that was just a wrinkle to be smoothed out of the fabric of the infallible system?

That day's meeting was particularly crowded. Aragon started the proceedings with a welcome address to Ehrenburg, who sat in the front row beside Elsa Triolet, and afterwards when the audience dispersed some of us – young authors and aspirants – moved into the adjoining room to meet the stars. Ehrenburg stood in a corner surrounded by friends and acquaintances. He had a slightly bent back, glassy blue eyes and unruly white hair. He spoke French well but he seemed mostly to be listening – especially to Triolet, who never stopped talking. If Aragon had dismissed my plea on behalf of the intelligentsia in Persia, surely Ehrenburg, a famous Soviet author, would take note and perhaps do something about it once back in his country? I put aside all shyness for the sake of duty and went up to him, delivering the little speech I had prepared, suggesting that Soviet Radio, which transmitted programmes in Persian, should start a campaign against our censorship. But he was bored: he had probably heard it all before from other exile groups all over the world who looked to Russia for support. He mumbled some excuse, saying he did not know anything about Persian literature – as if that were the issue – and returned his attention to his hosts.

That was that. But this time I was less disappointed than sad, and perhaps he knew that I was already out of date, that both inside Persia and internationally the situation had changed: the majority of our ex-Communists and fellow-travelling intellectuals were working for the Shah, who had meanwhile re-established 'friendly relations' with his country's northern neighbour. Ehrenburg knew all this, and rightly thought that I was an idealistic little girl ignorant of the machinery of big power politics. It was not until the 60s and 70s that the works of Pasternak, Solzhenytsin, Akhmatova, Natalia Ginsberg and others at last told the world the exact nature of life in Russia, 'the workers' paradise'. And after that Ehrenburg was reviled as an arriviste, a mediocrity who had survived by conniving with tyranny, by lies and distortions, while all around him genuine artists and great writers had perished for speaking the truth.

Yet in his youth Ehrenburg had indeed written a couple of satirical novels which had predicted all that would happen in Russia under Stalin, but luckily for him they had long gone out of print and been forgotten. Later he had been a correspondent in the Spanish Civil War and witnessed the elimination of the Anarchists by Stalin's agents, and he had said nothing; in 1940 he had seen Russia's allies, the Germans, occupy Paris, and had returned home and made no comment; then, when Hitler attacked the Soviet Union, he had joined the Antifascist Jewish Committee, whose members included many famous artists, writers and scientists – an organization earlier created in opposition to the Nazis, though in Russia anti-Semitism, which ostensibly had disappeared with the 1917 Revolution, was still very much alive.

The first wave of official Soviet anti-Semitism started before the end of World War II, with accusations of Zionism and 'cosmopolitanism'. By 1948 Stalin had rounded up and killed dozens of Ehrenburg's Jewish colleagues and friends in the Antifascist Committee, and had sent many more to concentration camps. Ehrenburg's reaction was to write an article in Pravda denouncing Zionism, and describing Israel as 'a creation of the Anglo-Saxons', 'a dwarf capitalist state', thus sanctioning his friends' murder. By the end of the 40s nearly all Ehrenburg's close friends had gone: Miakovsky and Maria Tsvetayeva had committed suicide, Isaac Babel had perished in a concentration camp, and Mandelstam had died at a transit camp while reading Dante's *Inferno*. Pasternak, Akhmatova and Paustovsky were spared, but only at the price of silence, fear, and despair. One survivor met Ehrenburg by chance in 1955 at Vienna Airport, and said: 'Your friends told me to ask you, if ever I came across you, to take some flowers to their graves.'*

In 1957 we ordinary people still knew none of this, and were not informed by those who did know. But to be fair even if they had told us, we would not have believed them – we would have branded them as renegades and treated them as pariahs, like Koestler and Gide.

Meanwhile Ehrenburg travelled abroad freely and returned laden with forbidden books and 'capitalist' goods. He could have stayed in Paris or Brussels, telling the world what was going on in his country. Why didn't he? Perhaps he did not have the courage to relinquish the comfort and luxury accorded to a 'People's Writer' for the uncertainty and humiliation of exile.

But our century has been shaped by exiles of one kind or another – from Picasso to Joyce, from Schoenberg to Beckett, and countless others, exiles who created new imageries, words,

*Claude Roy, a prominent author and friend of Ehrenburg's, who was expelled from the Party in 1957 for protesting against the invasion of Hungary, recounts this anecdote in his autobiography *Nous*.

and sounds that reflected the pain and dislocation of their condition, or perhaps of that original exile, from Eden.

Ehrenburg was definitely a 'survivor' of one kind, and our century has gone through such cataclysmic horrors that survival *per se* has become a virtue. We speak with admiration about someone being 'a survivor'. Yet all those hundreds of members of the Soviet Union of Writers who complied with its rules and published thousands of 'Socialist Realist' books in the decades of Terror have disappeared into oblivion, while Osip Mandelstam – whose name was crossed out in public records – is resurrected to glory. But who knows what any of us would have done in similar circumstances?

And there *are* circumstances in which just survival itself is a triumph: Primo Levi in his account of the Nazi death camps, *If This be a Man*, and Solzhenytsin in *The Gulag Archipelago* tell of the temptation to give up and die with other victims; but they refrained in order to bear witness, to hold a mirror of redemption to our century.

In her autobiography, Nadazhda Mandelstam tells that Ehrenburg was one of the dozen people present at the famous gathering where her husband read his poem against Stalin, which led to his subsequent arrest, deportation and death. One of them had denounced him, but she does not point an accusing finger at any of them, and so implies that it was not Ehrenburg, with whom she remained friends till the end. And by all accounts during the Khrushchev era Ehrenburg used his position to help others – writers, artists, and ordinary people, by pulling strings and giving advice. One of the them was my friend Anne, when she went to Russia – but that is another story.

All through the years following the Hungarian uprising French intellectuals cut their losses and left the Party, or were expelled. Only Aragon and Elsa Triolet remained unrepentant, yet they, better than anyone, knew what was happening in Russia: they travelled there frequently as VIPs, and they were sometimes petitioned by writers. Once Aragon told a friend: 'In Elsa's family alone nine people have disappeared.' Yet when I read that he had died, in 1981, I could not help feeling sad: it was like watching a boat on which I had once sailed sink into the sea on the horizon, carrying down its cargo of idealism, hope and youth.

Many of Aragon's poems were put to music and recorded by various singers, male and female – I too sing some of them, and the following lines are from one I have recorded:

> Nothing is given to man, neither his strength, nor his weakness,
>   nor his heart
> And when he opens his arms to life, his shadow is that of the Cross
> And when he hugs his happiness, he crushes it
> There is no love that is a happy love . . .

When asked who he believed was the greatest French poet of all time, André Gide replied: 'Victor Hugo – *hélas!*' The saying has become famous, and much paraphrased. If asked who was the greatest poet of that generation, one could answer 'Aragon, *hélas!*' For in the end poetry is indestructible, and long after the poet, weak and perhaps guilty of 'treason-of-the-clerks' has gone, the poem remains, pure and noble.

19

Gems and Stones

Le Poëte est semblable au prince des nuées
Qui hante la tempête et se rit de l'archer;
Exilé sur le sol au milieu des huées,
Ses ailes de géant l'empêchent de marcher
CHARLES BAUDELAIRE

One of the offshoots of the National Committee of Writers was the Group of Young Poets, whose patron was Elsa Triolet. She clearly enjoyed the adulation of the young men – for they were mostly young men who swarmed around her and her husband, and of course she had her favourites. Like any social group, the Young Poets' Group generated gossip – not all of it malicious – and partisanship. There were heated arguments as to who was 'better', whose poems were worthier, etc. The instructions came from Aragon, whose mastery of poetic form gave one vertigo: from the humorous free-verse of his Dadaist and Surrealist periods in the 20s and 30s, through his patriotic war and love poems, to his Communist effusions in Hugo-esque alexandrines, his poetry covered the gamut of verse forms with the ease of an ice-skater varying patterns. I remember Anne, Gilles, and several others arguing about the latest *consigne* – order – from Aragon: that there was nothing wrong with alexandrines, which we had been shunning for being monotonous, rigid – Paul Claudel had said: 'It is like watching telegraph poles appearing at regular intervals through a train window.' Suddenly everyone tried to write rhymed verse in classical metres – even Anne produced a sonnet in alexandrines which I can still recall.

Some of the young poets found their way into print, mostly in short-lived, small-circulation magazines that blazed and died like sparklers in a fairground. A few had a *plaquette* (thin booklet) published by Pierre Seghers, a publisher who specialized in poetry, and who had started life as a poet – when his poetic vein dwindled he had discovered a talent for business, and started a poetry publishing press. As he was extremely courteous and charming, and knew all the poets of his generation, he had no difficulty in securing the best writers for his firm. Soon he was successful enough to branch out into anthologies, illustrated books, poets' biographies . . . and before long was one of the most prestigious publishers in the country. To have a selection of poems, however small, published by Seghers was considered 'the consecration', the start of a literary career, and his *plaquettes* included volumes by Aragon, Éluard, René Char, as well as by beginners. Few of the hundreds of young poets who were published in the collection continued writing beyond a certain age, but that was to be expected, and did not diminish their value.

Having published poems in various magazines and a small book, Anne was beginning to gain a reputation. But everyone longed to be published, and there were not enough opportunities. Finally Gilles, Anne and a couple of their friends decided to bring out their own magazine in which to publish poems they liked, away from the dogmas and caprices of the pundits. They produced a manifesto and a charter, and received manuscripts galore, encouragement and moral support from famous poets – everything except the vital ingredient which would turn the project into reality: money. But who cared? Somehow it would be found! Everybody chipped in: Gilles' salary as a part-time teacher, Christophe's small grant as an apprentice radio producer, Yves' pocket money from his meagre Ph.D. allowance – even Anne produced something, hard-up as she was. Then Gilles took care of the practicalities, and found young printers and typesetters who gave their services free or at reduced prices, and the first issue came out, with a black-and-white cover of an abstract design (by Christophe), incorporating the name:

163

Gem. It contained thirty pages packed with passionate opinions, poems, articles, film and art reviews.

By the time I came into the picture three issues of *Gem* had appeared and Gilles was at the end of his tether. All hundred copies of each had been sold, mostly to friends and older bene-factors, but the proceeds had barely covered half the costs, and everybody's resources were depleted. Nonetheless Anne asked me to join the editorial board and come to its meetings, which took place in the café Boule d'Or, on the boulevard Saint-Michel. We would sit there all evening with just one cup of coffee each, and no one protested. How such cafés made any money I cannot think! Seeing papers and manuscripts spread over the little round tables, and hearing snippets of text as he went past, the waiter assumed we were writers and left us alone. I myself did not smoke, to protect my voice, but everybody else did, often heavily, and the air was dense with almost palpable grey fumes, like undulating veils. I had met Gilles and Christ-ophe before, at the National Committee of Writers' events and liked them: Gilles reminded me of a famous photograph of Rimbaud: blond, wavy hair, a tanned skin, and a wiry, very thin body. At the time he had a mulatto girl-friend (we thought: like Baudelaire!), and was deeply involved with African art and writing profusely about it, making pronouncements such as 'European Art will become Black or cease to exist!' He never produced his girl-friend at our meetings, wishing to be strictly professional, so in my imagination she was like Baudelaire's description of *his* mistress: dusky, voluptuous, colourful, languorously beautiful . . . Then one day I bumped into her, walking arm in arm with Gilles – a tiny mouse, barely coloured, with fuzzy hair straightened into a pony-tail, and huge teeth in a permanent good-natured smile. In due course she disap-peared, and Gilles married a pretty red-haired sound-engineer with whom he has lived happily since. But his involvement with African Art has remained, and he knows more about it than many professionals, like one of those amateurs on tele-vision quiz-shows who win all the prizes.

At one of our meetings Anne read a story I had written, which she liked. I can't remember what it was about – I discarded everything I wrote in early youth, or lost it through frequent moving – but it took place at the Flower Carnival in Nice, which I had never visited, though a boy from the South had described it, and the idea of a festival devoted to flowers appealed to me. To my amazement everyone else liked it, and it was accepted for publication in the fifth issue of *Gem*, the fourth having gone to press already.

I was wild with excitement: I had written it without any expectations, and it would be my first writing in French to be published – perhaps later I would dare to offer poetry, and songs too? But after its fourth issue *Gem* ceased to appear, having got into unrescuably heavy debt. So my story was never published. Anne was disappointed, as she had high hopes about the venture. It was then that she resolved to leave France, though it took some time before she did.

Taking advantage of Sergei's Russian origin, and despairing of ever finding somewhere to live, Anne and Sergei had decided to emigrate to the Soviet Union, and had applied for a visa several years before I met them. At first they had been told it would take at least six months; then after a year had passed and nothing had happened, they went to the Soviet Embassy and enquired, whereupon they were given more forms to fill in, asked more questions, sent more documents to sign, and told to wait. Every few months they went back to the Embassy and returned empty-handed. Years passed, during which Stalin died, Khrushchev came to power (and ushered in the thaw with his 20th Congress Report denouncing Stalin's 'Cult of Personality'), and things began to change in Russia.

Anne and Sergei more or less gave up on the Soviet Embassy and began yet another bout of house-hunting. They were promised a flat in a new dormitory suburb being built near Paris – another year or so and they would be settled. But such promises were slow to materialize, and one day Anne discovered that she was pregnant. Abortion was then a crime in France, she did not have the money to go to Switzerland, and the illegal back-street alternative was expensive and dangerous; besides, she wanted a second child.

Her mother poured a stream of lewd insults upon her, Anne responded with torrents of tears, and Sergei went back to the Soviet Embassy, explained their situation and demanded a yes-or-no answer. A secretary took pity on his plight and promised to pursue matters personally and let him know very soon. 'Very soon' lasted another six months, enough time for Anne's baby to be born – a little girl called Natasha. Then a letter summoned Sergei to the Soviet Embassy, and to his amazement he was presented with apologies for the delays – due to the 'old bureaucracy' – informed that their visas had arrived and that they could leave as soon as they wished: once in Moscow they would be taken in charge by the Soviet Government and presumably be given lodgings, jobs . . . Sergei rushed home with the good news, resigned from his job, packed his case, and left to hitch-hike to Moscow. Anne and the children would follow later by train, and his mother would join them once they had settled down.

I remember going to see Anne and her children off at the station. No one else had come to say goodbye, and I helped her find her compartment and an empty seat by the window. She had a good deal of luggage and the children were restless – how could she ever manage for three days and nights on her own? But Anne was far too apprehensive about the future in general to worry over such immediate practicalities. I made reassuring noises: Moscow was an exotic city, part-Asiatic and part-European, with a French colony, radio programmes and publications in French – surely she would find a far more interesting job than slaving away eight hours a day in an office. She was one of the Three Sisters whose wish had come true! We clung together tearfully, with promises of writing frequently and my visiting them once they were settled, perhaps the following summer . . . A whistle blew, doors were slammed, and the train pulled away laboriously. I stood and waved until Anne's head disappeared in the distance. On the way back to the Cité Universitaire I cried: my 'big sister' had gone – would I ever see her and Sergei again? It would be years, and perhaps we would have grown apart. Every departure touched a sore point, reminding me of my own from home in Persia, and foretelling those of the future with which I felt my life would be strewn. For I already knew that you can never go back, except in imagination, and that once you pull down that fragile, carefully wrought shelter in which humans keep loneliness and the fear of death at bay, you can never completely reconstruct it. Some part of the defence gets lost, and perpetual movement becomes a person's only escape. Pascal said that all man's troubles stem from a single cause – his inability to stay quietly in a room. But perhaps it is the other way round: that man's restlessness stems from the reality of his predicament – lost in 'the immensity of these infinite spaces' – what if they were empty of God after all?

A letter did arrive in due course, in which Anne told of her difficult journey. The three-day train ride had been exhausting: after initial excitement, the children had been uncomfortable and frequently sick; they had run out of provisions and water, and desperately short of money, she had not dared spend too much on food or the comfort of a couchette. The nightmare had been rendered bearable by the kindness of other passengers, who had shared their food and water, and taken turns with the children, allowing Anne to sleep – and all despite scarcely any verbal communication, since Anne did not speak any Eastern European language, nor they any French.

She and Sergei had agreed to look out for each other at various stops along the line, if he made it in time – hitch-hiking being unpredictable – so whenever they approached a major town Anne prayed that he would be there, but she was disappointed again and again, until she had almost given up hope. Then suddenly there he had been, on the platform in Prague, anxiously surveying the coaches as the train slowed to a standstill. The rest of the journey had been less fraught, and once in

Moscow they had been put into a hotel at the government's expense. It was an exciting, bewildering city, but she felt terribly homesick. I wrote back, giving news of mutual friends whom I continued to see, especially Gilles, who had 'adopted me' and become a caring friend, almost a brother – for we often fought, as siblings do without affection being impaired, mostly over mutual accusations of having our heads in the clouds (and *my* feet too). Then one day I received a letter from Anne saying she and Sergei were leaving Moscow, and that she would write again once they reached their destination. Two months later came a letter from Tashkent – Uzbekistan! To me the name was familiar, like those of Tibilisi, Dushanbeh, and the other capitals of Soviet Central Asian republics, for at school I had read how all those former provinces of the Persian Empire had been lost to Russia, in a series of wars at the end of the eighteenth and the beginning of the nineteenth century. I remembered discussing with teachers individual events of those wars, the intrigues and betrayals, mistakes and accidents, cowardices and heroisms that, as in all wars, had determined the final outcome of the contest – and had reduced Persia to its present size and humbled its people.

Then there were the literary and musical connections – for as so often, it was the spirit of the conquered that in the end triumphed: Lermontov, Tolstoy, Chekhov, Mussorgsky, Glinka . . . For them those remote mountainous regions were the Romantic *'ailleurs'*, the fount of inspiration, the loci of adventure and romance – indeed the essence of much that we now think of as fundamentally Russian. I wrote to Anne, excited that she was in my native world of 'Persia', and told her that now I would definitely come and visit them as soon as I could find the fare.

But that time never came. A year later Gilles married and went to work on a magazine in Marseilles. Christophe passed his exam and became a radio-producer in a provincial town – and eventually I left Paris too, married and settled in London. Then one day a letter came with Anne's familiar handwriting:

she was back in the attic at her mother's house in Gardennes, pending a move to a promised apartment in a new suburb, exactly as before she had left. She had returned to France sometime earlier, but had been so beset with problems of readjustment, housing, work and her children, that she had not been able to persevere in tracking down her friends, though she had looked. Finally she had found Gilles' address and through him mine. I telephoned her at once, but it was another year before I saw her, and then she told me about her odyssey.

Once in Moscow Anne and Sergei had been summoned to some office to be told that there was no question of them staying there – the city was so overcrowded that even Muscovites were being encouraged to leave, with promises of better jobs and homes elsewhere. The choice for them was between Siberia and Uzbekistan. *Siberia*! By then we knew all about the concentration camps, the connotations were too disturbing to be reasoned away, and they had chosen Tashkent. There they had been given an apartment, the children had been welcomed at the local crèche and nursery school respectively, and Anne had been snapped up by the university to teach French Literature, while Sergei was allocated an engineering job. Soon his mother had joined them, and given a small flat of her own and an old age pension.

It looked as though everything they had lacked in Paris was being provided for them, and that thenceforward their lives would run on an even keel. But it was not to be: Anne was not the stuff exiles are made of, she was firmly rooted in French soil, and cut off from her roots soon began to wilt. Perhaps in Moscow she might have managed, but in a Central Asian provincial town, among people whose language she did not understand, she was desperate. She had found cultural life rich, both in Tashkent and Moscow – Russian intellectuals were 'unblasé' and enthusiastic, and still belonged in the pre-Revolution tradition of broad, European culture, and many spoke English or French, read widely, played music, attended poetry readings and queued long hours for ballet tickets. But she missed France, and she pined for Paris inconsolably, despite the hardships with which her life had been fraught.

Her problems were compounded by her inability to learn Russian: 'I have no talent for languages, and that is that!' she decided. Like the Three Sisters, she constantly dreamed of Moscow – as a first step back to France. Far from blaming her for her lack of enthusiasm, her neighbours, new friends, and university colleagues expressed understanding of her plight. They offered to help her in every way – with money, the children, leave from her job. One day she felt so unhappy that she took the plane to Moscow and went straight to the French Embassy asking to be repatriated. Of course France would take them back immediately, but it was not as easy as it seemed. Her husband and children were now Soviet citizens and would have to apply for an emigration visa, which might take years. What to do? She was in despair!

Then she hit upon a bright idea: she would try to see Ilya Ehrenburg! She wrote mentioning their meeting at the National Committee of Writers, enclosed a copy of her volume of poems, explained her position, and was given an appointment by return. 'Why didn't you ask my advice before leaving? You can't uproot a tree when it is fully grown, and exile is a terrible thing, even in the best circumstances. I would have told you not to come!' Anne described Ehrenburg's large, luxurious and bright apartment, its walls covered with pictures by his Western artist friends Picasso, Léger, Marquet . . . his bookcases full of 'forbidden' European literature, which as a privileged author he could possess with impunity. Was it fear of exile or of losing all that comfort that made him choose survival above honour? At any rate he did not seem happy 'in his skin' – he was old and bitter, and tried to make amends by helping people; helping them to gather the remnants of their lives together, influencing the Writers Union to have certain suppressed books published. Perhaps it had been he who had secured the posthumous publication of Mandelstam's poems, hence Nadezhda's benevolence towards him? We shall never know: they have all gone with their secrets, and we survivors cannot sit in judgement on them. But that meeting remained vivid in Anne's mind: 'He was chain-smoking Gauloises, of which I had been deprived since I left Paris. I would have given anything for even a puff! He never offered me one!'

But he did offer her help: she should stay in Moscow for a while, put up by friends. He found her a job with Radio Moscow's French programme, and introduced her to *Moscow News*, a French newspaper for which she wrote articles and reviews. From what he said she gathered that had she gone to Russia under Stalin, she would most likely have been sent straight to Siberia as a spy. Now things were improving: Khrushchev allowed a measure of freedom to writers and intellectuals, to support his campaign against Stalinism; even the dreaded Writers Union had been forced to sanction the publication of works they had previously condemned: Solzhenitsyn's first novel, Nadazhda Mandelstam's memoirs, Akhmatova's poems, etc . . . It was a good time to be in Moscow – better than any for fifty years.

But Anne wanted Paris – at any price. So she pursued her request for repatriation, all the while going back and forth to Uzbekistan, teaching, writing, trying desperately to learn a little Russian. Finally after two years visas came for her and the children, but not for Sergei, because he was of Russian origin. And indeed he was much less unhappy than her in Russia, spoke the language well, and felt attached to the country and its people; or perhaps, having been an alien in France he was temperamentally better suited to exile.

So Anne decided to fight for him from Paris, though it proved so difficult that at times she despaired of ever seeing him again: 'I wept myself to sleep every night,' she told me. 'I even feared he might meet another woman and settle down with her.' It was only the personal intervention of Georges Pompidou, then President de Gaulle's Prime Minister, during Khrushchev's visit to France that finally secured Sergei's exit visa. It was lucky, for after Khrushchev Russia froze again for eighteen years under Brezhniev, dissidents were often dealt with harshly – sent to labour camps or psychiatric 'hospitals' – and frontiers were closed to all except 'official' intellectuals.

Anne's ordeals were not over even after her return to France. Back in her attic with two children, she worked eight hours a day in an office and freelanced as poet and reviewer. And as if her personal troubles were not enough, she was harassed by the French police, who interrogated her and kept her under surveillance. Yet looking back, she recounted her adventures to me as if she felt grateful for them. She had been helped by ordinary people as well as by officials in a way she had never known in France, her own country. Her stories tallied with my own impressions of travels in Eastern Europe – of the way in which Russians, Poles, Czechs coped with the harshness of their lives by personal acts of kindness. Less 'advanced', they had not yet traded innocence for cynicism, trust for suspicion, love for sophistication, generosity for monetary gain. They countered their bureaucracies' corruption and opportunism by individual probity and idealism.

Sergei's mother chose to stay in Russia, but her exile was not over: she pined for her native Moscow, and Tashkent was as far from it as Paris. Still, after thirty years of wandering she had a home.

I see Anne whenever I go to Paris. She has published several volumes of poetry and still writes children's stories and art reviews. Her son and daughter have grown up and left home, and Sergei is as gentle and innocent as ever. They are getting on, as I am, but when we reminisce or joke about the past, the burden of time lifts, and we know that our hearts are as full as all those years ago.

20

Autumn Leaves

Longtemps, longtemps, après que les poètes ont disparu,
Leurs chansons courent encore dans les rues . . .
CHARLES TRENET

When radio came to Persia one of the first people to acquire a
set was my mother's eldest brother, Uncle Alem, a well-known
lawyer fascinated by all things Western. It was one of those
large pre-war models in the shape of a bell-jar with a circular
speaker in the middle. At first our Nanny was sure that there
was a genie inside the box, who produced the sounds and
voices. When we explained to her how it worked she threw her
arms in the air, rolled her eyes to heaven, and exclaimed 'God
is Great!' – for creating Man so fiendishly clever. As I grew
older, newer designs came on the market, and soon my uncle's
anthropomorphic set gave way to a neater model. Whenever I
went to his house to visit my grandmother and aunt who lived
with him, I spent hours listening to music on it, as none was
available in our house. Finally my mother did buy a set – after
I had left Persia – but I noticed on a visit home that it was
switched on only at noon, to hear the Muezzin's call to prayer
followed by the recitation of a saying by the Prophet or Imam
Ali, his son-in-law and the Patron Saint of the Sufis. Otherwise
it sat silent and forlorn in its niche.

There were many musical programmes on the radio: Persian
traditional music with the best singers and instrumentalists,
Western classical music played on records imported from the
West and presented by an expert, and light music, which

173

included songs by American singers such as Frank Sinatra and Bing Crosby, French *chansons* by Tino Rossi and Danielle Darrieux, and above all by Umm Kolthum, an Egyptian star of sentimental tear-jerking musicals with happy endings, which were shown in down-town cinemas. She sang her lovesongs in a deep, dark voice, whose mellow tone was like that of a Stradivarius cello, and conveyed the whole spectrum of love's fluctuations, from its first stirrings to its final dissolution. Although she sang in a foreign language you understood it all, such was her intensity and pathos. She had her Persian counterparts, women with powerful, tellurian voices, who recounted the intricacies of emotional entanglements with exquisite trills and dazzling arabesques of sound, in classical modal forms. Listening to these singers lamenting the loss of a love gave their audiences a respite from their own sorrows.

Radio was beginning also to bring regional music and folksongs to a wider public. The first to make the songs of his native dialect widely popular was a singer from the Caspian region, said to be a Communist, who rapidly came into vogue among Leftist intellectuals, followed by a chorus that sang folksongs from the different regions, collected and harmonized by an Armenian teacher from the newly founded Teheran Conservatoire.

I loved these folksongs for their simple words and curvaceous melodies, and the French *chansons* because of the beautiful sound of the French language as well as the voices of the singers. Not knowing either our northern dialect or French, I learnt them parrot-fashion and sang them at school and parties ('provided no one knows', my mother would caution, because of the sinful repute of female singers). I had begun singing at nursery-school, where I had first experienced frowns of disapproval and threats of punishment that miraculously changed into smiles of approval and affection. Singing had become a shield, an act of propitiation and a pleasure, a part of me that was eventually taken for granted. As I grew up I was forbidden to sing in public, lest it tainted my 'reputation', so I only sang in private, among friends. But by the time I left Persia I had a substantial repertoire of songs in Persian, and in various other languages none of which I knew.

Those French singers of my childhood survived in Persia often long after they had retired and vanished from the scene in France, because their records were often played on the radio. Once in Paris, I found that the new idols were Juliette Gréco, Yves Montand, Jacques Brel, Léo Ferré, Georges Brassens . . . singers who carried forward a tradition that went back to the Middle Ages and the troubadours. France's great poets, from the thirteenth-century Rutebeuf through fifteenth-century Villon and the sixteenth-century *Pléiade* poets Ronsard and Du Bellay, right through to contemporaries such as Louis Aragon and Jacques Prévert, had written *chansons*: some, like Villon and Ronsard, had sung them themselves, but their tunes were lost, and now others put their words to music. To me the *chanson* seemed a unique expression of French genius, similar to the miniature in Persia, or flower-arrangement in Japan, it was part of the texture of life for all classes, and not just something limited to youth. Even a philosopher like Jean-Paul Sartre had written a song for Juliette Greco (as it happens not a very good one), and Antoine Roquentin, the protagonist of *La Nausée*, finds existence bearable only when he hears the voice of a black singer on record: Art redeems the absurdity of Life. (Edith Piaf, though a legendary figure, to us belonged not merely to a previous generation but to a different concept.)

But beautiful songs have been produced by people all over the world – not least in these islands, where Scottish, Irish and English songs revealed their richness in the folk-revival of the 60s. Singing is so natural a medium of expression that from the earliest times humans have been moved to sing their joys and sorrows, hopes and despairs, fear and defiance. At its best a song satisfies two elemental human needs, for poetry and music, and blends them together into a new entity that is immediate, compact, quintessential. It puts us in touch with our common human heritage: 'You are not alone,' say the Irish fisherman's ballad, the partisan's lament, the soldiers' morale-boosting march, the lullaby and the lovesong. And so the best songs survive and become 'evergreens', 'classics', even when their authors are forgotten. The separation between 'serious poetry' and song is a recent phenomenon, as if you 'catch' pop and rock as a teenager, like pimples or mumps, and grow out of them at twenty-one! But I loved songs and still do, and find a beautiful voice singing a beautiful song one of the great, simple pleasures of life.

'Les Feuilles Mortes' – 'Autumn Leaves' – written by Jacques Prévert with music by Joseph Cosma, was one of the most popular post-war *chansons* in France. Their collaboration produced many 'classic' songs, but none so universally popular. It was memorably recorded both by Juliette Gréco and Yves Montand, and by hundreds of singers all over the world in dozens of languages, including such *recherché* tongues as Hottentot and three Cameroonese dialects – so the poet told me later. Some versions, like that in English, had nothing whatever to do with the original words, but the song was still a hit, and the tune was played as Musak in airports, hotel lobbies, lifts, supermarkets and department stores, and is still in the repertoire of canned music everywhere. I too sang 'Autumn Leaves', but never dreamed that one day I would meet its author.

Like most poets of his generation, Jacques Prévert had been part of the Surrealist movement led by André Breton. But in the thirties the group had disintegrated as a result of ideological and temperamental differences, following endless acrimonious arguments and verbal fencing. The Communists, such as Aragon and Eluard, followed the Party line, while Jacques Prévert and his group, the 'Prévert Band', went their own way. They met at the Café Flore, while André Breton held court at the next-door café, Les Deux Magots. These groups were scattered even before the war, and afterwards everyone (except for the Aragons and their followers, who still formed a coherent group) went in a different direction. In the end what remained of Surrealism in poetry was a new freedom of expression, a primacy of imagination and fantasy, and in the case of Prévert a blend of pathos and humour, levity and depth, order and anarchy, which, together with his personal generosity and goodness, endeared him to everybody. His language was simple, his prosody varied, his humour logical yet zany, his epigrams instantly memorable. I have never heard anyone express anything but affection for him, but then he was invariably generous and tolerant in his assessment of others, an unusual trait in those days of ideological strife.

His book *Paroles* contained some of his most famous poems, including those put to music by Joseph Cosma that had become long-running hits. Part of it was translated into Persian, which I had read. Now in Paris I read the songs and poems again in French, and learnt many of them. Some were simple narratives which poked fun at pompous figures of authority, political and clerical, but the flavour of these had disappeared in translation, which could not cope with the rhymes and word-play.

If the symbiosis of Prévert and Cosma had produced many of the most beautiful *chansons*, the collaboration of Prévert with Marcel Carné resulted in several remarkable films, made in the 30s and 40s, which are among the classics of cinema, including above all *Les Enfants du Paradis*, which is shown regularly in art cinemas everywhere, and is rediscovered by each new generation. In Paris it was shown every year at one or other of the cinemas of the *quartier* which specialized in classics. In those days students of all nationalities and creeds seemed to share in two passions, politics and films. It cost the equivalent of one or two new francs to see a movie at the Cinémathèque (national film theatre) which was then in the heart of the district. There were three programmes each evening, showing three different films, and after each programme the auditorium was cleared and the attendants checked the tickets for although they were cheap, the cost of tickets added up and dented our tight budgets, and many of us cheated. We would buy one ticket and contrive to stay on for all three films through a series of stratagems and tricks – hiding under the wooden seats, passing tickets to each other surreptitiously, getting in behind the back of the attendant while she/he was being chatted up by one of us – usually of the opposite sex – and other undergraduate pranks. Strict adherence to morality did not come naturally to us, especially since we believed that most rules were designed to protect property, (and as Proudhon wrote 'property is theft'). I knew a student who systematically purloined all the books he wanted, under the vigilant eyes of the bookshop attendants – he was easily the most widely-read among us. Today all those cinema-stowaways and book-shoplifters are law-abiding citizens; morality grew on us as contact with reality made us realize that every society needs rules.

My first visit to the cinema was with my maternal uncle, when I was ten or eleven, to see *Conquest*, with Greta Garbo and Charles Boyer. Though made before the war, it reached Persia years later, and was thereafter shown periodically, its stars being popular and its romantic story much to the taste of the public. I instantly fell in love with both Charles Boyer and with the cinema, weeping profusely at the plight of the star-crossed lovers. Nor was I the only one so affected: more than any other single factor the cinema changed the attitudes of the educated classes in Persia, and in particular the relationship between men and women, and women's awareness of their position in society.

But in Paris cinema was an art form – perhaps *the* art form of our time, as it could express through one image what a thousand words could not convey. Georges Sadoul, who knew 'everything' about the subject and even ran an arts degree course on Filmology at the Sorbonne, was one of the greatest authorities on the subject. His course had ceased before my time, but I read his huge tome, *History of the Cinema*, his reviews in the Left-wing press. We all regularly read *Les Cahiers du Cinéma*, an avant-garde film magazine started by Eric Rohmer in 1954 around a contributing nucleus of young iconoclastic aficionados, critics and would-be directors, including Jean-Luc Godard, François Truffaut, Alain Resnais, Claude Chabrol. In time they became so influential in shaping public taste that by the end of the decade they had all made feature films, and were indeed acclaimed directors: *Breathless*, *Hiroshima, mon Amour*, *Les Quatre Cents Coups* were as popular with critics as with the public, while the stars they launched formed new constellations in the firmament of cinema.

For a whole year I went to the Cinémathèque with my friends, and covered the landmarks of film history from the brothers Lumière to the contemporary masters. Afterwards it was not difficult to keep up with the good new films. Even today going to the cinema and seeing a good film is as thrilling to me as in those far-off afternoons and evenings, sitting on hard-on-the bottom wooden chairs in the makeshift auditorium. Sometimes the Cinémathèque would show uncut versions of classic films, even their rushes: I sat with a friend through hours of Eisenstein's rushes of the *Battleship Potemkin* and of *Viva Mexico* – sometimes ten or more takes of the same shot – learning how great masters worked, what meticulous editing had gone into the final product. Similarly I saw all the Prévert–Carné films several times. Prévert's dialogues were pure poetry, his songs lyrical gems, and I learnt them through seeing his films over and over again.

Disillusioned by Aragon and Ehrenburg, I never tried to meet Prévert, lest he too differed from the image I had formed through his poems and songs. Several other well-known writers had made it clear that they were not interested in my brains or my political and artistic opinions, only in the potential I offered for exotic sexual adventure: perhaps it was a romantic dream to think an artist might embody his art? Unconsciously I decided that I liked my idols safely dead.

Time passed. Then a friend told me that he had seen an enchanting exhibition of Prévert's collages at a gallery near-by in Saint-Germain-des-Prés. I knew some of these through reproduction, and thought them just like his poems – original, fanciful, humorously irreverent. Many Surrealists, including Breton, had produced remarkable collages, but few had the humour and inventiveness of Prévert's. As it was only an hour before closing time on the last day of the exhibition, I immediately went to see it.

The small airy gallery was nearly empty, with just a few young people moving slowly around, looking at the pictures. At the far end the secretary, sitting at her desk, was talking to a white-haired man who was pointing out something to her in a book. I moved around looking at the pictures, and gradually became absorbed in their fairy-tale world, where winged horses flew over chimneys, ships raced through the clouds towards a full moon, a corpulent priest became the statue of Boboli, enchanted woods revealed their fauna through the trees.

'You are very beautiful – who are you?'

Turning, I saw standing beside me the white-haired man who had been speaking with the secretary a little while before.

'I am Jacques Prévert,' he added. I recognized him from his photographs, but his face was older than in them, and more worn – a face that reflected a life lived fully and enjoyably, but certainly not abstemiously. Heavy eyelids drooped over his pale-blue eyes, his chubby cheeks sagged down towards his chin-line, and his complexion was sallow. He was nearly sixty, which when you are twenty seems ancient. He held a cigarette between an index and middle finger, brownish-yellow from years of smoking – he had a reputation for chain-smoking and periodic drinking, though not for womanizing. This was indeed remarkable as he had discovered and launched beautiful actresses, such as Anouk Aimée, and possessed an irresistible charm.

'I am delighted to meet you – I sing your songs!' I said, blushing and astonished. We were such a long way from the bell-jar wireless in Persia that had first brought them to me.

'I can hear them in your voice. Come and sing them to me.' And he wrote his address and telephone number on a piece of paper. I hesitated to ring for a couple of weeks, thinking that he would not remember me, or be too busy to see me, but when I eventually did he recognized my voice at once:

'*Alors!* Where have you been . . . ?' and asked me to go and see him at his home the next afternoon. It was to be the first of many visits, for our friendship lasted until his death, of lung cancer, in 1974, though as I was living in England, and married with small children, I did not see him often in the later years. But my encounter with him is one of the '*brillants soleils*' of my youth, and of my memory – he became a father-figure to whom I could turn in moments of desperation, and tell everything, sure of understanding, sound advice, and affection.

Less than two years after our meeting I left Paris, but that period was the most adventurous of my Parisian life; it was largely due to Prévert that I found various jobs which enabled me to survive while deciding whether to return home to Persia or settle down in Europe. And it was through Prévert that I made my first record.

21

Persian Love Songs

I was a green tree in the forest,
They cut me down with an axe of pain
So that fire burns in my head forever
PERSIAN FOLKSONG

Many of our idolized post-war singer-songwriters (or poet-singers as they are called in French), such as Jacques Brel and George Brassens, accompanied themselves on the guitar in preference to the piano. It gave them more mobility, and seemed more in tune with their romantic image as latter-day Troubadours. By the time I heard them they had already moved up from the tiny clubs of the Left-Bank to large concert halls, and were backed by orchestras; but I have a photograph of Brel sitting on a stool with his guitar at *l'Echelle de Jacob*, a little club in rue Jacob, where he had started his career in the early 50s. I sang a cappella, or with a piano accompaniment by whoever was around. But everybody was taking up the guitar, or learning to play enough chords and picks to accompany a song, so I decided to learn also, to be independent.

Near the Benedictines' Foyer was the Schola Cantorum, in its heyday an important music centre, which since the war had lost some of its prestige as most of its well-known teachers had died or moved on. But it still had good young musicians, so there I went and enquired about guitar teachers. To my surprise I was given the name and telephone number of Ida Presti, a young classical guitarist who had been famous as a prodigy and solo performer since her teens. A few years before my encounter with her she had teamed up with a Spanish guitarist,

Alexander Lagoya (they were now married), to perform duets, and posters for their concerts regularly appeared on publicity pillars and walls all over Paris, showing photographs of a perfect couple – young, beautiful and talented.

That evening I queued with friends for hours to hear Segovia at the Wagram Hall, the smaller of Paris's two main concert halls. His shyness hidden behind thick glasses, he shambled shyly on to the stage, as if embarrassed by the rapturous welcome of the packed house, then bending over his instrument he played as if it were part of his very body. We were sitting in the cheapest area, at the back of the balcony, but we could hear and see him well, mesmerized by the nimble movements of his hands as they plucked and caressed the strings, producing at times an orchestral sound, as if several instruments were playing in harmony, while at other times he picked single notes and hung them in the air like candles, quivering to their dying fall. I can't recall how many encores we made him play, but each time he came back and bowed gently, sat down and played, as though he would go on forever if we insisted.

A few days later Presti and Lagoya were playing at the same hall, and again we queued and sat at the back. They were received with as much enthusiasm, and laced their repertoire with many of their own compositions, as well as their transpositions for the guitar of pieces written originally for other instruments. The next day I rang Presti up, and met her later at the Schola Cantorum. Petite, dark-haired and very pretty, she immediately put me at ease by laughing at my turning up for a lesson without an instrument: 'Let's go and buy you a guitar first,' she said. I told her that I had only about 10 pounds – all that was left of the proceeds of some English lessons I had given to an America-bound Greek at the Cité Universitaire.

'That won't get you far!' she warned, 'but we'll see what we can do'. I sang her a song and off we went to a little guitar shop she knew by Place Mouffetard, whose owner was a musician and a friend of hers. He was not in the shop, but his assistant, evidently thrilled by the star's impromptu visit, brought out several instruments which Ida tried. The ones she liked invariably turned out to be expensive. I was beginning to despair, when the assistant suddenly remembered that they had just acquired very cheaply a hand-made guitar from a Spanish student who needed money quickly to go back to Spain. As soon as Ida picked it up and began to play I knew it was the one for me, not only on account of its price, but because it was small and light, and had a deep, mellow tone like that of a cello: 'This is just right for your voice,' she said, to my delight. I took out all my fortune and gave the assistant the ten pounds, promising to return with another seven Francs for the dilapidated case as soon as I could. From his smile it was obvious that he expected us to forget about the extra money the minute Ida and I walked out of the shop.

After some rudimentary lessons with Ida I knew enough chords and runs to practise by myself and make up simple accompaniments for my songs. That guitar has been with me through the years, often neglected, at times even forgotten, but always there when needed, like a faithful friend. Several times it has been damaged during travel, once so badly that I thought I had lost it forever. But a repairer worked on it for a month, sticking the shreds of wood together like broken limbs, until it looked and sounded as if nothing had happened to it.

Ida Presti died tragically young, from a fatal illness. The day I met Jacqueline Rolland at the Conservatoire I remembered her, for as I waited in the hall I looked in the glass windows where the set-pieces for the examinations in various instruments were announced, and for the guitar saw that there were several Ida Presti compositions. Jacqueline told me that in her short career Ida had been a prolific and original composer, and had enriched the repertoire with her own works as well as those written jointly with her husband or transposed from other instruments.

That afternoon when I first went to see Jacques Prévert, I took my guitar. He lived above the Moulin Rouge, in a little cobble-stoned alley by Place Clichy, appropriately called Cité Véron

– one of the vintage Prévert–Carné films is a contemporary *Romeo and Juliet* called *The Lovers of Verona*. Jacques opened the door dressed in grey trousers and a pale blue pullover – the shade of his eyes – soaked cigarette butt at the corner of his mouth, which he took out to greet me and once inside used to start up another cigarette. He led me to his study, a large light room opening on to a flat terrace. From it you could see the motionless red sails of the Moulin Rouge silhouetted against the grey wintry sky – a familiar landmark in pictures and posters, home of the Folies Bergère, and associated with such artists as Toulouse-Lautrec, and now almost close enough to touch.

A long refectory table stood in the middle of the study, covered with papers, drawing pads, bouquets of coloured pens and pencils in glass vases, objects and artefacts . . . The walls were adorned with pictures, drawings, collages, postcards; and on another table near the partition wall were a stack of records, and a record-player. A grey cat lay beside it in a pool of light, lifted its head and miaowed disdainfully, as if only reluctantly accepting my presence: 'If she doesn't like a record, she jumps on it and scratches it,' said Jacques. 'Luckily we usually share the same taste.'

He showed me some of his coloured drawings, and auto-graphed a few copies of his books for me, with pictures and words. Then I took up my guitar and sang him one of his songs – not 'Autumn Leaves' or any of his famous hits recorded by countless professional singers, but one of his poems that Cosma had put to music, and which had been sung in his films, 'Night Visitors'. Set in the Middle Ages, it is an allegory of France under German occupation, which somehow miraculously had escaped the censor:

The tender and dangerous face of Love
Appeared to me one night after a very long day
It was perhaps an archer with his bow,
Or a musician with his harp,

I can't remember . . . all I know is that it wounded me;
Was it with an arrow? Or was it with a song?
All I know is that it touched me and wounded me to the heart, and
   for ever:
The burning, searing wound of Love . . .

'Beautiful, isn't it, Janine?' Behind me a small, frail woman stood in the door, smoking – Jacques' wife Janine. Then a blond, rosy-cheeked, chubby little girl of about ten or twelve appeared, carrying the cat which had left its sunny perch unnoticed. 'This is Minette,' said Jacques and introduced me. 'I'm glad you accompany yourself with the guitar rather than the piano, which I think is like a tank – you can't carry it around with you.'

We all sat down to a cup of coffee prepared by Jeanine and talked. It was obvious that Jacques adored his daughter, and that he spoilt her, while Janine was quiet and anxious. I wondered what troubled her, since they seemed a harmonious family, but in those days many people of their age looked like this, having been through the war and the occupation, and not yet quite adjusted to the new era of relative ease and prosperity. The Préverts then asked me to sing a Persian song, and I chose an old folk melody, 'The Water-Pipe', and told them how even the simplest Persian popular quatrains were imbued with the whole tradition of mystic poetry, and indeed used the same metaphors.

They asked for more, and finally Jacques said: 'I have an idea! A friend of my brother Pierrot has a record company – we must introduce you to him. Perhaps he would make a record of your Persian folksongs. It would be unique, and a good start for you.' (Pierre Prévert, a year or so younger than his brother, was a film-maker, and had founded 'The Fountain of Four Seasons', a club famous after the war and in the early fifties.) Jacques then immediately rang him up, wrote down the telephone number of the record company's director, telephoned him and spoke about me in flattering terms, and made an appointment for me to see him the next day.

186

I was reminded of my father pulling strings in Persia – 'fixing people' as my mother called it – with the same unfussy efficiency, for there nothing ever happened without such a personal push. But I did not expect it from a stranger in Europe, where democratic institutions were supposed to have dispensed with nepotism – or so I thought. Later in life, experience showed me that generous men and women everywhere help others whenever they can; that indeed 'the kindness of strangers' is a human trait which redeems many less laudable characteristics.

At any rate it seemed that Prévert had decided to adopt me as a protégée, and thereafter I often went to see him, though never as often as I wanted, fearing that I had nothing to give him and that I would be wasting his time. Now that I am older I regret this, for I realize what a pleasure it is to have young friends, to share their enthusiasms and hopes, how gratifying it is to help them if they need it, and how much one learns from them, if only through remembering one's own youth.

The record company to which Jacques and Pierre Prévert introduced me was B.A.M. (the initials of La Boîte-à-Musique – The Music Box), in boulevard Raspail, on the corner of a cross-street. You could see its sign, hung above its entrance, from every direction, and when you entered you found yourself in a long medium-sized warehouse, its walls covered with record-shelves, its spaces filled with cardboard boxes and packaging for records to be packed and despatched by two young men. The office at the far end consisted just of a large desk strewn with papers and files and telephones. A tiny cubicle on one side provided an enclosed private space for Madame Lévi-Alvarez, while half way up the shop at another desk, almost hidden behind boxes, sat the owner's aged mother, who took care of the book-keeping – a tall, imposing figure, extremely *soignée* on account of an 'invisible net' protecting her elaborate hair-do from the vagaries of the wind, which you only noticed if you got close to her

The company had a reputation for excellence incommensurate with its size, and regularly won the music industry's highest prizes for its remarkable recordings of classical and folk music by renowned interpreters. Long before any other record company, B.A.M saw the commercial and artistic potential of folk music and began to produce and market ethnic songs and instrumental pieces from all over the world, including France itself. One prize-winning artist, Jacques Douai, had collected songs from various regions of France and sang them accompanied by the guitar, modelling himself on the troubadours of the past, dressing appropriately in white shirts and black velvet trousers, and singing with such feeling in a mellifluous tenor voice that he soon won a large following and became France's top folk singer. Later others followed his example, uncovering a rich seam of long-forgotten French music.

While Madame Lévi-Alvarez managed the finances and the personnel side of the business, her husband André was in charge of the artistic side. This was just as well: he was intelligent, sensitive, and very gentle, yet you had the impression that financial considerations were not his strength, and that he could easily embark on ventures that would get the company into trouble. His family was Jewish, originally from Spain, but that was a long time ago and little beside his aristocratic allure, hyphenated name and cosmopolitan taste remained of his Sephardic background. His wife by contrast was forceful, down-to-earth, and everyone, not excluding her husband and mother-in-law, was a little afraid of her. By turns she was fearsome enough to keep the employees on their toes, protective of her husband, and charming to artists. Always dressed elegantly, she wore more make-up than was usual in those days, and was followed everywhere by a lingering trail of strong, spicy scent.

I arrived one afternoon just before closing time. André and I talked about Persian music and poetry until the two employees had left, and then he asked me to sing some of the songs I wanted to record. They both seemed to like my renditions, and suggested that we meet the following week, by which time he would have contacted a Spanish classical guitarist whom he felt sure would provide the best instrumental accompaniment for me.

In the meantime he suggested we should go and hear a couple of American folk-singers whom he had recorded at the Abbaye, a tiny club in Saint-Germain-des-Prés, by the church. It was packed with a cosmopolitan crowd, mostly Anglo-Saxons judging by the language, who sat on stools at round tables. Presently two male singers appeared – one black, tall, hand-some and deep-voiced, and the other white, small, with a thin, high-pitched voice that was clearly not meant for singing. Both played the guitar, and together they had arranged some agree-able harmonies for voice and instrument. Because the club was small, after each song the audience clicked their fingers instead of applauding, creating a serious and almost reverential atmos-phere, though perhaps this was due as much to the novelty of the offering. This was the beginning of the folk revival which was so marked in the 60s, but in fact started in the late 50s. After the show we went to congratulate the two performers, and they signed a copy of their record for me, which I still have. Some of their songs were recorded by Joan Baez at the same time, on her first record in 1957, but I had not yet heard that.

The accompanist chosen for me was F. Fernandez-Lavie, a Spanish exile who taught classical guitar at a music school and at the Conservatoire. I worked with him for a whole week, arranging simple accompaniments for the Persian songs we had selected, until we were ready to go with André Lévi-Alvarez to a huge sound studio and record the songs. Some time later I signed a contract that was put in front of me. I had never expected any payment, so eager was I to have the songs on record, and when Lévi-Alvarez mentioned the sumptuous sum of 30,000 franc (£30). I thought that *I* had to pay it! I felt tears welling up in my eyes. 'Oh dear! I'm afraid I haven't got it!' He reassured me that he meant I would be *receiving* the sum, and hoped that I would find it fair.

I was so thrilled to receive my first 'professional' cheque that

I immediately invited friends to dinner, bought some flowers for Prévert, and a pair of shoes and material for a dress for myself. I even felt guilty at being paid for doing something I enjoyed! After all, I had not gone down a mine, or made fifty beds in a hotel – I had just stood up and sung for pleasure and love. And that feeling remained with me even when I worked in much tougher conditions in the 70s and 80s. I remember once touring England with Brian Patten, he reading his poems and I singing my songs, when every evening before the show, I would panic, suffering agonies of stage-fright and uncertainty as to the audience's reception. Brian was placid and reassuring: 'Remember you are going to sing for your supper!' And I thought it was also my children's supper and my two musicians', but still it did not seem like 'work', which to me is something unpleasant done reluctantly.

I never read through that contract, being incapable of understanding such documents and implicitly trusting Lévi-Alvarez. But years later when I did the same, signing up with a major multinational record company, I was accused of madness by my musicians: they told me that artists never ventured into the shark-infested waters of the 'music-business' without an armada of lawyers, managers, and other 'minders'. Yet over the years the only contracts on which I have been swindled have been those arranged by managers and vetted by lawyers!

That first record of 'Persian Love-Songs' was considered for a major prize and became something of a classic, or so I was told by the Lévi-Alvarezes, who kept it in their catalogue till the demise of their company many years later. Among the songs was 'The Water-Pipe' that I had sung to Jacques Prévert, a quatrain which had been sung to me many years earlier by my old nanny, and whose tune I had forgotten and had to rearrange from memory.

I have only one copy of that first record, which I keep in a box containing memorabilia. I looked at it the other day to remind myself of my accompanist's name, which I had forgotten, though I remember vividly the rehearsal sessions, his kindness and patience, and the true artist's humility with which he tackled a hitherto unknown music. Over the years whenever I went to Paris I would call in at the Boîte-à-Musique to say hello to the Lévi-Alvarezes, until one day the old lady was not there any more – she had died the winter before. André Lévi-Alvarez contracted Parkinson's Disease and his capable wife took over the business, although he continued to sit at his usual desk, his hands trembling, his sallow forehead perspiring. Finally one day he was not there, and eventually their Music Box disappeared.

All those visits to Prévert are jumbled in my memory, though individual images, words and incidents remain vivid. For example, how that first day Jacques played me a record of Ella Fitzgerald singing Cole Porter songs, and said: 'I learnt English from her!' and gave it to me to take home and play. I learnt all the songs on it, but it was over a decade before I recorded two of them. Another time he asked me if it was true that Persian carpets were made by little girls aged five to fifteen, and said indignantly: 'I don't care about art; I want children to be happy.' We had then argued whether art was worth the suffering that it often entailed, and he thought not – his own art was joyous, hopeful, compassionate, and as far as he knew had hurt no one. Once he told me that years earlier he had gone to a party on the second floor of a tall building. He had drunk a little too much wine, and sitting on a window-sill for a breath of fresh air he had leaned back and fallen out on to the pavement below: 'I would have been killed sober, drunk I didn't have a scratch!' Years later an incident occurred which I have never been able to fathom: one day I dialled the number of a friend in Paris, but instead of her voice I heard Jacques' – which I recognized at once. He said he was in Normandy, where he had a country house, and that he was not well – in fact he was in the grip of terminal cancer. Whether he himself knew it or not I never learnt, but it was in character that he should not wish to alarm me. Although telephone lines do sometimes get crossed, it was a chance in a million that I would dial a number in Paris and get through to Normandy, and stumble upon him, and it seemed somewhat spooky in view of his death soon after: perhaps fate wanted me to hear his voice once more before it became silent forever.

I read his obituaries in the press and wept, bitterly regretting that I had not been to see him more often, nor made any record of our talks – his jokes, epigrams, comments. But at twenty you don't believe that memory weakens, that time smoothes away even feelings whose intensity seems to engrave them on your soul, or that you can forget the names and faces of those you love deeply. Then I recalled Jean Cocteau's saying: 'Poets don't die, they only pretend to.' They live on in their poems, songs, voices, and today it is not just Jacques' songs that 'whirl in the streets', but his stories and anecdotes too, which have become part of his legend. One day for example he had came across a blind beggar sitting on the pavement in a town in the South of France, his hat in front of him on the ground to receive coins, and a placard saying: Blind Man Without a Pension.

'How is it going?' asks Prévert.

'Oh, very badly. People just pass by and drop nothing in my hat, the swine!' replied the beggar.

'Listen, let me turn your placard round and I guarantee you a fortune.'

A few days later he sees the blind beggar again, and asks how he is faring:

'Fantastic! My hat fills up three times a day.'

On the back of his placard Prévert had scribbled: 'Spring is coming, but I shan't see it.'

He was the epitome of an authentic artist at one with his art, setting an example as hard to achieve as it is rare to encounter. I sing many of his songs, and sometimes in a public place I hear a line of 'Autumn Leaves':

Mais la vie sépare ceux qui s'aiment . . . 'Life separates those who love one another . . .'

192

22

The House of Tania

C'est au théâtre qu'on trouve la vérité
ALBERT CAMUS

Western theatre had arrived in Persia partly through my
father's younger brother, Uncle Emad, who had translated,
produced and directed Molière's *The Hypochondriac*, using his
innumerable children and domestic staff as actors. My mother
took me to see it, and the excitement and fascination have
remained vivid, although I was much too young to remember
the occasion in detail. Later I acted in school plays, perhaps
because I could sing and the shows invariably contained songs.
I enjoyed these diversions and relished the popularity they
produced among my teachers and classmates.

At the *lycée* I was one of the prime movers of theatrical events
and usually the main actress as well. Then someone informed
my mother, by way of unsolicited compliments, of what I was
doing, and I was ordered to stop: if she heard about it, then
others might also, and what would happen to my 'good name'?
I pleaded and cried and promised discretion, but it was no use:
her interdict was irrevocable and I had to comply.

In Paris I was free to see as many plays as I wished, at the
reduced prices given to students, and it was a time when the
theatre was flourishing: Sartre, Camus, Anouilh, and a host of
others were writing important and original plays using traditional forms, while Ionesco, Beckett, Adamov, and their
younger followers were changing the very language of drama,

and creating new forms, including what has since been called the Theatre of the Absurd. Again, others like Albert Roussel and Marcel Aymé were nourishing the *boulevard* theatre with clever comedies and farce. Beside this rich home-grown crop there was an abundance of foreign plays: English, Spanish, Russian, German . . . both classical and contemporary. Private investors helped by government subsidies provided the financial backing for productions, but above all the impetus came from personal enthusiasm and initiative. And every year there was a season of world theatre to which famous companies from other countries were invited: Laurence Olivier and Vivien Leigh brought Shakespeare from Britain, Brecht's Berliner Ensemble played Brecht, The Moscow Arts Theatre Chekhov. We queued for hours, pulled strings to gain tickets and saw everything we could.

Our Mecca was the Théâtre Nationale Populaire or TNP, on the Right Bank. It was created in the early 50s as the third National Theatre in Paris – the others being the two theatres of the Comédie Française on either side of the Seine – and was subsidised by the state. Le Français, founded by Moliere in the seventeenth century, represented traditional theatre and was largely devoted to the classical repertoire. It was connected to the Conservatoire, from whence it replenished its garrison of actors, whose acting style, with its emphasis on technique, verse declamation and stylized gestures, guaranteed continuity. But we the young believed that the whole institution was 'bourgeois' and 'old-fashioned', whereas by contrast the TNP was progressive and innovative, conceived to appeal to those sections of the public who would not habitually go to the theatre. Accordingly tickets were cheap, and concessions were made to students and groups from factories and work-places. The auditorium was like a concert hall – you could see and hear perfectly wherever you sat – and the programmes contained the texts of the plays and photographs of the company in rehearsal.

The TNP owed its success largely to the energy, enthusiasm, and organizational talents of its first director, whose brain-child it had been, Jean Vilar. He had started life as a jobbing actor without any apparent outstanding assets, developed into an actor-manager of genius, and become one of the most influential and celebrated personalities in post-war French theatre through sheer steely will-power and dedication. He was small, thin and wiry, with a face that would melt in a crowd and an ordinary voice. Yet once on the stage he commanded respect and attention by his extraordinary presence and the intensity of his acting: you had no difficulty believing that this plain man was indeed Don Juan, capable of stealing the heart of any woman, or that this tiny Henry V could indeed win battles against all odds.

Vilar combined managerial and financial know-how with artistic acumen, and personal charm with total commitment to his vocation. Actors are well-known for their devotion to their profession, but Vilar seemed more driven than most. He so inspired other actors with his faith and idealism that several of France's top film stars relinquished the vast fees they commanded to join the TNP where salaries were minimal – among them such popular idols as Gérard Philipe and Jeanne Moreau, and the tragedian Maria Casarès. As a result his was the finest company, and some of his productions among the most memorable of the decade.

Similarly he secured contributions from artists in other fields who had not been connected previously with the theatre. Famous writers were moved to give him new translations and adaptations of foreign classics, renowned painters and sculptors designed his décors and costumes, and distinguished composers wrote original scores for his productions, all for little material benefit.

One such artist was the American sculptor Alexander Calder, whose colourful mobiles and stabiles provided the set for some of TNP's contemporary plays. Calder was already celebrated in America when his one-man show at the Museum of Modern Art in Paris made him the object of a cult in France, while his décors for the TNP spread his reputation further afield to a wider public. Not being able to afford genuine Calder mobiles, everybody picked up his idea and began to make his or her own version: Sergei had produced one for Anne which hung from the ceiling above their bed, Gilles had made a few with coloured cards.

The plays Calder had designed were before my time, but in their texts, which I bought, there were photographs of him: a huge, white-haired teddy-bear in scarlet shirt and baggy jeans dwarfed by his sculptures, or in the company of the actors laughing and drinking wine, exuding geniality. I was told that he now lived and worked half the year in a village in the Loire Valley.

'He is a great friend,' said Jacques Prévert, when I mentioned him. 'He lives near Tours, in a little village called Saché; if ever you are in the area, call on him.'

I never did, and when I moved to England I thought I never would. But one day my husband wrote an article about him in an art magazine, as a result of which we all met and became close friends. Thereafter I often took my two small sons to stay with him and his wife Louisa in summer. He had converted an old farmhouse in a copse near an arm of the river Loire, with a studio opposite. The road, then a quiet country lane, meandered between the two. Inside, the house was filled with objects and utensils he had made from tins and wires and pottery, transforming materials ordinarily discarded into orig- inal works of art. The stone floors were covered with colourful rugs made to his designs, with moons and stars and moths and birds, floating happily in space. Everything he devised conveyed an affirmation of life's sanctity in all its manifestations, a pan- theistic joie-de-vivre. He worked like a child, inventing as he went along, yet his patterns were subtle and sometimes sophisti- cated, and often conveyed mathematically precise relationships.

Later in life he designed and built a larger house and a huge studio on high ground amid and overlooking rolling fields and vineyards, where friends and admirers from all over the world came to see him, and where he welcomed with the same warm hospitality the village carpenter or stone-mason who worked on his house as his neighbour Max Ernst, or Arthur Miller and Marilyn Monroe, his neighbours in Connecticut.

Today, more than a decade after Calder's death, Saché is marked with his presence. In the middle of the village square, named after Calder, stands one of his huge mobiles, flashing in the sun. In the mediaeval church on one corner of the square a tapestry and a plaque commemorate his art and contribution to the community's life, the little local café opposite sells post-cards of his house and studio – now given to the Beaux Arts for the benefit of sculptors who live and work there for a year – and tourists stop their cars to ask the way to them. Not far from the square is Saché château, where Balzac used to spend long periods. From the window of the room where he wrote *Le Lys dans la Vallée* the view stretches over the lush valley with the munificent river Indre meandering through it, and up to the high ground where you can see Calder's huge mobiles and stabiles – colour dots on a green patchwork.

Although, by the late 1950s, in Persia economic and political changes were escalating, especially with regards to women, it was still inconceivable that I would be able to appear on the stage there. But I would be free to produce and direct, or work for the newly established television – so I decided I should learn some of the necessary skills, while 'lingering' in Paris.

Apart from the Conservatoire, there were several reputable drama schools or 'courses' in Paris, which provided the training for most young actors and actresses, and which were also win-dow-cases where film and theatre directors looked for new talent. Many of the younger generation of celebrated actors came from the school run by Tania Balachova, a Russian émigrée who had come to Paris with her parents after the Revolution of 1917, and who was now considered one of the greatest dramatic actresses and teachers of her generation. Russian émigrées had considerably influenced French theatre between the wars: their ideas were new and had brought a breath of fresh air into the stuffiness of conventional French dramatics. Tania Balachova's teachings were basically Stanislavsky's, although her method was more eclectic than the 'Method', made fashionable in America through the Actors' Studio and its golden pupils, Marilyn Monroe and Marlon Brando. She emphasized the authenticity of feelings and emotions, but not at the expense of clarity of diction and solidity of technique. Nonetheless she was controversial, and provoked extreme reactions: for her students and admirers she was an exemplar and they adored her, while others – usually those who had not experienced her charm – criticized her for encouraging introversion and morbidity in her actors and pupils.

How had she risen to such prominent professional heights with so many handicaps, not as a character-actress, but playing leads, parts written for and usually played by beautiful women? Her own story was a remarkable example of the triumph of human will over fate. At the age of ten she had suffered an illness that had resulted in a complete loss of hair, including eyebrows and eyelashes. Her Jewish mother and aristocratic father had despaired that she would ever marry, or be able to do anything except work in an office, or as a governess. Instead she chose a glamorous profession, in which it was difficult to succeed even if you had all the required assets.

How had she risen to such prominent professional heights with so many handicaps, not as a character-actress, but playing leads, parts written for and usually played by beautiful women? She took advantage of her disadvantages to enhance her appearance: the wigs she wore framed her lovely bone-structure and fine complexion better than her own hair would have done, the long black false eyelashes shaded her deep blue eyes with a soulful expression, her pencil-thin painted eyebrows were drawn at exactly the right angle, and altogether she looked ravishing: 'She looks like Greta Garbo,' they said of her. And the resemblance in her photos was indeed striking. She was tall and statuesque, moved regally, and had a mesmerizing presence which, together with her low, expressive voice made her the focus of attention as soon as she entered the stage.

The stage is the chalice of illusions, and the stratagems she had used are after all part of the actor's tools, but what of her private life? It had been equally remarkable: three famous husbands and a score of lovers had loved her passionately and been broken-hearted when she had 'moved on'. In later years her men were considerably younger than herself, and her male students were all secretly in love with her. Now in her sixties she wore a suitable grey wig, a small hat with a voilette, and elegant but subdued clothes. She had a boyfriend, but he did not appear, except rarely to collect her at the end of the day. How could she fail to be an inspiration and a role-model for her female students?

Gilles suggested that I follow her drama course, as he knew and admired her and thought that being Russian she would be closer to me. He himself sometimes attended her classes and offered to take me with him. The course took place twice a week in a dark, cavernous storage hall behind a café, off Place Mouffetard, in the Latin Quarter. You entered through a little door with a tattered velvet curtain protecting against the light of late-comers entering. A bluish cloud hung in the air, compounded of cigarette smoke and stagnant air. There were some fifty or sixty chairs arranged in rows and a makeshift stage at the far end, two spotlights, and a black backcloth.

That first day a young couple were presenting a scene from Chekhov's comedy, *The Bear*. Occasionally they were interrupted by Tania (everyone called her by her first name), who enquired, explained, corrected, and guided them back, before they were allowed to resume and play till the end of the scene. Afterwards lights came on, she turned round and called another name.

You prepared a scene from a play and auditioned. If Tania liked you and believed in your potential, she accepted you. Otherwise she would find some excuse – that she had already too many people – but without brutality, and recommending some alternative. With the robust memory and eagerness of youth I had learnt many poems, scenes from plays, and even passages from novels by heart. Yet when Tania asked me 'What do you have for us?' all I dared do was a couple of poems by

Baudelaire. It was a long time since I had been on a stage at school, and I was frightened, though I managed to conceal it. The stage is the natural home of a performer, providing the 'roots' and the sense of belonging that artists in general and 'rootless' artists in particular lack. Tania seemed pleased, for she asked me what I wanted to do and assigned Jocelyn, an ex-pupil who was now a professional actor, to work with me to present the scene the following week. Many of Tania's former students would occasionally attend classes long after they had become famous, as if drawn by nostalgia, or simply to see her and her new 'stable', or to limber up.

How did Tania manage her finances? She had a friend, an old retired actress, who appeared from time to time and collected the fees from the students, but as far as I remember only those who could afford it paid, and Tania did not seem to mind at all. She herself spent all she had earned on theatrical ventures: putting on plays no one else wished to finance, appearing in 'fringe' productions because she liked the plays or the directors, backing her protégés in their débuts as producers and actors. The cinema was a good source of income for actors who subsidised their meager earnings from the stage with films and television work, but Tania was terrified of it and had always refused offers that others would have accepted with alacrity. Her life was entirely devoted to the theatre; in its loftiest form, so that she hardly ever appeared in money-spinning commercial or *boulevard* plays.

Tania lived the authentic *vie de bohème* at a time when artists were beginning to expect and receive decent material rewards for their work. She had no home and no possessions, and although she was shrewd and had an acute economic sense when it came to producing a play, she herself exhibited a queenly disdain for money which harked back to the Romantics. For years she had lived in a little none-too-glamorous hotel in the popular district of Batignolles, on the Right Bank. On the corner of her street was a café where she spent all her time when she was not working, and where she played bridge – her second passion after the theatre – sometimes till the small hours. As the café was also a bistro, she took her meals there as well. When she was working, the café nearest her rehearsal rooms, classes, or theatre became her headquarters. She was approachable, but her courtesy ensured a reasonable distance even from her closest friends and associates. She never addressed anyone in the second-person singular: no one was *tu*, everyone was *vous*. Only once did I hear her use the intimate form: when her lover, a handsome younger middle-aged man came to join her in the café next to her hotel: '*Ah! C'est toi!*' she said, with the blushing seductiveness and enthusiasm of a young girl at her first meeting with a potential suitor.

Similarly nobody ever saw her room. Only once did I visit her at her hotel: I was married and living in London, but I was passing through Paris and rang her up. Being in bed with a cold she suggested that I call on her. Had I not been out of her professional life I am sure she would not have received me there, preferring to maintain the barrier of illusion. High up on the sixth floor, her room was small, with a window overlooking the street covered in lace curtains that had gone grey with age. Overflowing with clothes, toiletry, wig-dummies, hats, it was a cross between an actress's dressing-room and a gypsy's caravan. A worn screen with pink panels partially hid the hand-basin and a little gas-stove with two burners near the window, and in the bed she was lost beneath a profusion of colourful cushions. Without her usual props – her head was covered in a scarf, her eyelashes were removed – she looked old and frail. I sat on a chair by her bed and talked about life in England. 'Never mind your foreign accent, English theatre is the best in the world – get into it,' she advised me. 'I am sure your husband is as wonderful as you say, but you never know about men – when they love you they are saints, but when they stop loving you they become cruel beasts. You must have something to fall back on. Singing, acting, writing – keep up everything you can do, just in case.'

Not the desire to be different, but the outsider's reluctance to trespass on another's territory, the fear of inviting unfavourable comparison, has always impelled me to choose 'the path less trodden'. So instead of a scene from a play, for that first appearance before Tania I adapted a dialogue from a favourite seventeenth-century novel: Madame de Lafayette's *La Princesse de Clèves*. It is a love story in which the heroine's own sense of duty and moral rectitude stands in the way of her fulfilment. It rang an atavistic bell – even though I had ostensibly rejected my puritanical upbringing – and I wept profusely as I learnt the part.

'Imagine weeping like this every night for a year!' said Jocelyn. 'You must learn to harness your emotions with technique, and use them at will.' That was, and still is, beyond my power, as was making long-term plans, such as what I would do if and when I returned home. I was on leave from reality – *en sursis*, as they said of soldiers – and never planned beyond the day.

Encouraged by Tania and my fellow students I was soon absorbed in what Camus called 'the great fraternity of the theatre'. So for the next year or so, until I left Paris, I was immersed in a new world, made new friends, had fresh and unusual experiences. It was a short period that coloured the rest of life, shed a harsh light on dark, shadowy areas of the human soul that I had not wished to probe before, and shattered the few illusions I still naively clung to. It opened new vistas on reality which would have otherwise remained closed – for you never get to know a society so well as when it gives you your daily bread.

23

Characters in Search of an Author

We are such stuff as dreams are made on
SHAKESPEARE

I liked the company of my new friends: actors were an interesting brood – sensitive, instinctive and generous. It seemed to me that the professional jealousy and rivalry which exists in all professions was superseded by their love of the theatre. It was only when someone undeserving or unsuitable was cast in a role for reasons other than talent that they unleashed merciless venom. And then what a demolition job they did!

Perhaps because my own life was always 'temporary', 'moving on', I was less committed than my fellow apprentices, so that I could never fully understand the ruthlessness of their condemnations.

Helped by Tania I worked on plays with my friends, and presented them in the tiny backroom which was our school. Drama was a new world, a new territory to explore, and I read the classic and modern repertoire. If sooner or later I went back home, I thought I would translate certain plays into Persian and stage them, or from English into French; and inevitably certain authors became favourites: Racine, Chekhov, Lorca . . .

The Russia that Chekhov depicted was exactly my childhood Persia, his characters members of my own family, their predicaments the same, while Lorca's passionate, oppressive Andalusia was painfully reminiscent of the interdict-ridden society I had escaped from, his poetic language full of Persian speech patterns. But like so many adolescents what engaged my mind and soul completely was tragedy.

'There is no need for blood and corpses, so long as the story is noble, the characters heroic, passions are aroused, and everywhere we sense that Majestic Sadness which is the essence of Tragedy,' wrote Racine, and his own plays supremely expressed the truth of this. It was no accident that all his 'heroes' were women, incarnations of that 'Majestic Sadness' of Tragedy by their very condition, and their destinies – prey of the capricious gods, particularly Venus: *C'est Vénus tout entière à sa proie attachée*, says Phèdre, abandoning herself to an illicit and fatal passion for her step-son Hippolyte. I learnt all these great tragedies, and still remember whole sections by heart, while I cannot recall familiar names or the events of yesterday!

Cocooned in this cosy, hopeful new milieu of young thespians, I lived day by day, stalling my parents' enquiries about when I would be returning home. I was quite happy, though had no money to live on. But the young somehow survive through kindness and chance: Gilles found me some translation work for the radio; Prévert sent me to a friend for a small part in a film about contemporary youth – I worked for a week and ended up on the cutting room floor, but earned enough money for a couple of months.

Then in a street market I found a black-and-white striped jersey and bought a length to make a dress. I had never done any sewing, so the result was a tight shift utterly at variance with the contemporary fashion for full-flowing skirts. It had sleeve-seams coming half-way down the arms, and the rolled collar turned into a hood.

'You look like a zebra colt!' said a young man in the street as I was rushing to catch the Métro. 'Hang on one second for a photo!' People were always approaching young girls on the Boul' Mich' and in Saint-Germain-des-Prés, asking them to pose for photos, offering them bogus film contracts and modelling jobs. We were warned against such strangers, usually sinister middle-aged men with shifty eyes, and ran from them a mile. But this was a fellow student – I had noticed him in the Cité Universitaire where I lived . . . *Snap, snap*! . . . He said he would show me the pictures if I called on him at the International House – wasn't that a ploy too? I never did. But a while later I bumped into him near his House, and he ran upstairs to his room and brought down a large photo, which I still have. He said he had already sold it to a magazine, that he was sure it was going to start a whole new vogue for tight short clothes, and that if I would give him a proper session he would try to get me modelling work.

I had several friends who were models in couture houses – Balmain, Balenciago, Dior. They worked from nine to five while clothes were created on them by the master couturiers. It was hard, boring, unremunerative work and culminated on the cat walk at the beginning of the season. The big money was made only by the freelance photographic models whose faces you saw in fashion magazines – usually very tall and thin American girls flown in from New York – whereas I was only five foot four, a midget in comparison with the Anglo-Saxon girls. Nevertheless I did get a few modelling jobs through friends, and many more later on in England. I have kept some of the photos, but names and occasions are all jumbled in my memory, or lost.

One day I had my guitar with me and sang a few songs for Tania and my comrades: 'You are mad not to sing in a *boîte*!' said Tania, and suggested that I go and see André Schlesser, whose club L'Ecluse was one the best on the Left Bank. He was a minor actor with the TNP, playing mostly the singer-guitar-player when this was called for, but he was a clever impresario. Frequented by intellectuals, his club had the highest artistic reputation, and had launched many a famous comedian and singer, including Barbara, who was then little known but soon became a star. Several of the TNP actors would come straight to L'Ecluse after the theatre and present comedy and satirical sketches, while Schlesser himself compèred the show.

With an introduction from Tania I went to see him and sang for him. Inundated as they were with requests for auditions and 'spots', people in his position often put up a barrier of hardness. But he was unexpectedly warm and gentle – he liked my songs, especially the Persian folk songs, because they were 'unusual and exotic', and said that although his club was devoted to French poetry and song I could have a spot there with a few Persian, English and French folksongs. He suggested that I go and see him immediately after the summer break, as he was booked up for the next six months. I agreed to go back nearer the time, happy to have something to fall back on – but I could not begin to think so far ahead.

In fact I next saw him nearly twenty years later, when he came to London with a show in which he dressed up as a troubadour and sang a few folksongs between sketches. It turned out that the director of the show had started his career at L'Ecluse, and was now in a position to pay back Schlesser's kindness by devising a small part for him in their tour. I saw him after the show and surprisingly he remembered me: 'You never came back to sing at L'Ecluse, did you? I wondered why, then I heard that you had left Paris.' We sat in a corner and reminisced. Old acquaintances had died or retired, others had continued their rise in the theatre firmament, while yet others, such as Philippe Noiret (who had had a 'comedy turn' at L'Ecluse) had abandoned the theatre in favour of cinema, and were now international stars. L'Ecluse itself was no more, for after years of struggle against rock 'n' roll he had finally conceded defeat: 'Now it is all discos and ten-thousand-crowd gigs.' He himself was married, very happily, to the Spanish-born actress Maria Casarès, but aside from small assignments such as the current one, did not work much – he was content to look after his marvellous companion. Both their lives had been so fraught with stormy relationships and tragedy – his as a Jew in occupied France and hers as a Spanish refugee after the Civil War – that their union was a haven of friendship, a homecoming after a long and hazardous voyage. He gave me their address and asked me to call on them when next in Paris, and later I received a postcard from him. But he died shortly after, and with him went the legend of L'Ecluse, so many of whose gold sparks grew into twinkling stars. Maria Casarès has continued her exemplary career and is one of the *grand dames* of the French theatre.

I was soon among Tania's protégés, and adored her like a mother. I felt that I could tell her everything, that her understanding and tolerance were based on her own vast experience and intense sufferings. 'You know that whatever hell you may be going through she has traversed many times before,' Joceylyn said of her. As I had no money she waived her fee, and often invited me to join her when she and some of her more prosperous pupils went for lunch after class to a nearby café-bistro, knowing that food was an irregular affair with me, way down my list of priorities.

Sometimes one or two of her old students who were now famous came to see her. Then the star-studded meal would go on for hours, with heated debates about current shows and other topics. The greatest arguments centred round the comparison between the merits of Brecht's theories of 'Alienation', and Stanislavsky's 'Method' upon which Tania based her teaching, and which was self-evidently highly successful, since a large number of the best actors on the French stage had been trained by her and evinced her influence. Tania had seen the Berliner Ensemble, and admired some of its actors, especially Brecht's wife Helen Wegel in *Mother Courage*, a role she could have played herself, and she maintained that they were the living proof that theory was irrelevant to an actor's work, which had to do with the creating of a character, complete with a life-story, a body and a soul. 'The truth of character comes from within, not from theory,' she would say.

I had returned to Tania's drama course after the summer holidays, and had plunged immediately into new plays with renewed enthusiasm. Then one day she told me that she was going to play Bernarda in Lorca's *The House of Bernarda Alba*, and that she would arrange for me to audition, as the play had an all-female cast and many small parts. She said that the most suitable for me would have been that of Adela, Bernarda's youngest daughter who runs away with a lover and kills herself at the end of the play (a part I had once played for her and knew by heart). Sadly that part was out of the question, being taken in advance by an actress whose husband was putting up money for the production. Whatever my part, it would be good experience for me, and earn me enough money to live on for a while if the play became a success and ran a long time.

I loved Lorca's works – indeed, just to read his poetry I would later learn Spanish – and of all his plays *The House of Bernarda Alba*, based on the true story of a family he knew in his native Granada, is considered the most substantial and accomplished. In addition, this tale – of a tyrannical widow who keeps her five daughters incarcerated at home and turns them into frustrated spinsters, culminating inexorably in a tragic dénouement – had always had for me a special significance: for it reminded me of a similar family I had known in Persia, except that the tyrant of the Persian family had been the father, an ignorant fanatical mullah who demonstrated his religious zeal to his congregation (on whose tithes he depended for his living) by locking up and brutalizing his wife and five daughters.

His poor wife had died young, but for his girls there was no escape: 'I don't like marrying my daughters,' he would say to anyone who approached him for their hands. The eldest, deciding that she had missed the boat herself, helped three of her younger sisters to run off with husbands that they found with the help of local marriage-brokers. Sadly it was out-of-the-frying-pan-into-the-fire for them, as their husbands proved almost worse than the father, but at least they had children to love, and some measure of material fulfilment. As for the youngest sister – she contracted meningitis and went stone deaf, and no effort to find her a man bore fruit. My mother knew them, and the two spinsters occasionally came to visit us, especially at religious ceremonies; and although their lives had been ruined in the name of religion, they were devout, and did not even blame their father for destroying their hopes. Indeed in old age he had become gentle and loving, and the two spinsters had responded by looking after him devotedly. It was the married three who resented him, blaming him for turning down their respectable suitors and thereby forcing them into marriages 'beneath their station'. 'You explain the vagaries of the human heart,' our wise Aunt Ashraf would sigh, telling their story; 'the ones who have homes and children and money curse the old man, the ones who have nothing give him their blessings.' Years later, after he died, the youngest, deaf daughter would visit his grave every Sabbath eve, to distribute alms and pray for the salvation of his soul. 'He certainly needs it!' we used to say.

The common complaint among actresses is that while their number in the profession by far exceeds that of men, there are very few female parts in plays, ancient or modern. So when the word got round that *Bernarda* was being cast, the whole of Paris applied for audition: recommendations, string-pullings, supplication and gentle coercion inundated the director, Jean-Baptiste Dellor. The applicants were sorted out and their number reduced to four times the available parts – and then these were seen by the director and the two lead actresses, Tania Balachova and Diane Blaire.

The backstage area where we waited was full of actresses none of whom I knew. Smoke from cigarettes hung in the air; everyone was tense but friendly, some volunteered introductions, others wished each other good luck as they were called in. You could hear snippets of dialogue wafting from the stage, followed by a hush before the stage-manager came in to fetch the next person. I remember thinking that the place was like a cross between a brothel and an abattoir! Luckily I was with

Elena, a classmate whose parents were Russian émigrés and who was also a protégée of Tania's.

'Imagine doing this all your life!' she said. 'That's why I want to produce my own shows, so that if I want a part, I can just cast myself!' And indeed she became a well-known and respected 'fringe' actress/manager.

I was paralysed by stage-fright and would have just bolted had I not thought that I would be letting Tania down. Finally my turn came, and I followed the stage-manager like a sacrificial lamb to the stage. The auditorium was empty and dark, and you could just discern a few heads in the penumbra of the stalls seats. To exorcise panic I took off my high-heeled shoes and bent down to put them in a corner, accidently showing my underwear. This produced hilarity in the 'audience' and reduced the tension. 'Go ahead,' said a male voice and with shaking legs and pounding heart I did 'my bit': the nocturnal confrontation between Adela, Bernarda's rebellious youngest daughter, and her crippled jealous sister.

'Thank you. Next,' said the same voice from the orchestra, and my ordeal was over. Everyone in the waiting-room was solicitous and smiling, and when the last auditionee had finished the director came in: 'You, you, you . . .', he pointed to the selected few. 'The rest, sorry, next time!' Amazingly I was one of three out of several dozens to be retained. At first I was elated at the thought of the fantastic experience ahead, of being on the Paris stage and having some income – and relieved that I could postpone deciding to go home or not for a while. Then I felt guilty about those who had been rejected, every one of whom was better and more experienced than I.

I was to play the young maid who had been seduced by Bernarda's dead husband and left with a child, and at the same time to understudy Adela and the two youngest of her four sisters. Tania was pleased with me, as only two of her protégées ended up in the cast.

On the first day of rehearsals everyone met everyone else and everyone was charming to everyone – it was only later that venom built up, behind her back, against the leading lady, Diane Blaire. She had been picked as a teenager by a film director, and had starred in a movie that had since become a minor classic. She had married a rich industrialist by whom she had two children, and they lived in a sumptuous apartment off the Champs-Elysées, with starch-aproned maids, a chauffeur and an English nanny. How different from the rest of us, who belonged to the various echelons of Bohemia, and lived in make-shift homes that ranged from Tania's little hotel to small flats on the Left Bank.

Diane Blaire was tall, blonde, elegant and soignée. She spoke with a clear voice and measured her words carefully. There was nothing whatever primitive, passionate, or Andalusian about her, and she was totally miscast in the role of Adela – indeed she was in the wrong play altogether. But she longed to play the part, and her husband had made it the *sine qua non* of his financial backing. The director had struggled hard to find alternative funds, but had not succeeded, and rather than aban-don the project, had decided to go ahead and do his best to make Diane fit into Adela. But she remained an outsider, and must have noticed that there was something blatantly false in most of her colleagues' stiff amiability. The play was a success, but she did not enjoy the experience. Once Tania interrupted the flow of criticism by saying, 'Don't be too hard on her! Remember that it is only thanks to her that we are playing at all.'

The theatre is an enclosed world; night after night you are thrown together with a group of people in a limited space, and forced to communicate with them. When harmony prevails the company becomes a supportive, loving family, better than most families in 'real life', but otherwise backstage life is claustropho-bic and unhappy. I was the youngest and least experienced member of the cast, and I watched from outside, protected by Tania. Besides I liked Diane – she was kind and encouraging to me, and once or twice invited me to her home. I did not mind her playing the part I coveted and for which I was 'a natural', though I sometimes did wish she would catch a cold and disappear just for a couple of evenings and allow me to enjoy myself playing Adela. She never did. On the contrary, she always arrived at the theatre before anyone else, closed the door of her dressing-room to put on her costume and make up, and 'to prepare herself'.

Only once was Diane late. We delayed the show for ten minutes, after which the director in panic asked me to take over. I was ecstatic, already dreaming of lovely notices in the next day's newspapers – for surely some influential critic would be in the audience! But just as the curtain was being raised, Diane rushed in, breathless and flushed: there had been an accident and a road-block, hence her delay.

I learnt more during those four weeks of rehearsal than in several months of the drama course, as Tania and Monsieur Dellor directed us – explaining, analysing, demonstrating, repeating, until each character was born, grew and assumed an authentic independent existence. Your character followed you everywhere, like a shadow, and visited you in your dreams. Tania managed to bring out hitherto unknown features in her own part, humanizing with floods of tears at the end (when Adela kills herself) the monstrous heart-of-stone Bernarda, who had tyrannized her household and slave-driven her dependants. She had complete emotional control, and could conjure up true bitter tears at will from the depth of her psyche. At such moments you could see that her habitual good-humour covered deep reservoirs of sorrow which she tapped for the benefit of her role.

At the end of four weeks the play opened to rave reviews, and settled down to a six-months' run. Like the rest of the cast I knew how lucky we were to be in a successful play in one of the city's best theatres, and how this would open other doors. I felt particularly fortunate for being accepted as a professional actress after only a few months of training, while so many others more experienced than me languished for long periods of 'rest' – especially since in those days not being French was a formidable handicap, and the slightest trace of a foreign accent excluded any entrée into the mainstream theatre. I relished the expressions of admiration and affection I received from friends and strangers, the visits of stars who came backstage to see Tania and graciously extended congratulations to me as well, and I liked the way of life (being by nature a night bird), going to restaurants and cafés after the show with friends, never giving a thought to the future. But I was conscious always of being in the play by fluke, a lucky respite from anxiety, hunger, decision-making.

Of the many new friends I made among actors and writers, some have stayed with me until today. Others I have lost touch with, and yet others have died, young as well as old. All were different from the intellectuals and artists I had previously known. Some were more intelligent than others, but they were not cerebral; combining fragility with resilience, they were sensitive and more in touch with their instincts. Generally a-political, though vaguely to the Left like everyone else in those days, they had a tendency to live very much within the profession, whose enclosed world provided them with ample pleasure and variety. Because the profession is so hard and an actor's life is so precarious, they were often superstitious. They tended to believe in astrology, palm-reading, fortune-telling – and thereby reminded me of my Persian relatives.

It was while in *Bernarda* that I began to look for a flat, as I had to leave the Cité Universitaire: I could no longer be considered a student, and my room in the United States House was needed, although the director kindly suggested that I stay until I found a comfortable alternative. Living there had always been somewhat inconvenient: to catch the last Métro home I had to leave after the show, instead of being able to linger with friends over a meal in Saint-Germain-des-Prés, unless some friend with a car was at hand. I wanted a room of my own in the *quartier* – that square mile between the Seine and Montparnasse that has to this day remained *my* Paris. Hotels were out of reach. Indeed, as Prévert said one day: 'In the old days you had to be poor to live in a hotel. Now you have to be rich!' – his own early life had been spent largely in dingy hotels.

Eventually I did find a studio-flat in rue Gay-Lussac – and that made all the difference.

24

The Poet and the Gypsy

On sait bien que l'on se damne,
Mais l'espoir d'aimer en chemin,
Nous fait penser, main dans la main,
A ce qu'a prédit la Tzigane
GUILLAUME APOLLINAIRE

For foreign students summer holidays were as much part of
their education as their studies. Some went home to their own
countries if they could, others stayed in Paris. By the mid-
sixties Persia had become prosperous enough for its national
Airline to give Iranian students substantial discounts so that
they could return home, but in those days we all stayed in
Europe and travelled around or took holiday jobs – fruit-pick-
ing, potato-harvesting. As a result we never saw our families
and became more and more cut off from our roots.

By the end of June most students had left Paris and the
quartier was depleted, but it was in August that the major
holiday exodus took place, and the city became empty, with
fewer cars and less noise. Tourists wandered around the commercial centre of town and visited the sights, before hurrying
to the sunny South.

'France is the most beautiful country in the world,' said the
French, and most French people took their holidays within the
country. And indeed with its Mediterranean Riviera, its Atlan-
tic coast, its Alpine lakes, and the Pyrenees, France catered for
every taste – only adventurers and romantics ventured abroad.
But with the development of the European Community and
better communications the number of French families who holi-

dayed abroad increased dramatically until, by the end of the decade, it almost matched that of other European countries.

Perhaps the turning point was the Coronation of Queen Elizabeth II in 1953, which, watched by the whole of France on television, ushered in the age of Eurovision. Similar events followed – royal weddings, papal coronations, grand funerals – through them the average French citizen 'discovered abroad'.

I spent my first summer away from home in the mid-fifties in Germany, where my eldest brother was a junior diplomat. He had a German girlfriend, Angela, whose father had been a major industrialist in the Third Reich. The Nazis, needing his services, had decided to turn a blind eye on his 'unfortunate' choice of a non-Aryan wife, so her Jewish mother had been 'officially dead' during the war, hiding 'somewhere', and re-emerging only with peace. It was painful for Angela to talk about her war experiences as a child, but from bits of conversation and allusions I could guess at her suffering. Together we travelled around Germany, through the Black Forest, and visited several famous beauty spots. So much had already been rebuilt in the decade following the war that entire cities, such as Düsseldorf and Frankfurt seemed brand new, yet here and there the charred skeletons of buildings, moon-craters of bomb sites and rubble-fields indicated the extent of the former devastation.

Only the forests, hills and lakes remained unblemished. We would drive along country roads and stop at a lakeside restaurant for lunch, in an Edenic setting – glassy aquamarine water dotted with sailing boats, green hills and chalets, silence broken only by the sudden cry of a lone water-bird. In the restaurants sombre elderly Germans sat alone or in pairs and consumed their meals quietly, gazing dreamily at the lake: how many sons, daughters, friends had they lost in the war, I wondered, and for what purpose?

The following summer my friend Michelle invited me to spend a couple of weeks with her parents at their home in the Pyrenees. She and her mother met me at the station in

Perpignan, and we drove through rolling fields and vineyards to their house – an old stone building tucked away in the folds of the hills, and half hidden from view by tall poplars and willows. A stream meandered through the valley, and across it a tiny arched wooden bridge led to the house. It reminded me of our country home in Persia, an impression enhanced by the interior. Michelle's father had been a colonial officer, and her parents had brought back from their various posts the rugs, vases, chests, screens and objets-d'art with which it was now furnished. My little room upstairs was decorated with a Persian screen depicting the meeting of Joseph and Zuleikha, a Chinese lantern, a four-poster bed from Provence, French mirrors – heterogeneous items that cohered to make a cosy whole. My window overlooked orchards and vegetable fields that sloped uphill behind the house. There was no other building for miles around, and no sound save the murmur of trees, the songs of birds, the drone of crickets.

Michelle's father, Monsieur Guillemin, was in his sixties, but still tall and vigorous. He spent most of the day outdoors, inspecting various parts of his estate and talking to his men. We would come across him on our walks, sitting on his shooting stick and surveying the view, rapt in thought. His last post had been Indochina, and he had retired 'just before the mayhem'. For years he had 'seen it coming' and warned the French Colonial Office, but no one had listened to him. Perhaps for that reason he was now taciturn, and even at meals barely exchanged pleasantries. By contrast his wife – petite, round and vivacious, with regular features, red hair, and a freckled complexion – was garrulous. She was a devout Catholic, and would argue passionately about politics, religion, literature, even farming.

We spent our days walking in the hills, digging up potatoes, picking beans, swimming in the river at noon. In winter the water rose and broke its banks to flood the fields, but in summer it skipped over white stones or formed shallow pools in the hollows. It was an ideal place for learning to swim, and

Michelle's mother showed me how to float along with the current and feel its buoyancy, which enabled me to get over my fear.

On the Sunday we drove some three miles to the village church for Mass, where Michelle's parents, being the local grandees, had their personal pews, with their names on brass plates nailed to the back. I was perplexed by such an emblem of class division in the House of God, and we had a heated argument about it afterwards at lunch. Like all such discussions it led to no conclusion, but Madame Guillemin decided that I was a mystic, and understood nothing about the temporal side of religion and its role in social organization, but that one day I would 'see the light'.

The highlight of the season was the music festival in Prades, a nearby small town, which ran for a fortnight and was organized around the exiled Spanish cellist Pablo Casals – the region's most illustrious resident. Celebrated instrumentalists and chamber orchestras came from all over the world, and tickets were sold out months in advance, but Madame Guillemin had secured some for an evening when Casals himself was to play Bach's Cello Suites.

The small open-air auditorium, already full when we arrived, was loud with the sound of a crowd speaking a babel of languages, and vibrant with expectancy. Except for a single chair in the middle, the stage was bare. Suddenly all eyes turned towards the front and applause broke out, as a short, tubby old man shuffled onto the stage carrying a cello. He bowed gently, sat down on his chair and adjusted his instrument. Presently came the starting notes of Suite Number One, and then there was nothing but a ladder of music straight up to heaven. The crepuscular light faded, a young moon rose and stars appeared in the indigo sky, as if they too had come out to listen. Then as Suite Number Six drew to its close we were back to earth, and calling out for Casals! He returned for several encores, and then reluctantly we dispersed into the night and back to our homes.

I have a recording of Bach's Cello Suites by Casals, and when I see his photograph on the cover of the box-set, it is exactly as I remember him that night – his eyes hidden behind thick spectacles, his expression impassive, his body at one with his instrument, a humble messenger from the Gods.

Another summer I went to Florence. The tiny *pensione* where I stayed was the three-room apartment of a young couple with two children, a toddler and a baby who was always in his mother's arms, whatever she happened to be doing. Whenever she put him down he howled with such anguish that she picked him up again immediately. But he did not really mind whose arms he was in, for I sometimes carried him to relieve his mother, and he was equally content. My landlords seemed a perfectly happy couple, judging by their constant laughter and conversation, and the love-sounds coming through the thin partition between their bedroom and mine, yet she did all the work. She got up early in the morning, cleaned, shopped, cooked, while her husband reclined on a divan in their sitting-room, with doors and windows open to create a draught, reading a newspaper or dozing. He would sit up and say '*Buon giorno, Signorina,*' as I went past, invariably complaining about how much work he had to do and how hard life was: '*La vita è difficile! Laborare! Molto laborare!*'

In two weeks I saw as much of Florence as I could, walking everywhere map in hand, alone or with other students I had met, going into churches, museums, galleries, palazzi – shrines to be visited again and again on subsequent pilgrimages over the years. Every visitor to Florence finds soul-mates among the artists of the past, and mine was above all Fra Angelico. I spent hours at Saint Mark's Monastery looking at his pictures, as I still do whenever I am in Florence. The Virgins and Angels and Babies of his pictures seemed all alive, ready to step out and join us in a feast of hope and joy.

The summer before I left Paris I went to spend a couple of

weeks with Simone, a fellow student at Tania's drama course, at her home near Montpellier. We decided to stop at Avignon, where the Théâtre National Populaire held an annual festival. It was the most prestigious drama event of the year, and aficionados came from all over the world to attend the shows, staged at the Palais des Papes, so called because it was the papal seat for a brief period in the Middle Ages. The high walls and ramparts of the palace lit to form a spectacular backdrop for the stage, which was otherwise unadorned, and a vast open-air auditorium was created in the court outside. It was a grand setting worthy of the classical plays for which Avignon had become famous. During the month-long festival the small provincial town became a fairground – the population increased tenfold, houses turned into *pensions* to accommodate the influx of actors and tourists, restaurants and cafés spilled their customers over on to the pavements, souvenir shops did the business of a year. Walking in the central square towards the palace you could bump into Gérard Philippe, Maria Casarès, Jean Vilar – idols usually glimpsed across the chasm that separates the stage from the auditorium, 'illusion' from 'reality'.

Simone had met one of the stars of the TNP earlier in the summer, when she had auditioned for the part of Julie in Racine's *Britannicus*. She had not been given the part, but had been complimented by a famous actor in the cast, who had invited her to dinner to talk further 'about her career', and later they had started an affair. He was her first lover, and she was radiantly in love with him, believing that he appreciated her 'surrender' and reciprocated her feelings, and that any day he would propose to her. She had woven a dream of a long happy life with him in the theatre, working together, perhaps one day setting up their own company, becoming a legendary theatrical couple. Meanwhile she would surprise him by turning up in Avignon, and he would certainly welcome her into his grand hotel.

She never wondered why a man twenty years her senior who had never married and was well-known for his amorous exploits would suddenly change his way of life, but each new female victim of the Don Juan syndrome believes she will be the last, the one who will 'change him'! It is true that occasionally a seducer is caught in his own trap, but it is rare, and never predictable. But then love is not a reasonable sentiment: 'To know that it is all over and still to hold on' was Kafka's definition of love, and if you have not experienced that, you are lucky indeed. Simone believed that her lover would respond to her devotion and innocence, and that 'the others' had been unworthy of him.

Anyway, first we had to get to Avignon. We had little money, and I was nervous about hitch-hiking. Luckily a Persian carpet-dealer living in Germany was going south to buy himself a villa and through my brother he offered to give us a lift in his large Mercedes.

In Avignon I had managed to find a tiny attic room in a makeshift *pension* off the central square, while Simone planned to join her boyfriend. She sent him a billet-doux announcing her arrival and whereabouts, and we waited for him to arrive, doubtless with a bunch of flowers. Instead a note was delivered by the landlady, in which he said that he was with his 'fiancée' and could not see Simone; he wished her a happy stay and enclosed a couple of tickets for the evening's show – *Britannicus*.

Simone was inconsolable. I see her clutching her stomach as if she were stabbed, her beautiful face undone with grief, her eyes begging rescue, weeping, weeping . . . Our friend Jocelyn had a part in *Hamlet*, and I rang him to come and help me look after Simone. He arrived within minutes: 'But everyone knows what he is like with women,' he told Simone. 'What made you think he would behave differently with you? Fiancée my arse! I know the girl, she is a so-called model looking for a break in films, and he has picked her up just for the week he is here. They deserve each other – she has slept with everyone in every company.' It took a couple of days to calm Simone, and I believe she never recovered from the shock completely – from then on she was suspicious, affected cynicism and took several lovers: 'You must drop them before they drop you,' she would say. In the end she married a Moroccan diplomat, a devout Muslim who treated her with devotion and respect. They travelled around the world as I did, and we lost touch, but I still remember the harrowing scene in our little *pension* room.

Simone never set foot outside, lest she would see the man who had so callously ditched her. The landlady felt sorry for her and gave me a mattress to sleep on the floor while I gave Simone my bed, as there was not an inch of space left in town. I went to see Jocelyn play Laertes in *Hamlet*, with all the energy and emotional commitment of a young actor in his first important role. The next night Simone's boyfriend was magnificent in *Britannicus*. The Palais des Papes was illumined from all sides in a subtle arrangement of light and shade. The stage was bare save for a single throne in the middle, but the sumptuous costumes glittered in the limelight. Simone never played the virtuous Julie, and eventually gave up the theatre.

From Avignon we took the train to Montpellier, where Simone's parents met us at the station and drove us home in a taxi. They lived in a modest flat in the old, populous part of town, a criss-cross of narrow streets and old buildings teeming with children and stalls which reminded me of the Middle East. As they had no room to accommodate me comfortably, they put me up in the house of friends who were away on holiday, in a backstreet round the corner. Simone would keep me company, and we would go to her parents for meals.

She was her parents' only daughter and the apple of their eyes. Her father was small, thin and bald, with watery bespectacled eyes and a genial expression; her mother was plump, with a round face and a loud voice. Both were fairly plain, and they regarded it a miracle to be blessed with a daughter who was truly beautiful, like Botticelli's *Primavera*: thick, long, wavy blond hair, large green eyes, ivory complexion, and a sunny temperament – when her heart was not broken. In his youth Simone's father had been a violinist with the local orchestra,

222

but later had developed epilepsy and been forced to give up playing. He earned his living as a piano-tuner and sometimes played for pleasure. On my insistence one evening he brought out his violin and began to play – Schubert's Serenade, as I remember. He closed his eyes and played with his heart, and although he was clearly out of practice, he had a good tone and a sure touch. We asked for more and he played for us all evening – melodic pieces from the Romantic repertoire which suited our mood.

Simone's mother took in alterations and repairs to help their finances and support their daughter while she studied drama in Paris, convinced that she would be a successful actress and film star within a year. In view of their circumstances I had taken useful presents and insisted on contributing towards the housekeeping.

In the days that followed our arrival Simone and I went for long walks in the town, visited the sights, sat under the trees in the parks and read poetry. Simone spoke good Italian and recited long passages from Dante's *Paradiso*, while I translated Hafiz and Khayyám for her, and recited Baudelaire.

Montpellier had a large population of gypsies who lived on the edge of the town in camps and caravans and makeshift homes. Their men worked seasonally on farms and building sites, while their women took on menial jobs or worked in factories. You recognized them in the streets from their looks – dark complexions, curly hair, thin wiry bodies – and strong accents. They were said to be primitive and hot-headed, prone to petty crimes and violence. You could see some of their women, dressed in long, full skirts and colourful scarves selling bunches of flowers, or offering to read palms, in the shopping areas. Simone's mother knew a few of them, but she thought it wiser to keep them at a distance, as they were shifty and capable of casting evil spells if they were thwarted. Some were known to have killed their rivals-in-love with witchcraft, while their men were believed to be unreliable and promiscuous. Once a year gypsies from all over Europe went on pilgrimage to the shrine of their patron-saint at Saintes-Maries-de-la-Mer, in the south. This annual gathering was an occasion for festivities, trade, alliances, and many returned with material as well as spiritual gains.

I was attracted to the gypsies and their way of life which reminded me of nomads in Persia, and I wanted to see them in their own quarters. Simone and I were particularly intrigued by the fortune-teller her mother knew, who was supposed to be uncannily accurate. I did not believe in predictions, but Simone did, and to prove the point she persuaded her mother to take us to see the old crone.

The gypsy area on the border of the town was littered with shacks and caravans, rusty old cars and station-wagons, with clothes-lines in between. Only the few old-fashioned wagons conformed to our romantic notion of gypsies as children of the gods, living on their bounty. In the dusty spaces between the vehicles and shacks children played, chickens pecked and cackled, dogs and cats chased each other. The clothes-lines swayed in the evening breeze, naked bulbs glared from wires. Here and there camp-fires glowed despite the summer heat, surmounted with pots and tin kettles, and the smell of cooking pervaded the air. At our approach dogs barked and ran towards us, only to be called back by their owners, while children rushed to inspect us, touch our clothes, ask for sweets. Simone's mother was greeted by her acquaintances with warm embraces and we were welcomed and led to Old Marie, as the fortune teller was called. Chairs were produced and we sat at a distance from the fire. It was a dark, moonless night, with only the pink glow of city lights on the horizon. Gradually our circle widened as others came to join us, including some men, but Old Marie had to be treated tactfully and allowed to 'get into the mood' before she would offer to read your palm. She had a face so wizened and wrinkled that she seemed a hundred years old, and when she smiled her teeth were a set of black stumps, broken by hollows, with only one incisor miraculously intact, shining like a piece of ivory. She wore a black scarf, and a white jacket tucked into a full black skirt – she looked like a huge black-and white bird of prey.

A guitar appeared from somewhere and a young man began to play and sing, then foolishly I picked it up and sang a song, whereupon they asked me for more, and more . . . Then at last Old Marie was asked by Simone's mother to look at her daughter's palm, and mine. She took Simone's hand and examined it carefully, then told her that her heart was sore with a 'chagrin d'amour', but that the pain would pass, and she would marry a tall, dark southerner from across the sea. To me she promised a handsome man from the North – not East or South as might have been expected: 'You will get what you want, but life is not easy . . . not easy at all . . .,' she concluded, shaking her head. But what *did* I want, apart from love? In truth nothing, as everything else I cared about – music, poetry, drama, art – emanated from it and nourished it in return. Perhaps that was the 'difficulty', and I was reminded of Hafiz's line:

Come, Cup-bearer, and pour forth the Wine,
For Love appeared easy at first, then proved fraught with difficulties . . .

But at the time I was in love and happy, and I had no reason to believe that things would change. We left and walked back to our home and slept late. In the morning I opened the shutters and looked out, and there was a gypsy in the street, leaning against the wall opposite. He was carving a piece of wood with a small knife, looked up and sketched a smile, then went on working. I recognized him from the night before: he was one of the men who had joined our circle as we sang, not uttering a word, just listening. He was about thirty, with a dark, weather-beaten complexion, huge burning black eyes, and wavy hair parted on the side and smoothed back with brilliantine. I shut the window and went to get dressed. Later when Simone and I came down to go over to her parents' home, he said hello and began to walk beside us. I thought the object of his interest was Simone, but it soon became apparent that I was the one he wanted to see. He did not talk much, and just shrugged and smiled when I asked him what he wanted to say to me. I remembered Simone's mother saying how difficult it was to shake a gypsy once you drew his attention, and I decided to ignore him.

The next morning he was there again, leaning against the wall, carving away. After a few days I began to worry seriously and wondered how to get rid of him. I thought the best strategy was to talk him out of pursuing me. I told him that he was wasting his time, and that my heart was completely taken by another man whom I was to join after the holidays.

'Oh, you'll soon forget him if you come with me,' he said confidently. Did he not have a job? 'I do, but I am on holiday,' he said without further information. What did he do? He would not say, but implied that he was a car mechanic in winter and a farmhand in summer. Above all he was a wood-sculptor and sold his artefacts for 'good money'. And indeed after a few days he gave me the piece of wood he had been carving: a little guitar, beautifully finished and painted with frets.

'I don't want to get married, anyway,' I told him.

'That's all right, you can just live with me.'

'What if I turn out to be fickle and unsatisfactory?'

'Oh I'll get rid of you. I'll sell you to someone else, or perhaps I'll just kill you.'

Now I was really scared! So were Simone's parents. We agreed that I would move to their flat, sleep on the floor, and leave one day without warning. But he knew the flat and the next morning he was there, standing by the door as I came out. When I left a few days later, Simone's mother told him that I had gone back to Persia and that I sent him my good wishes. Apparently he had just spat on the ground and walked away, never to be seen again.

A few years ago I found the little guitar my gypsy had carved for me and remembered that last summer in France. Then I wrote a song, 'The Poet and the Gypsy' – I had chosen the former.

25

Peter and Paul and the Second Sex

L'amour a remué ma vie comme on remue la
terre dans la zone des armées
GUILLAUME APOLLINAIRE

My best friend at the School of Oriental Languages was Paul.
He already had degrees in philosophy and law, and was studying Arabic preparatory to entering the Ministry of Foreign
Affairs. Less endowed with beauty than brains, he was of average height and stocky, wore thick glasses, and had curly dark
hair which was already thinning in the front, making his convex
forehead seem out of proportion to the rest of his face. But his
gentleness, attractive smile, ironic sense of humour and luminous intelligence more than made up for his lack of good looks.

He reminded me of Schubert in his famous portrait, and I
told him so soon after we became friends: 'I would rather
sound like him!' he said, with a twinge of bitterness at my
'compliment'. A devout Christian, his interest in Arabic and in
Islamic culture generally had first been ignited when he had
read Massignon's *magnum opus* on Hallaj, the eighth-century
Muslim mystic. But unlike many of my Catholic friends his
was essentially a mystical attitude to religion (hence his attachment to Sufism), and not political, though he was strongly anti-
Marxist. 'It leads inevitably to barbarity, concentration camps,
and general stupidity. Long after Marxism has become a foot-
note in history books, the light of Christianity will shine over
humanity like the sun, and illumine the hearts of men,' he
would say matter-of-factly. Others were saying and writing

similar words in those days, but amid the roar of the flood that swept the cultural life of the Left Bank their voices were unheard – at least not by young rebels from the Third World with dreams in their heads and fire in their hearts. I wish that Paul could have lived to see his predictions come true all over Eastern Europe, where the old order has crumbled and the churches are full.

After our language classes in rue de Lille, Paul often accompanied me to the Foyer – or at least part of the way, to boulevard Saint-Michel, when he would take the Métro back to the 15th Arrondissement where he lodged with an old aunt, as his parents lived in the south-west. We would walk along the backstreets of Saint-Germain, talking, arguing, Paul keeping me on my toes and teasing me whenever I strayed from rationality towards 'poetic flights' or 'utopian clouds'.

I became gradually aware that Paul's feelings for me were more than fraternal, but I pretended not to notice, being unable to reciprocate them, and taking advantage of his shyness and my own *pudeur*. No one was more worthy of love than Paul, and I adored him and depended on him, but only as a friend.

However rational we try to be, our lives are mostly governed by mysteries, of which desire is the most intractable. If only 'worthiness' determined the vagaries of the heart, the world would be a happier place: no oceans of tears, no burning flames of jealousy, no tortures of uncertainty – but also no sublime poetry, prose, music, art, inspired by love's torments. '*Rien ne vaut le malheur d'aimer*' – nothing is more precious than the sorrow of love – wrote Éluard, and we quoted it whenever one of our friends had 'heart troubles'.

And it is no less true for being a truism that we never understand other people's loves: 'what does he or she see in her or him?' we ask, and we ask ourselves the same question after our own love for someone has died. There are of course 'sensible' people, who organize their lives rationally and whose other interests overshadow the arbitrary dictates of the heart, but they are few and, alas, I was not one of them.

So I did not fall in love with good, honest, loyal Paul, but with his friend – beautiful, clever, shady Pierre.

I was often admonished by my friends for being 'naïve' and 'romantic', and confused. My ideas about relationships between the sexes were formed first by the sometimes contradictory influences of my background, limited education, and experience, and then by all that I read and observed. Yet there were basic instincts I knew I should never defy. I was constantly amazed at the conduct of my first friends at the Foyer: these were the middle and upper-class girls, usually Catholic, who believed in the conventions of 'bourgeois' families, and whose one aim in life was finding a husband. There were the 'progressives' and Communists who were almost as rigid in their approach to love but without the excuse of religion. And the 'Existentialists', who rejected all conventions for the sake of hedonism ('life is absurd, enjoy it!') before – often – settling down into ordinary marriage and children. Whatever the 'philosophy', the ultimate aim, the Mecca, was getting your hooks into a man and dragging him to the altar!

All this contradicted every illusion I had about Western women's freedom of spirit and social mobility. Paradoxically the most natural independent behaviour seemed to be that of my Jordanian friend Jamila, who as a Muslim was expected to be more cautious and restrained than any Western girl, yet who recklessly fell in love with a cripple without any thought of the future, abandoned herself to passion, and in the end paid the price for it.

For myself as far back as I could remember I had hoped that all my dreams and longings would be realized in a single love, whose radiance would illumine my whole life in freedom and harmony, and that until I found him I would accept no compromise, nor settle for any second-best. But I did not want to get married – at least so long as the laws and attitudes concerning women in Persia remained unchanged: 'You give away your life when you say "yes",' my Aunt Ashraf, our household's philosopher, would say; and indeed all around me I saw women suffering abject misery, locked in hopeless marriages, 'just putting up with it' for the sake of the children whose custody they would automatically lose if they divorced. Of course there *were* happy marriages, and women *did* wield considerable power over their families and through influencing their husbands and sons (my own parents being an example, and they had not met before their wedding night). My mother did run our lives, but she was a relic of another era: I and my girl friends were the daughters of women's emancipation, of the abolition of the veil, and of modern education; we had been to the movies and read books, and we wanted something different.

Persian society had changed in many important ways. Yet somehow its basic laws regarding marriage and divorce and children's custody remained unaltered, and the discrepancy between women's expectations and the law created anomalies and a social malaise. As a teenage revolutionary in Persia I believed that women's lot would improve only when poverty and exploitation were abolished and justice reigned – as in the Soviet Union! Many years later, reading about the predicament of Soviet women in Andrei Sakharov's books, and speaking with Soviet feminist exiles, I was dismayed by how naïve and optimistic I had been.

Now, in Paris and no longer a 'believer' in that utopia, I wondered what the answer was. Paul had brought me Simone de Beauvoir's *The Second Sex* to read: a huge tome that I meant to skim through. But as I read on I became more absorbed, until by the end I was as if thunderstruck. It is said that this book has changed more women's lives all over the world, particularly in traditional societies from Asia to Italy, than any other. It looks at the problem of woman comprehensively, from the viewpoints of philosophy, sociology, psychology, anthropology, and biology, in the light of Existentialism. For me, it focused and organized feelings and thoughts, and cleared away much confusion and dead wood cluttering my mind. I was not experienced enough to question some of its propositions – notably about women's sexuality – but its socio-psychological

231

findings, seemingly solidly built on facts and statistics, appeared beyond doubt.

So I swallowed every word of *The Second Sex*, without any caution and admired the authenticity with which the author followed her precepts in her own life – being tied to Sartre in a complete, lasting love, without jealousy, eschewing marriage in order to remain free and keep their attachment uncontaminated by the quotidian (the Romantic's *bête noire*). Surely she was the paradigm, the example to follow?

Rereading the book recently, I found myself as much in profound disagreement with several of its essential tenets as in awe of its pioneering sweep. Despite the wealth of writing on women since the sixties, it is still a landmark, and today, at least in advanced countries, women have achieved some measure of the sovereignty it proclaimed over matters such as divorce, abortion, adoption, and custody.

It was at that moment, full of de Beauvoir's ideas, buzzing with new-found understanding, that I first met Pierre. One day Paul and I were walking down rue Jacob when I noticed a tall young man in a navy duffle-coat on the other side of the road – I thought I had seen him before, but could not remember where. Then he smiled and called out to Paul, and crossed the road.

'Ah! You are the mysterious Persian girl he has been hiding?' he said, shaking my hand as Paul introduced us.

'It is you who have been doing one of your vanishing acts. Where have you been all this time?'

'Oh, the usual, the mountains . . . Let's have a cup of coffee and hear your news.'

The café on the corner of rue Bonaparte was full and we stood waiting for a free table. It was clear that the two friends were close, though very different from each other. Pierre had dark blue eyes shadowed by long black eyelashes, high Asiatic cheekbones and hollow cheeks, and a tanned complexion. His light brown hair was cut longer than was usual in those days – though the style would soon become fashionable among the young, through the Beatles and American folk-singers. When he laughed, which was often, he threw his head back, and you saw his thin, long neck encased in a slightly large collar, with a neat tie in a reddish pattern. He reminded me of some members of my mother's family, Northerners who 'looked Russian'.

I listened to their conversation fascinated, while Pierre tried to draw me in from time to time. 'Have we not met before, somewhere?' I finally asked, having searched my memory in vain.

'I would remember if we had!' he said, and laughed at his own conventional answer.

Paul told me afterwards that Pierre was one of the most brilliant people he knew, that they had been at the *lycée* together and become best friends. Pierre had suffered a great deal from lung illnesses – though not tuberculosis – which together with his passion for winter sports explained his prolonged stays in the mountains, near Chamonix: 'Women love him, but he is a Don Juan, and never lasts more than a few months with anybody, if that . . . luckily nowadays girls can handle it,' he said. 'French girls, that is,' he added with a note of warning.

After that first encounter I sometimes asked after Pierre: 'Oh, I saw him last week,' or 'last month', or 'I haven't seen him for ages, he must have gone away,' Paul would answer.

It was my last Christmas at the Foyer des Bénédictines. In a couple of months I would be offered a room at the Cité Universitaire and move – *quel miracle*! Meanwhile I spent a lot of time with my friends who lived there. I was tired of the Foyer's suffocating rules and broke them as often as I could.

Christmas Eve was particularly cold; a mean wind blew fitfully, sharp enough to penetrate the bones, but without bringing on the snow which would purge the skies. I was always freezing, and being wary of crowds, I decided to stay in and read instead of going out with friends. The Foyer was quiet, most students having gone home for the holidays. Dinner on Christmas Eve being traditionally a family-and-friends

233

occasion, most foreign students were left to their own resources and gathered in restaurants and cafés.

Around eight o'clock the bell rang, followed by Mademoiselle Mori's shrill voice calling my room number. Who could it be? I wondered, and rushed downstairs to the waiting-room. A tall man in a navy duffle-coat was looking out of the window; I recognized him when he turned round and smiled – Pierre. I was surprised. He had a single red rose, with a long stem, wrapped in transparent paper in his hand which he put on the table as we sat down.

I had not seen him since that first meeting, and now suddenly here he was in the monastic little waiting-room of the Foyer.

'I had a hunch you'd be in, unlikely as it was,' he explained.

'I should be out, because it's my birthday . . .'

'You see! I must have guessed something. Very many happy returns of the day and all that . . . *Mademoiselle!*' And he gave me the rose with a gentle bow in mock formality. But why was he in town? 'It's my little half-sister's birthday too, and I am about to go and have dinner with her at my father's. She is fourteen. How old are you, if this is not an indiscreet question?'

'Nineteen.'

'*Mon Dieu!* How dare you be so young?'

'Oh, sometimes I feel so old. How old are *you?*'

'Twenty-four; now that *is* old, when you think that Lermontov died at the same age, Rimbaud was finished a year younger, Raymond Radiguet, Buchner. But my father who is fifty-nine says that life begins at sixty – and he can't wait!'

Why was he in Paris, I enquired, when every other keen skier was away in the snow? He would go after the holidays, he said. He then asked me to dinner the following evening, and left.

I went back to my room and my book, but my concentration had vanished and my mind kept wandering. The next evening the weather was milder. The wind had abated and a brief snowfall had cleared the air. I put on my red skirt and black top, which was my only *chic* outfit, made for me by a seamstress in rue Gay-Lussac. A quiet, shy young woman, with permed honey-coloured hair, a whey complexion, and a gentle smile. She worked in a dry-cleaning-and-alteration shop, and I used to see her sitting in front of her sewing-machine by the window working all day. I thought how in the nineteenth century pale dreamy seamstresses and laundresses like her were sometimes picked up by rich men and 'settled' as their mistresses – like Marie Duplessis, and other 'Dames aux Camélias', the modern equivalent being getting 'discovered' by a film producer, with your face on every magazine cover (having originally been 'spotted' by the producer's wife as a shampooer in a hair-dressing salon). But most *midinettes* – thousands and thousands of them – just stitched away their lives reading pulp magazines, dreaming of a man who would come along and save them from drudgery. My seamstress at least was married, had a child and seemed content – that was something.

I remembered Paul saying that Pierre was always late and unpredictable; some of my friends had complained of being kept waiting or even 'stood up' by their boyfriends, and I had been outraged, saying that they should not tolerate such bad behaviour. But 'Love has no pride', says the song, as sooner or later we all find to our cost. Pierre was on time.

We went to a little Russian restaurant nearby, La Poule Dorée, A metallic golden hen, surrounded with the letters of its name hung from a rod above the entrance door, and inside was a small room, with square tables covered in red-and-white gingham. Each table had a candle stuck into a liqueur bottle and a small vase of carnations; the waiters wore black trousers tucked into riding boots, red satin Russian shirts with the neck opening at the side, and black belts. They seemed to know Pierre, for the MD saluted him warmly and kissed my hand, before leading us to a table in a little arched niche by the wall. Pierre told him that I was Persian:

'*Ah la Perse*! Omar Khayyam! The wine of Shiray! A dream-land! I was there in 1919, you know...' He moved away to greet other clients coming through the door, and Pierre told me that he had been a junior officer in the White Army, and had retreated to the Caucasus with his regiment before crossing into Persia. 'My mother was Russian,' added Pierre casually, which explained his Asiatic looks – now I knew why he had looked familiar that first day.

Soon a middle-aged duo, a fiddler and a pianist dressed in dark suits, appeared, and the exiguous space filled with the sound of gypsy tunes and Russian folk melodies. I thought eating, like most quotidian functions, was unromantic, and I ordered what was easiest to toy with and swallow; then afterwards we went for a walk by the Seine, crossing the bridge to the Ile Saint-Louis. The majestic silhouette of Notre Dame stood against the wintry sky, the glittering bridge lights were reflected on the dark water, and vagrant clouds played hide-and-seek with a cold new moon.

I told Pierre that I was somewhat obsessed with Russia, first as 'the Great Bear in the North' who had swallowed half of Persia in the nineteenth century and was ever a menace, then as the Ideal, the country of Socialism, and now as the *illusion perdue*. But above all through its literature, many of whose characters seemed to come straight from my own family.

He told me about his family. His mother had come to France with her parents when still a child, after the Revolution of 1917. They had belonged to the landed gentry and had not been able to bring out anything except a few pieces of jewellery. They had lived among the other émigrés in dire circumstances for a long time, until in the 30s her father's business as an antique dealer had started to produce an adequate income.

Perhaps as a result of those early traumas Pierre's mother was fragile, but she was beautiful and a sensitive pianist and her death, when he was twelve, had affected him deeply. In due course his father, a lawyer, had remarried a Frenchwoman, but Pierre did not get on with her at all, and after many quarrels had left home to live with his paternal grandmother. Later she too had died, and now he lived in the attic servant's-room of his father's apartment building (to which he referred as 'my official residence'), and in 'borrowed' accommodation of various degrees of luxury. It was part of his 'mystery' that no one knew exactly where he was at any given time – it was always assumed to be the grand homes of his international skiing contacts, who were often away from Paris.

I was too inexperienced to realize that those early bereavements, which to an adolescent felt like 'abandonments', had caused deep wounds in his psyche, or that the experiences of the Russian exiles and the émigré community was what my own family would go through many years later, after the 1979 Revolution in Iran – poverty, alienation, internecine conflicts, pain and nostalgia – or that one day I would recognize in my two sons his ambivalent emotions towards his country, France, and his mother's, Russia. Perhaps those conflicts and disappointments explained his 'Don-Juanism' and cynicism. It is not easy for a child to accommodate a 'foreign' mother; she is different at an age when children want to be like everyone else. The resulting malaise can cause deep problems, or be the grit that produces the pearl – children of mixed marriages are often said to be more 'interesting', and not only in their looks.

We did not arrange to meet again, but I had no doubts – does the sun 'arrange' to shine every day? – and I returned to the Foyer on the dot of midnight. He found me working at the library a couple of days later, and we went for a walk in the Luxembourg Gardens, entering by the boulevard Saint-Michel gate and walking down the main alley to the row of statues of the Queens of France. 'French kings ruled over their people through their wives or mistresses,' he informed me. 'With their Cartesian minds they were too divorced from ordinary people and practical life, and without their women they would have lost touch with reality. Poor Marie Antoinette! Being a foreigner she could not fulfil this most essential of her functions, and so she lost her throne and her head.'

'You mean she could have stopped the Revolution?'

'Who knows? What a pity – France has never recovered. French history should be rewritten through the wives and mistresses of the men who were supposed to have shaped its course.'

Then he asked me: 'Which would you prefer to be, the wife or the mistress?'

'Of course, the mistress!' I said. 'Between love and the crown I would chose the former any day, wouldn't you?'

No answer – just an amused quizzical look.

Pierre's father had insisted that he read Law and join his family firm, taking it over in due course. But he liked neither the subject nor the practice: 'The only reason for becoming a lawyer is to learn the Law so that you can break it with impunity,' he would gibe. 'And I already know how to do that! Real Justice is not accomplished by lawyers.'

To postpone working as a lawyer he had gone to *Sciences Po* – the Institute of Political Sciences – after his degree, and was now writing a doctoral thesis on some arcane aspect of International Law, which he was dragging out indefinitely. He only liked literature (in particular poetry) and painting, and combining the two: writing about it in the tradition of such poet-critics as Baudelaire, for whom he felt a veneration akin to my own passion.

He considered his own poetry futile and unworthy of publication to the point of spurning the offer of a Seghers' *plaquette*. He destroyed most of his output, but occasionally quoted a line or two in the course of conversation, and when I asked who the author was, answered 'nobody'. Yet we spent many happy hours reading and reciting poems together – Racine, Apollinaire, Éluard, Breton, Aragon . . .

Politically he considered himself an anarchist: 'After a brief flirtation with Communism I have gone back to my Russian roots' – he meant the nineteenth-century Anarchists. Paul told him that he was a mixture of all the Brothers Karamazov – except the murderer. 'Don't be so sure!' he retorted. To me he was Dimitri – wild, tormented, passionate, noble – the brother with whom I had instantly fallen in love when I had first read the novel in Persian.

There was a playscript of *Karamazov* in French, and Grouch-enka was one of the first parts I played for Tania (Jocelyn was Dimitri). I later confessed to her that I dreamed of being cast for the part in a theatre production one day: 'You will be, you will be,' she had reassured me, and as she was not given to idle promises or encouragement, I believed her. Later, when I had plans to start a drama group should I return to Persia, an adaptation of *Brothers Karamazov* was my first idea, as the audiences would recognize themselves and their friends in the characters. Every time I re-read the novel I still have the same emotions, yet I know now that the likelihood of encountering a Dimitri is remote, because he is the creation of supreme imagination, and has a reality more enduring than that of 'real' people. But at that time I completely identified Pierre with Dimitri: he was as I had envisaged him after that first reading.

When I told Pierre that I was moving to the Cité, we celebrated at the *Poule Dorée*. He still could not visit me in my room, but we often sat in the large communal reception room, sometimes with my Persian friends, or walked in the grounds and saw events at the International House. Periodically he would go away to Chamonix 'to write his thesis' or 'give the lungs a break from Paris air', or just because he missed the mountains. We wrote often and sometimes telephoned. Once he rang to say that he would be back the following week on the Thursday, and would I meet him underneath the Pont Neuf at eight o'clock, in the *Vert Galant* since he would come there straight from the station. The place had acquired for me a sacred dimension – for it was there that our student camaraderie had first blossomed into something that had hitherto been only an adolescent dream. Since then it seemed that I had always known Pierre, that he had always been there, and would be always, however long we lived. So I went to our appointment, even though something told me he would not come, as a previous letter had informed me that he was unwell and might not be able to return to Paris for a while.

It was a cold, windy night, with intermittent gusts of icy rain blowing at different angles like showers of needles, and a black sky hanging down in tatters. The square was virtually empty, and the benches, usually occupied by promenaders and court-ing couples, were soaked and uninviting. I walked up and down to keep myself warm, looking at the dark languorous river, the boats, the traffic on the Embankment, the whole drenched city spreading all around to infinity, pulsating with life yet empty for me: '*Un seul être vous manque et tout est dépeuplé.*'

There was a telegram in my pigeon-hole when I returned home, drenched and frozen through. It cancelled our appoint-ment, 'Letter and roses follow.'

'I have not told Paul that I have been seeing you,' I informed Pierre after a few months. 'Why not? Aren't we *innocent*?' he laughed. When I did tell Paul, he looked worried, and reacted with a smile of resignation. Thereafter sometimes the three of us would meet in cafés and talk, but after he finished his exams Paul went home and soon began a job, and we saw less of each other.

One evening I walked with Pierre to his attic, his 'temporary' home when in Paris and when he had not secured a borrowed flat. It was like a small hotel-room, with decent non-descript furniture, and few personal effects except books and one or two items of clothing. Through the window you could see the upper part of the Eiffel tower glittering in the far distance. He said that his stepmother used the room when he was out of town to put up friends, and for that reason he could not give me a key, but that when he was 'in residence' I could always stay there. I did, and when he was not in, I used to wait on the stairs, reading, until he arrived.

Some months later one night I missed the last Métro back to the Cité and turned up at Pierre's without warning. He was not in, and as I sat waiting on the stairs, I fell asleep, only to wake up when I heard steps walking up. It was one of his neighbours, a middle-aged nurse back from her night-shift. She had a 'soft spot' for Pierre, he had told me, and she asked me into her room for a cup of coffee: '*Ah, Monsieur Pierre! Quel numéro!*' she commiserated.

I thanked her and declined – it was dawn, the Métro was working, and I wanted to get back home. I was stiff and tired and depleted, and I made up my mind to find a room in the *quartier* as soon as I could.

When I was jolted out of my stupor by the early morning Métro, I began to worry seriously about Pierre, lest something had happened to him, a car accident for example, or a sudden attack of asthma. He had 'crashed out' at a friend's, he told me when he rang. It never occurred to me that he could have been with another woman, any more than I would dream of looking at another man, ever, as long as I lived. Then one day as we were crossing the Luxembourg we heard a woman call out his name. It was someone he had known in Chamonix, he explained later – a tall, blonde French woman in her late twenties or early thirties, her hair pulled back and gathered on the nape, with tanned skin and blue eyes. She was dressed expensively in beige-and-brown tones, and sported slightly tinted glasses which enhanced her elegance.

Pierre asked me to wait and walked towards her. As they greeted each other warmly, spoke and laughed, just out of my earshot, I became aware of a completely new sensation which I had never experienced before: my stomach began to churn with nausea, my head swelled, my heart pounded against my temples with acute anxiety. Fires flared in front of my eyes and tears welled up into my eyelids, while blind anger gripped me like the teeth of a shark. As I waited there I discovered possibilities in myself I had never imagined, such as murdering, maiming, digging someone's eyes out, applying Chinese torture! . . .

'Why didn't you introduce me?' I asked Pierre, furious, letting go of the tears.

'Well, well! What would Simone de Beauvoir say to that! I thought jealousy was possessiveness, that Love was freedom, etc . . . etc . . .'

I had never been jealous of anybody. My older sister was much prettier and more sought after than me, yet I had not been jealous of her, nor had I experienced rivalry at school or since, but this was a new area, and clearly I was fiendishly and inordinately jealous in love. Perhaps because jealousy is the fear of loss, and people are only jealous of what they really care about and wish to keep. At any rate there it was, I was ashamed of it, but I could neither hide it nor quell it – from then on it was a virus that lay within me and would flare up whenever the psyche's immune system was weakened.

In time I realized that the only solution was to avoid situations and people whose behaviour triggered off an attack. I have tried to do that ever since – I'm afraid not always successfully.

For the remaining time that I lived in Paris Pierre was the centre around which my whole life revolved, in relation to which everything was measured, the rock on which existence was built – indeed the main 'reason' for my lingering on there, since I should have returned home immediately after my exams, as my friends did.

He encouraged me to be an actress and singer and praised everything I did. And because he was so hard on himself, so astringent in his judgements on artistic matters, I believed him, or did he just want to keep me in Paris? 'Thou art Peter and on this Rock I build my house.' Does a name confer an obligation or influence an identity? He thought so, and for my sake tried to change, since concessions had to be made to my Muslim background, with its emphasis on chastity and modesty, and my temperament, but it was only a temporary solution. Perhaps no mere human can be 'the Rock', on which to build the house, only Love itself – with all its mansions.

Unlike the rest of us Pierre always seemed to have enough money, since he never mentioned the subject. He was forever hailing taxis, or turning up in cars borrowed from friends – usually English models fashionable amongst the gilded youth.

He would come and pick me up after the play, and we would go to fairly expensive restaurants in Saint-Germain-des-Prés or Montparnasse, meet friends and talk till late. Once day he borrowed a scooter 'just for fun', and we went for a long ride across Paris in the early hours of the morning when the town was empty. I had not learnt to ride a bicycle (girls did not do anything so unbecoming) nor had I ever been on a motor-cycle before, and I was terrified. I clasped Pierre's waist, hid my head in his back and closed my eyes. No one wore helmets in those days, and we tore down the boulevards and turned corners at full speed, but somehow we never crashed. I remember the exhilaration, the intoxication of speed and warm summer wind, and the hallucinations caused by the city gyrating past like the patterns of a kaleidoscope.

I liked the unpredictability of our life – everything was temporary, surprising, a step in a perpetual pilgrimage. I had thousands of years of nomadism behind me, and perhaps that part of Pierre's Russian heritage which was Asiatic contained some of it too. 'You never know what he'll be up to next,' Paul had once said of him when we first met, 'he is *insolite*' – unusual. But I was used to wild young men in Persia, and did not find him so different. Then someone said that I was *étrange* too, and it was reported to me, which made me worried, as I wanted to be considered completely normal.

Why do lovers part? 'Explanations' do not really explain anything. We blame Love for what is Life's doing – or undoing. Prévert knew: *La vie séparent ceux que s'aiment*, said his song. Pierre and I did not quarrel, because I had witnessed too many violent scenes around me as a child and had a horror of them, but we argued. He blamed me for being uncompromising, naïve, ignorant of the world and people, not made for the rough and tumble of life in a competitive metropolis: 'Get thee to a nunnery,' he would quote. 'Your parents surely brought you up for that!' or 'You are a century too late, *ma chère demoiselle*! You should have been born around 1830 and died by 1850!'

243

and other similar taunts I have forgotten, but which hurt. In reality I was indecisive, torn between East and West – between going home and trying to fit into Persian life, or staying in Paris and being free but rootless and insecure.

I thought that marriage to Pierre would make our relationship mundane and prosaic, that my parents would be heart-broken if I announced that I was marrying a Frenchman and settling down in the West for ever. Everything led to a black tunnel with no light at the end, it seemed. I wanted to die. I thought I could get hold of some sleeping-pills and swallow enough never to wake up, as Jeanette had done. I was dis-Oriented – and it would take me half a lifetime and much pain to be re-Oriented again, and to return to that Orient of the Spirit to which all pilgrimage aspires, and to become whole, eventually.

Only Paul was let into my 'secret', and he was gentle and level-headed, as always. Too delicate to say 'I told you so' or 'Why don't you marry me and be safe forever?' he was just amusing, strict or soothing by turn. 'I will never love anyone, ever again!' I said – a rash pronouncement, aged twenty-one. 'Nonsense!' he said. 'It's like Paganini saying he'd never play a violin again because the first one was not a Stradivarius!'

Meanwhile I had at last found a studio-flat and was about to move into it. Having hardly any possessions, it was not a difficult operation, and Paul helped me carry my books and clothes there, in taxis. 'It is the beginning of a new life,' he said cheerfully. I was not so sure – perhaps it was just another turning on a twisty hairpin road.
Meanwhile, through Pierre I had become an *habituée* of Saint-Germain-des-Prés.

26

Saint-Germain-des-Prés

Le choix libre que l'homme fait de soi-même s'identifie
absolument avec ce qu'on appelle sa destinée
JEAN-PAUL SARTRE

Dans une époque de mauvaise foi, l'homme qui ne renonce
pas à séparer le vrai du faux est condamné à une certaine
sorte d'exil
ALBERT CAMUS

The legend of Saint-Germain-des-Prés as the intellectual centre
of Paris had reached Persia by the end of the 40s and gradually
spread among the young progressives. Through articles, photographs and films we learnt the topography of the area: a maze
of cobblestoned streets clustered around the square, dominated
by the abbey and its graceful eleventh-century tower – the
oldest in the city. We knew of the cafés Flore and Deux Magots,
where Sartre, Simone de Beauvoir, Albert Camus, and many
other authors had written the books we read in translation, We
had heard about Le Tabou, where Juliette Gréco had first sung
the songs of Jacques Prévert and Raymond Queneaux, and
launched the fashion for a pale complexion and disillusion. All
you had to do was hop on an aeroplane and disembark in Paris,
and there they would all be, waiting for you!

In reality by the mid-50s the writers, singers and actors had
mostly disappeared, having moved from their dingy hotels to
apartments acquired with their earnings, while the developers
and financiers had moved in. But many of the old *habitués* still
lived in the district, and sometimes went to the cafés and
restaurants they had made famous. It was not unusual to see
a short, tubby man, with balding head and strabismic eyes
behind thick glasses rush down the boulevard towards his home
in the square – and recognize Sartre; or to see Simone Signoret

245

and Yves Montand having a drink with friends at the Flore. But if the stars appeared occasionally, those in supporting roles – writers and poets of various nationalities living in Paris, actors and film-stars, chanteurs and impresarios – were regular visitors, and you could count on seeing them if you went to the cafés at certain times of the day, or at night after the shows.

All this was enough to attract intellectual tourism, and put prices up beyond the reach of students, who increasingly favoured the less expensive establishments further down the boulevard, in the back streets, or in the Latin Quarter nearer boulevard Saint-Michel. By the 60s many of the small food shops had become boutiques, the rundown hotels where impecunious writers and artists had lived were refurbished into three-star hotels, and the apartments had been bought up and restored – yet another twist in the fortunes of a district which had fluctuated from commercial prosperity in the Middle Ages to dilapidation at the beginning of this century, when its derelict buildings had become the abode of students from the Beaux Arts and other university annexes. Yet despite it all, the area retained something of its village atmosphere, as it still does, with crowded street-markets, food-stands and flower-sellers suffusing the air with varied fragrances, antiques and exotica shops, while the presence of important cultural institutions such as the Institute and the Academy, and of major publishing houses ensures its continued intellectual prestige.

But Saint-Germain was a mental space far more than just a geographical district, for it symbolized the triumph of France's spirit after collapse on the battlefield. Germany had aimed its guns against culture, and lost; France had used culture as its weapon and won, wiping out the shame of military defeat. Jean-Paul Sartre (whose name more than any other was associated with the district) was one of a group of extraordinary French men and women in the forefront of European thought, who shaped their epoch: Simone de Beauvoir, Raymond Aron, Claude Lévi-Strauss, Simone Weil, Albert Camus. . .

Out of their writings here, in Saint-Germain, was born the

philosophy of Existentialism, a philosophy popularized above all by Sartre's fiction. Each generation of students has its particular vocabulary, based on the prevalent ideas of its time. Ours was compounds of Existentialism, Marxism, Psychoanalysis . . . At that time in Paris the majority of young people who called themselves 'Existentialists' had no more read Sartre and Camus than most Communists had read Marx, but the ideas were in air, and the post-war climate propitious for their spread.

I was given Sartre's lecture 'Existentialism is a Humanism' by Paul, and later ploughed through numerous volumes of Sartre, as well as Camus. Philosophical choices depend on temperament and circumstance, and at the time Existentialism, as I understood it, suited mine: it was an expression of exile. It proposed that man is alone, 'abandoned' in the universe; and free, and that the price of his freedom is perpetual anxiety; that there is no pre-determined destiny, since we choose what we wish to be and thereby make our own destinies; that life has no meaning save what we give it; and that art and literature can redeem existence, which is fundamentally absurd. Most people, it says, refuse their freedom and take refuge in fantasy and self-deception, which leads them to 'bad-faith' and 'inauthenticity'. But freedom is exercised within a 'situation' which can change by 'action' (notably political action), and this makes commitment unavoidable.

Existentialism was a hard philosophy to live by, as it put the responsibility of life squarely on man's own shoulders, offering him no alibis and no comfort. Amazingly Sartre himself found it too hard to bear: he tried to reconcile Existentialism with Marxism – an attempted 'squaring of the circle' which led him to compromise and to personal 'inauthenticity'. He and Simone de Beauvoir aligned themselves with the Communist Party and became staunch fellow-travellers. They established a kind of intellectual terrorism by declaring 'all anti-communists are swine', broke with their friends – Camus, Aron, Koestler, even the suave Merleau-Ponty – and surrounded themselves with

247

younger cronies, many their ex-students. By 1957, after the Hungarian uprising and the Khrushchev Report, most Communist intellectuals had left the Party or been expelled, but Sartre continued to 'believe'. Later, when asked why he had concealed the existence of concentration camps in Russia, about which he had known for a long time, he replied: 'One should not drive Billancourt [ie the Renault car workers] to despair' – a quote that has become famous since as a supreme example of 'treason of the clerks'. Towards the end of his life, when he was ill and almost blind, and history – to which he had sacrificed truth – had moved on and left him behind, he declared: 'I'm not a Marxist.'

Sartre was not alone in this political trajectory; countless other Left-wing intellectuals and fellow-travellers followed it. Disillusioned with Russia, they kept finding promised lands, in China, Cuba . . . 'Something in them aspires to slavery' is how Camus described their attitude.

By contrast Camus remained honourable and true to himself till the end of his life. He and Sartre had quarrelled after the publication of Camus' *The Rebel* in the early 50s – a dispute chronicled in numerous volumes since. Suffice it to say that Camus contrasted man's continuing metaphysical and political revolt with the banality of 'revolution': the one a refusal of injustice and an affirmation of human dignity, the other a suspension of human values for the sake of a 'programme', a hypothetical better future. 'I rebel, therefore we are' against 'the end justifies the means', which sanctions violence, deceit and terrorism.

More than a decade before it became a commonplace, he understood the nature of totalitarianism and denounced it – the irrational totalitarianism of Fascism as well as the rational totalitarianism of Communism. Not wishing to align himself with either the Left or the Right, he became increasingly isolated, a lone voice crying in the wilderness. Stoically he stood his ground, won the Nobel Prize in 1958, and died in a car crash in January 1960. And then, what posthumous triumph over his persecutors! All his predictions came true and by the time that Eastern Europe collapsed in 1989–90 not a single intellectual of note was left in the French Communist Party.

Camus embodied a temperament both rebellious and mystical, but always on the side of life and joy. Unable to endorse a philosophy which says that moral principles have to be sacrificed until they can be resurrected in a 'better future', I found myself more and more drawn to his position.

Although married with two children, Camus was known to have extra-marital love-affairs. His two marriages and major relationships have been chronicled in his biographies as well as in contemporary *romans à clef* – notably in Simone de Beauvoir's *The Mandarins*, published in 1954. At that time Camus' main 'companion', was an ex-pupil of Tania's, a celebrated actress, whom I had met and admired greatly. But so many beautiful women came into his orbit: young aspiring actresses, would-be writers, society-hostesses. Clearly he had no trouble making new conquests, and in this he was no different from countless other writers and artists; Saint-Germain was always rife with gossip about love-affairs among intellectuals.

'There are absolute loves and contingent loves', Sartre had told Simone de Beauvoir, assuring her that theirs was of the first variety while his and her other affairs were of the second. The formula had become famous and provided a model for their followers. The American writer Nelson Elgren, with whom de Beauvoir had a long affair, commented: 'How can love be contingent? Contingent upon what?' I agreed with him: this was surely promiscuity dressed up in philosophical garb? And it was not for me: I was truly innocent, and I did not see any reason to change my behaviour – it would be inauthentic!

One of Camus' conquests was Antonella, a student at Tania's who was among the first to befriend me. She was of Italian origin and very attractive – tall, slim, with a dark complexion and grey-green eyes which seemed to be always moist with tears. She had studied Italian at the university, then married a fellow student and produced a son, while writing short-stories and fairy-tales, a couple of which had been published. One day she had written a fan-letter to Camus, which had led to their meeting and later to an affair. For Camus it was evidently a short, inconsequential encounter, like grabbing a chocolate bar on your way home to dinner, but for Antonella it was serious. She had fallen hopelessly in love with him. She had left her husband and taken her little son to live with a schoolteacher girlfriend, hoping that Camus would make a commitment to her.

Instead gently and politely he had made it clear to her that he had no intention of doing any such thing, telling her that he was incapable of love in her sense, and that he would always be her friend, as he was with many other women. But no more. Antonella was heart-broken. She was now twenty-five, and had built a whole emotional edifice on very little, certainly no pledge. She lived for the rare occasions when she saw him – taking up acting was one of the ways in which she sought to remain in his life.

She confided in me and wept profusely, and I was sad not to be able to do anything about it. Despite being so influenced by his thought, I resented Camus for being the cause of her suffering. Then Tania, my drama teacher, cast me as Olga, the revolutionary heroine of his play *The Just*, and later when he came to see *The House of Bernarda Alba* I was introduced. He was courteous and charming, paid me the usual compliments, adding some specific remarks that made me believe them. He hoped to set up his own company, he said, and suggested I audition for him. To be part of a group of actors under his direction was to acquire a family security in doing worthwhile work while earning a modest living – it was a dream! But because of my feelings about what he had done to Antonella I never took up his offer to audition, and eventually left Paris a few days before he died. It was one of those 'missed appointments' with which life is pock-marked, part of that mass of regrets that we accumulate.

Not that we did not meet again – once. One day I bumped into him on the boulevard Saint-Germain, coming out of a café near his publishers' offices, and we stopped for a chat. He said he had an appointment, but would see me the next evening at six o'clock in the same place.

I believed that we would talk about the theatre, his plans, ideas and books, but when I told Pierre he laughed: 'How can you survive with such naïvity? Is it not possible that he might like you as an actress *and* an adventure?' and he gave me a lecture about Camus' philosophy and how it tallied with his way of life – *joie de vivre*, multiplicity of experience, Mediterranean equilibrium and clarity – all as remedies against the angst and feeling of the absurd. So I did not go to my appointment, and never saw Camus again, but instead wrote and told him honestly that I was afraid of him, and had been warned against him. He sent me a gentle, kind letter, and we exchanged a couple more. I threw away most of my letters, diaries and notes when I left Paris, but his are among the few I have kept.

I was told that when he died, apart from his widow and the actress who was his acknowledged companion, many other unknown 'widows' appeared in Paris, all claiming to have been great loves of his. Antonella was one of them.

I became a regular visitor to Saint-Germain-des-Prés only in the last eighteen months of my stay in Paris. Some of the friends I made have remained close ever since, and their memory imparts a rosy glow to days which were often darkly bleak. Others were fortuitous but brief encounters. These make up an important part of life's education, and I had gone to Paris to be educated! One of them was José Bergamin, the Spanish exiled poet and sage. He belonged to that scintillating group of Spanish poets known as 'the generation of 24', which included Lorca, Alberti, Hernandez and several others. They had sided with the Republicans in the Civil War. Lorca was assassinated, and, when Franco won many of them went into exile, mostly to Hispanic countries in South America. Bergamin had opted for Mexico, where he had taught at the university and written his books – poetry, essays, criticism. In the mid–50s he had retired from teaching and come to live in Paris, to be near his children who had remained in Spain.

Now he lived in Mexico House at the Cité Universitaire. He could not afford a place of his own, and it was a great honour for Mexico House to accommodate him. Kind, gentle, elegant, he was also, despite his limited resources, very generous: he never allowed anyone to pay the bill at the Flore, where he usually met his friends. And when he could not help his fellow exiles financially, he pulled strings for them – with publishers, theatre- and film-directors, and whoever else was in a position to employ them.

Bergamin sometimes invited me to snack lunches and English teas at Flore, where other friends would often join us. Listening to them talk made me aware of their plight, scattered all over the world, trying not to lose their roots, language, customs until the time came when Franco would be gone and they could return to Spain.

He educated me in the rudiments of Spanish literature, by talking about it and giving me books of poetry by Lorca, Machado, Hernandez, Alberti, saying that poetry and songs were the best way to learn a language – through pleasure. He encouraged me to return to Persia: 'Exile is the most terrible predicament. When you are young and busy coming to terms with the world you don't notice it as much, but as you get older it gets worse.' There was no political impediment to his living in Spain, as, unlike Alberti, he had never been a Communist – he was a democrat, profoundly tolerant and civilized, and a natural Christian mystic. But he had vowed not to set foot there so long as Franca lived, and he kept his word, putting up with hardship and longing, until the day when, old and frail, he went back at last to become a revered elder statesman of Spanish letters in the republic. I wanted to go and see him, and indeed arranged a trip to Madrid, but he died before I could go – covered with honours and surrounded by affection. I have kept the few books he gave me – Lorca's *Quatrains*, Saint John of the Cross, Saint Teresa of Avila: none of them believed in death.

Another Flore *habitué* was the Egyptian writer Albert Cossery, whom I met through a Persian friend. A Coptic who wrote in French, he had come to Paris after the war with his first manuscript, 'just to see' – and had never left. Like Sartre and Simone de Beauvoir, and many other French and expatriate writers, he had found a room at the Hôtel Louisiane, in rue de Seine, but unlike them he never moved out. Though the hotel is now renovated and expensive, enjoying the prestige of its past inhabitants, to its credit the management has not forced Cossery out, indeed is rightly proud of his presence.

Cossery was not a prolific writer, and his reputation rested on the excellence of three novels, all about his native Cairo. He was hailed as France's Henry Miller, whose praise of his books had contributed to their international reputation, but the comparison was not fair – to Cossery. His novels, unlike Miller's, were short, compact, classically constructed, contained no verbal incontinence, no obscenities, no misogyny, and no humourless earnestness – indeed are imbued with humour and irony tempered with compassion.

His sexual philosophy was that women were solely for pleasure and comfort, not intellectual intercourse, that they had to be cherished and looked after, and that only a degenerate man would expect them to earn a living. These attitudes would have won him a lynching by even the mildest feminists, had his humour not saved him. It was all provocation, mischievous anti-conformism, surely? For in reality he understood and greatly appreciated intelligent women, preferring their company to that of *any* man. He had been briefly married to an actress – just long enough to realize that he was not made for marriage – and since then a succession of beautiful women had loved him, none expecting any lasting commitment. His affairs died natural deaths, in their beds so to speak, then metamorphosed into friendships.

How Cossery earned a living was a mystery, and when you enquired, his answer was: 'but I don't earn a living!' His literary output was small, journalism was hard work and beneath him, and teaching the same. Yet somehow enough money 'happened'. He told me many stories about occasions when he had completely run out of money, and suddenly something had materialized out of the blue, such as a cheque from an American admirer who had been urged by Henry Miller 'to send Cossery some money'. His wealthier friends 'lent' him some too, with which he was in turn generous towards others – he behaved like an Oriental grandee, without a *sou*! He had a profound contempt for striving after material gain, his only digression from hedonistic enjoyment being writing, or doctoring the occasional filmscript, at which he was very good, and could have become rich had he not found the preoccupation with money unworthy, a distraction from the serious business of *s'amuser* – having fun.

As can be imagined, Cossery's own company was as rewarding as his books. He was observant, funny, and underneath his caustic humour moved by pity for his fellow humans. He chainsmoked, but did not inhale (or so he claimed). When in his seventies he developed cancer of the lungs, his surgeon told him to give up cigarettes, advice he ignored: 'Doctors will say anything to stop you having fun!' he told me, when I upbraided him.

In those days you could find him around two o'clock in the afternoon having breakfast at Flore, alone or with friends. 'Sit down and have something,' he would say, in a deep voice with a heavy Arab accent. 'Breakfast' could take between one and several hours, depending on who was around. For genuine talent and intelligence he had the traditional Oriental respect. But he could be ruthlessly and hilariously sarcastic – the pretentious, the phony and the intellectual bully were usually the prime targets – given the right audience. In the evenings he went to dinner with friends, and sometimes ended up after hours at bars or back at Flore.

When did he write? The truth was that he did not have much time to write, hence his small output. Several years lapsed between books, but when they appeared they were received with rapturous reviews, and today on the strength of a few novels his reputation has grown all over the world, his books have been translated into over a dozen languages and several have been made into films. In France where he always enjoyed a cult following, he has received official recognition and important literary prizes. In his native Egypt he is the subject of veneration and pride, even though he does not write in Arabic. I see him whenever I am in Paris; he is in his late seventies, but age has not changed him much nor dimmed his wit – his assessment of current fads and fancies is as hilarious as ever. Beneath all this facetiousness lurks a fastidious perfectionist, a vocational writer for whom literature is indeed too serious to be confused with the mundane business of earning a living.

One of the writers you could sometimes find talking to Cossery was Lucien Goldman. Born in Rumania, he had lived in Vienna, Switzerland and Brussels before settling in Saint-Germain-des-Prés with a French wife. A real cosmopolitan, he could speak in several languages on a variety of subjects including criticism, sociology, cultural history and philosophy. He had become famous in intellectual circles for his acute intelligence and vast erudition long before he had written a single line – he just talked! Then one day someone told him that instead of wasting his brilliance on the air he should put it down on paper. He did, and from then on he wrote a considerable amount, leaving an impressive oeuvre when he died.

Goldman was a disciple of the Hungarian Marxist critic Georg Lukás whose theories he helped to spread in France. Today he is described as a major 'theoretician of French Marxist structuralist criticism', but in those days structuralism had not yet become the latest fashionable 'ism' – that happened in the 60s – and we just read him for his original insights into a world of which we knew little. His magnum opus, *Le Dieu Caché*, was a study of Jansenism, and its relationship to Pascal's *Pensées* and Racine's tragedies. Later a shorter, easier book on Racine and Jansenism brought him a wide readership, and many students were influenced by his theories.

I had become interested in Jansenism, first because of the oppression the Jansenists had suffered at the hands of the Church and the State, and later because their tragic vision of human condition – the arbitrary nature of Grace, the injustice of sin, the centrality of guilt – seemed to make sense in view of all the human suffering I witnessed and experienced. What political solution could ever change this state of affairs? How could the world be transformed so that innocent children did not die of disease; so that love was always requited, virtue rewarded? That did not mean that we should stop striving to alleviate the burden of human suffering, but that we should remember always where we stood. The Jansenist Pascal summed it up by comparing human beings to prisoners condemned to death, 'who look at each other in sorrow, without hope, waiting their turns'.

'Here is someone who has read your books,' Cossery introduced me. Goldman was kind: instead of showing boredom at a mere student's half-baked 'philosophy', he gave me an exposé of his newest ideas, and whenever we met thereafter he gave his unstinted attention to whatever subject we discussed, doing all the talking, which was instructive and enjoyable. Then I lost touch with him, and read with sorrow in the newspapers about his death after I had left Paris. When Hungary officially gave up socialism I thought of him and his friend Lukás and wondered how they would have reacted: I should think with a sigh of relief.

Saint-Germain had a large floating population of actors and actresses, many of whom have achieved successful careers since. Among those I met one became a life-long friend, despite our age difference. Loleh Bellon was considered one of the best dramatic actresses of her generation, particularly appreciated for her interpretations of the Russians classics – Chekhov, Turgenev, Dostoevsky – as well as the heroines of Racine and Claudel. I first saw her in Chekhov's *Ivanov* playing the protagonist's consumptive, victimized wife. The audience was so enthralled by her dramatic intensity and so moved by the pathos of her presence that there was not a dry eye at curtain fall. As I was with a friend who knew her we went backstage to congratulate her. In the place of the distraught heroine of a few minutes earlier, we found a gay, vivacious, beautiful woman laughing with friends. She had to rush home to her little boy, but we agreed to meet at the Flore for tea the next day; although she lived on the Right Bank and did not often come to the area. And so we became friends.

Older than me, esteemed by critics and public alike, with a wide range of interests outside the theatre, she was a perfect role-model. She had married young an exiled Spanish writer, George Semprun (Spain's present minister of culture) and though the marriage had been brief produced a son. Now she had to support herself and her child. That anxious juggling between acting in the evenings, often working during the day as well in radio and television plays, and looking after her child was something I would know a decade later, when I with two small children had to earn a living touring the country. Like most actors she was often out of work, despite her fame, yet she never lost her optimism, gaiety, or her open-handedness: whoever she was with, she insisted on being the hostess, fighting over the bill and usually winning. Such generosity is rewarded by fate, and somehow she always managed to earn enough.

She had joined the Communist Party in her teens after the war, and as a successful young actress had soon become one of its assets in the theatre. You could see her on the rostrum at meetings, in the company of other celebrities the Party paraded, hear her read poetry, sign autographs, and generally enhance the Party's prestige with her presence. You recognized her deep, warm, distinctive voice on the radio, and saw her name on posters. But by the time I met her she too had left the Party.

Her mother was Jewish, but her family were so assimilated that she had only become aware of her origins when her uncles had been forced to wear the Yellow Star during the German Occupation. Since then she had learnt to recognize antisemitism however well-disguised, and she had first begun to have doubts about the Soviet Union at the time of the Jewish Doctors' Plot, which had revealed Stalin's anti-semitism. But faith being stronger than reason, she had persisted in her beliefs until the Hungarian uprising and the Khrushchev report finally dealt the *coup-de-grâce* to them.

Having tea with Loleh at Flore was an occasion for meeting other actors and writers, among them Claude Roy, a prolific writer who had been one of Aragon's close associates and whose defection from the Party had dealt it a severe blow. I had read his poems and articles, and seen him from afar at popular festivals and book-fairs. His output was formidable both in range and variety – poetry, criticism, fiction, travel . . . 'He has read everything,' friends used to say, and yet it all seemed effortless, and he always had time for sociability. It did not come as a surprise that he and Loleh became friends, married and set up home in Saint-Germain. Luckily theirs is a genuine case of 'and-they-lived-happily-ever-after'.

Because I married an Englishman, and lived in the English countryside with two small children, I inevitably lost touch with many Paris friends and acquaintances during the 60s, but Loleh and Claude somehow kept in touch – they came to England to see friends and to watch plays, some of which Claude translated into French. Then one day Loleh wrote her own play. It was produced, received rave reviews and ran two years. A second followed, then a third. She won prizes and was produced all over the Continent: her transition in middle age from actress to playwright was smooth and happy – and she has not looked back.

As the centre of Bohemian life, Saint-Germain had always attracted expatriate and exiled artists and writers, from South America, the Middle-East, Africa . . . Following in the footsteps of their illustrious predecessors – Joyce, Hemingway, Fitzgerald, Gertrude Stein – whose ghosts still haunted the Left Bank and the establishments they had made famous, a number of writers and artists from Britain and America had come to live and work in Paris after the war. The Anglo-Saxons (as the British and Americans, lumped together, were called) formed a large group, and gathered in their own cafés and restaurants, the favourite being Café Tournon, in the street of the same name that runs from the boulevard Saint-Germain to the Odéon Theatre.

It was a Persian acquaintance, Hesham Shahini, who one evening first took me to Café Tournon. He had been a 'professional' Communist Party activist but was now retired, because of a heart ailment which eventually killed him. He had remained a Communist even after Hungary; he admitted to Stalin's 'mistakes' but used the famous old excuse of you-can't-make-an-omelette-without-breaking-eggs. No one then could foresee that by 1990 the unscrambling would begin, that the eggs would have to be retrieved from the omelette, and that that would prove a great deal harder than the initial 'cooking'.

Shahini and I were greeted by a group of his friends, sitting at the back of the café where two small tables were joined together to make a wider circle: an American writer, a West-Indian mathematician and his wife, an East-African actor and an English poet, as well as a couple of decorative young intellectual groupies. A heated argument was in progress, in English, which was not easy for me to join in as I then did not know the language at all well; but as a newcomer I excited some interest and they made an effort, repeating in French the words I did not understand.

The American writer was Richard Wright, who had been one of the first 'Anglos' to arrive, back in 1948. A protégé of Gertrude Stein's, his best-selling novel *The Black Boy* had been

259

serialized in Sartre's revue, *Les Temps Modernes*, and Sartre had encouraged him to come to Paris, where he had been received with open arms. Such infatuations are usually short-lived, and when Sartre wrote an anti-racist pamphlet in which he said that a white skin was obscene, Wright warned him against 'inverted racism' and their relationship cooled.

Although he had been a Communist in the 30s, Wright had gradually become disenchanted and left the Party. Inevitably he was accused of becoming 'bourgeois' and *passé*. The fact that his later books had not matched the success of his first and most famous novel did not help, but he was still respected and listened to by a loyal entourage, until eventually he went back to America and died in 1960.

Wright and James Baldwin were often at the Tournon, surrounded by compatriots and friends and fans of other nationalities. Among them were two young Americans, Robert Silver and George Plimpton, who had set up a literary magazine aptly called *The Paris Review*. Foreign, especially English-language, publications abounded, but they usually had short lives, starved to death by lack of money and other practical causes. Not so *The Paris Review*. Thanks to the enthusiasm and know-how of its founders, who managed to find backers and persuade prestigious authors to contribute for little remuneration, it took root. Its interviews, in which celebrated writers like Hemingway, Faulkner, Wright and others talked in depth about the genesis of their works and lives, soon won the magazine a largish readership, and later the best of these were selected and published in book form. In 1956 Silver and Plimpton moved back to New York and took *The Paris Review* with them, keeping its quarterly format and style. Silver later became editor of the *New York Review of Books*, while Plimpton remained editor of *The Paris Review* and wrote his own books. Baldwin moved on too. But that was all before I was taken to the Tournon.

On that first evening Christopher Logue, the English poet, dominated the discussion, speaking in a gravelly, unusual voice, but with a clear diction which made it easier for me to understand. He had published two books of poems which had been well received, and he contributed poetry, his own and in translation from French and Spanish, to a number of publications. Paradoxically his French was sketchy and his Spanish non-existent, but working from word-for-word translations which he transformed into original poetry, he produced eloquent versions of Villon and Neruda, among others. These were preludes to his grand project, only to be realized two decades later, of translating Homer's *Illiad* – which when it came out was hailed as one of the best renditions ever. But at that time he was a young poet at the start of his career. He was also interested in the theatre and had been to Berlin to see the Berliner Ensemble, where he had made friends with Brecht and his wife Helen Weigel. As a result he was one of Brecht's first disciples in Britain and held forth with fervour about his theories of alienation.

On my next visit Richard Wright brought me a copy of his novel, *The Black Boy*, and Christopher gave me his book of poetry, both of which I have kept. I turned down Wright's invitation to dinner – by then I knew that such expressions of interest were preludes to other demands, the tacit or overt process of refusing which was disagreeable, and to be avoided. But when Christopher asked me later I accepted because with him I felt safe, knowing that we had both emerged from broken relationships and were too emotionally battered for anything save gentle, affectionate friendship.

We each had contemplated suicide – and he had nearly succeeded in carrying it through. I had heard the story from Shahini: apparently at the time Christopher lived in the same derelict hotel as a friend of his who claimed to be a Nietzschean Nihilist, and advocated suicide as the only 'authentic' solution to existence. But instead of committing suicide himself, he encouraged Christopher to do so. In despair over the fiasco of his love-affair, Christopher agreed, and went to Barcelona to ponder the matter, leaving his jubilant hotel-mate rubbing his hands at the success of his 'philosophy', and telling everyone! Upon hearing the news, George Plimpton and a couple of other friends panicked, found the money to despatch someone to Barcelona, who found Christopher sitting on a deserted, wind-swept beach, about to walk out into the sea. Gently he was talked out of his resolve and brought back to Paris, since when time and the publication of his books, together with their success and the affection of his friends had helped the slow process of healing.

Christopher was interested in my singing and acting, being passionate about the theatre and writing songs himself – one of which I recorded twenty years later on an album of poets' songs.

Some of the Anglo-Saxon expatriates were well-off, as the dollar was strong and life was relatively inexpensive, but Christopher Logue was not one of them – he had no money. Yet with the poet's generosity he spent prodigally any small sums he made. 'I've sold a poem, I can take you out to dinner,' he would say, as soon as he arrived, and take me to a nearby restaurant. He would order a substantial meal for me, while he himself toyed with a small portion, his stomach having shrunk from prolonged lack of food. One day he came to see me and announced that he was going back to London for good. I was sad at losing him, but knew he was right to go: he had sowed his wild oats, had experienced hardship and heartbreak, and now he had to go home and get on with the serious business of his work and earning a living. I went to see him off at the Gare du Nord and found him waiting for me at the barrier. Someone else was coming to say goodbye too, but he was late and we began to hurry along the platform towards the coaches. 'Christopher! Christopher!' a voice called out. A tall, thin man was rushing after us; he had short, greying hair and intense liquid-blue eyes dominated his gaunt striking face: Samuel Beckett. The success of *Waiting for Godot* and his two subsequent plays had made him famous, but at that time had not produced substantial material rewards. Nevertheless he had helped Christopher to leave and settle in London by giving him some money (I heard later that Beckett, despite his reclusiveness and diffidence, performed such gestures of generosity as a matter of course). And he was the only one of his friends, apart from myself, who had come to see him off – the others had said farewell at the Tournon.

We had time for a short exchange before the whistle was blown and Christopher had to get on to the train. Beckett said goodbye and walked away with long strides, turning round at the end of the platform to wave, but I stayed on: 'You promise to come to London before going back to Persia, won't you?' I promised. Then the whistle blew, the train screeched and began to pull out. I waved till it swerved round a bend, enabling me to glimpse Christopher at the window of his compartment once more before it disappeared.

27

Leaving

Between us and death there is sometimes only the width of
one single person
MARGUERITE YOURCENAR

One morning I was woken up by the alarm clock, and for a
moment did not know where I was. This momentary amnesia,
common to travellers on the move, usually lasts only a few
seconds, but it provokes the awareness of deeper layers of
impermanence. A shaft of light came through the crack of the
almost-closed shutters, was deflected by the book shelves, and
rested on the bed at my feet. Then I realized I was in my new
studio flat, in rue Saint-Jacques. It was on the ground floor
overlooking a concrete courtyard, and consisted of one largish
rectangular room, a kitchenette and a little entrance where
there was just enough room to install a shower in due course.
After the noise of the Cité it was a haven of quietness, hence
my disorientation.

The building belonged to a government-sponsored housing
company with properties dotted about the city. The company
had a huge waiting-list, and priority was naturally given to
desperate cases – homeless couples with babies, old people –
which meant that only a miracle had secured it for me. A friend
of my family had come to Paris, and he had brought his old
pal the Marquis of C., the President of the housing company,
to see me in *The House of Bernarda Alba*. Afterwards we went for
a drink and the old marquis, learning that I was desperate for

a place to live, asked me to go and see him at his office to discuss what he could do for me.

On the appointed day I arrived at the premises of the housing company and was welcomed by a secretary who led me to Monsieur le Président's office: a long room furnished with antiques and Persian rugs strewn over the fitted carpet, Old Masters on the walls, and a view over the avenue de l'Opéra and the Opera House. The marquis – in his sixties, tall, slim, and slightly stooping – was standing behind his gold-and-mahogany Empire desk, smiling benignly. His thinning hair was smoothed back, with a faint off-centre parting, as if a wilful trick of the comb had divided his scant crop slightly to one side. He came round to kiss my hand and offer me a seat, and speaking in a quiet patrician voice asked after our mutual Persian friend, spoke about the theatre, for which he confessed a soft spot, and finally told me that there was in fact just then a little ground-floor studio available in the *quartier*, but that I might not find it worthy of me. I did not tell him that after the Foyer and the Cité a room of my own in *my* area was beyond my dreams:

'It will be fine', I said, 'for the moment,' trying not to betray my enthusiasm and planting the idea of a better offer at a later date. As I got up to leave, he came to accompany me to the door and shake my hand, but instead of letting go of it, he held on to it, then tilted my chin with the other hand and made as if to kiss me.

I panicked, parried by pretending that it was not happening, pulling away and laughing: 'No, thank you!' No good. Presently I was rushing round the desk, trying not to run, still treating the situation as a joke. Eventually he gave up and said: 'All right, Mademoiselle, good luck,' opened the door and once again bent down over my hand for a *baise-main*. Oof!

I walked over the bridge to Saint-Germain, where Pierre was waiting for me in a café, feeling relieved but somewhat nauseous and despondent.

'*Alors?*' he asked.

'I don't think I've got it – the usual story!' And I told him what had happened.

'You never know, you might still get it. But maybe you shouldn't have gone looking like a zebra colt, inviting predators.'

'That's all I've got. Anyway, I would have had even less of a chance dressed as a nun, unless he is kinky!'

'He probably thought he would try you with the studio before installing you in a proper apartment as his mistress.'

'*Quelle horreur!*'

But the marquis did turn out to be a gentleman, for to my surprise the studio did materialize and I never saw him again. The previous occupant had left behind a clean and comfortable divan-bed, which together with a little table, a trunk covered with Persian printed cloths, and a Moroccan pouffe contributed by Elena, made up my entire furniture. Bricks collected from a building site and planks were used to make extensive bookshelves – just as solid as built-in shelves, they were more decorative, the red bricks, creamy planks and books forming a colourful pattern against the bare white walls. My little radio and a cheap record-player with some records were legacies from Cyrus, who had returned home, and provided me with music. I had everything I needed and was content.

All that was a few months prior to my momentary amnesia when I woke. During the intervening period the play had ended, I had run out of money, and started doing odd jobs: modelling, translating, writing notes for a Spanish record-producer – a kindly exile married to a French woman who was forever creating jobs for young people who needed them – and all the while waiting for another play which Tania was planning to produce and in which I was promised a substantial part. Whatever happened, I would soon have a regular income – for a while – by singing at L'Ecluse. But long days were spent mooning around in a state of uncertainty, or hiding like a sick cat, oscillating between elation and melancholy.

266

For Pierre was gone. That it was 'my fault', that it was I who had broken off our liaison did not assuage the pain, nor abate the fear and anxiety above the gaping abyss of loneliness. 'Where do tears come from?' apparently I had once asked my mother, for they seemed inexhaustible, unlike the springs of water that in Persia one day gushed forth from under rocks, then dried up leaving nothing but thorns and stones. Now I knew the answer.

'I am going home,' I thought that morning, as I opened the shutters and the sun poured in like liquid honey. A pall had suddenly lifted, the far away wintry sky shimmered blue, immense and unblemished, the grey concrete courtyard glittered yellow, even the tingling icy air was pleasant, like a cool hand caressing a feverish brow. From the cabin of the concierge opposite the smell of cooking wafted across, rousing the tabby cat who, miaowing in anticipation of a juicy morsel, left the sunny spot on my window-sill and slunk away towards his mistress.

Like a swimmer in a sea of grief who suddenly sees the contours of an island, I knew that I was approaching terra firma, however bleak. 'I'm going home,' I repeated aloud, as if to the receding cat.

The decade had ended: de Gaulle had come to power and established the Fifth Republic in 1958–59. 'The Sixties' in their various manifestations were still round the corner. My Persian friends had all gone home and were flourishing in their different fields, the élite of their generation. They wrote urging me to return, saying that everything at home was changing, that the country was taking long, quick strides towards cultural liberalism, encouraging creativity in every artistic field, and that there were infinite possibilities for doing worthwhile work.

Persia was a 'developing' country, my friends assured me (the term 'under-developed' had proved offensive to some sensibilities and was changed to a euphemism). 'Europe is fully squeezed, all possibilities are exhausted, because thousands of other people want the same thing as oneself, whereas here everything is waiting to be created – theatre, films, TV.' Hormoz wrote to me. His first-class degree from the Beaux Arts had secured him the job of restoring an ancient city, and its further architectural development. 'In Paris I would be bent over a drawing-board in some famous architect's office for years, and end up building a villa in the suburbs, *maybe*! Here I have a whole town to restore and expand with new buildings – a university, hospitals . . . '

My past political radicalism would be no handicap, for after an initial crack-down on Communists and their sympathizers some years before, the Shah had co-opted the educated élite, of whatever political tinge and they were now in positions of responsibility, working enthusiastically in their fields.

The picture was alluring, even if only half true, and I had been thinking about it for a while. So that morning I decided to go home and face the music. Although it would still be impossible for me to be a performer of any kind, sufficient progress had been made for a girl of my background to work as a director or a producer. One of my closest friends was now running the arts department of the new national television, and he wrote to say that I could work in the drama and music section, making any programmes I wished. I could build up a repertory company and put on all the plays I admired, I thought.

Having decided, my first telephone call was to my brother Nasser, who had now come to live and work in Paris. Always considered the most gifted of my parents' four children, from early childhood he had drawn, painted, produced cartoons, made filigree objects with soft plywood. Aged sixteen, he had painted a picture of my father (now hanging in my room, one of the few relics of the past) which was pronounced outstanding by the country's foremost academic painter, who had then taken Nasser under his wing as a private pupil. He was already well-known as an artist by the time he reached the School of Fine Arts at the university. Thereafter master and pupil went their separate ways, the one remaining traditional and the other becoming modern, but their devotion to each other remained unimpaired.

A few years after university he had come to Paris, because at the time there was no possibility of being a professional artist in Persia – you had to 'do' something else, and paint in your spare time. The situation would change by the mid-6os, with galleries and an art market, but at the time possibilities were limited, 'being an artist' meaningless.

Paris was then the art capital of the Western world, some of the greatest artists of the century lived and worked there, many of them exiles and expatriates themselves, who acted as magnets and exemplars for the younger generation. Nasser had no money and nowhere to live. He worked hard and suffered much, damaging his health in the process, until at last he was given his first exhibition and recognition followed. Soon he was declared by critics the leader of the *nuagistes* – a small group of painters whose 'cloudy' imagery led to their name. Within a few years he was representing France at international bienn- iales, and having regular exhibitions. But in those early days in Paris sadly I was in no position to help him.

Now at last I could give him something: my little flat. Though too small to be a long term proposition (and indeed he moved to capacious studios a while later), it was his, for as long as he wanted it.

Packing was easy, as I had few possessions except books and records, and these I packed into two crates to be shipped by a maritime transport company. My clothes and personal effects fitted into two smallish suitcases – but my real baggage was my love for France and her language, and they could never be lost or stolen.

The following few days were spent in saying goodbyes. My friends' and acquaintances' responses to my departure ranged from disbelief to discouragement: 'Oh, you'll be back!' they mostly said. 'You are used to freedom now, you won't fit in there.' Prévert wondered: 'How could so modern a girl ever

269

live in a Muslim society with all its restrictions?' 'I'm not that modern and Persia is no longer that Islamic,' I reassured him. Only Tania was encouraging: 'Keep your flat, and come back if you don't like it. But you may be able to set up something good there.'

Several chance encounters and incidents have kept those last few days vivid in my memory – some in retrospect seem as if 'arranged'. I had been away five years and my parents, who had been anxiously but gently pressurizing me to return home, had asked a Persian businessman to buy my air ticket whenever I asked him, 'one way'! We agreed that I would travel first to London by boat to see my sister, then take the plane from there (she had married a young diplomat and they had recently arrived there on their first post abroad, with two little boys, aged eighteen and six months, whom I had not seen). The businessman's office was off the Champs-Elysées, and a couple of days later I went there to collect my tickets.

It was a bright, crisp winter day, with already the promise of spring in the still air, and the night frost made the pavements sparkle like a thousand glittering mirrored lark-lures. The fountains at the roundabout soared high and cascaded down into their basins in crystal chandeliers, sending a fine rainbow spray around. In the surrounding gardens the bare twigs on the trees and bushes quivered with the promise of new growth, of impending bud-burst. People walked unhurriedly, looking at the shop-windows.

'Mademoiselle! . . . mademoiselle, excuse me . . .' The chance of meeting anyone I knew in the middle of the day on the Right Bank was remote, but I turned my head, and saw an old black man approaching me, smiling. His face was familiar: 'Excuse me, mademoiselle, will you have a cup of coffee with me? I'm Sydney Bechet.' And he held out his hand. I was in too optimistic a mood to refuse – what did it matter, since I was leaving in a couple of days? – besides I liked his music, which was played on juke-boxes everywhere. In the café-bistro opposite the Cité Universitaire where we sometimes took refuge from canteen food, there was always someone pressing the button for 'Petites Fleurs', a beautiful tune, and a hit for years, played on clarinet by Bechet. For us students he was a far-away idol whose music resounded in cafés and glided across the busy boulevard to our rooms at the Cité. His picture was everywhere, playing his clarinet, or smiling at the camera, his hooded eyes, squashed nose and round cheeks giving him the expression of a mischievous child. Like Louis Armstrong, he had a far wider appeal than most of the other jazz musicians who played in Left Bank clubs.

Jazz, banned by the Vichy government during the war as an expression of decadence, had consequently become an anti-bourgeois symbol for the young after it ended, and among Left-Bank intellectuals it was fashionable to know about and listen to jazz. Indeed a few became professional players, chief among them being the writer Boris Vian, who was said to have com-piled a jazz record collection for Sartre and de Beauvoir. Black players were particularly appreciated, since the struggle for racial equality was on the agenda of the Left, and many famous American jazz musicians were invited to play on the Left Bank in the late 40s and 50s. But Bechet had settled down in Paris, where I believe he remained till the end of his life.

He led me to the first café-terrace on the Champs-Elysées, and I told him that I heard his records every day, and that all the students loved his music. But he had more in mind than a fan's admiration, and was not interested in discussing the subt-leties of improvisation in jazz, classical and oriental music – he thought he had picked me up, since I had accepted his invi-tation to coffee. I told him I was thrilled to meet a living legend, but I was just about to leave Europe, and would never again have the opportunity for such a fortuitous encounter. When he realized I was not swayed by his compliments, he changed tactics and offered more: 'You see that Cadillac?' he asked, pointing to an American car as big and slick as a motor-boat. 'I'll buy it for you!' 'I don't like American cars!' I parried. 'Ar' right, I'll buy you a Citroën Déesse,' pronouncing the last word 'day-yes'. Next he offered me a house, trips to America, South America . . .

It was getting late for my appointment, and I was not a little bored, so I said goodbye, leaving him to look for another quarry, and I only remembered this episode recently, when I heard a man in the street say to his toddler daughter: 'Come along Little Flower . . .' Memory, like God, works in mysterious ways. But my next encounter, a few yards further up the avenue, changed all my plans and the subsequent course of my life.

It was a meeting with Curtis, the only American among the Anglo-Saxon expatriates whom I knew who lived on the Right Bank, in his parents' Parisian home. From an old New England family, he had come to Europe, after graduating in America, spent a couple of post-graduate years at Oxford where he had made a number of English friends, and then in the mid–50s had settled in Paris to write, while contributing occasional pieces to a number of American literary publications and researching for a book. I had met him at a party in his grand apartment a year earlier, but had not seen him since, and now here he was, walking down the Champs-Elysées! When I told him I was going back to Persia via London, he at once wrote down on a piece of paper the names, addresses and telephone numbers of two of his Oxford friends who were in London, and promised to write to them that very day, telling them to expect me.

I doubted that I would have time since my stay would be brief and I would be involved with my family, and I wanted to fit in my own only English friend, Christopher, but at least I could ring them and convey his greetings. One of his two friends was a German diplomat, a protégé of Churchill's because of his family's anti-Nazism during the war – for which they had suffered – and the other an Englishman: 'Try and see him at least, if you can; he is an explorer and rather unusual – you'll like him. *Il est beau comme le Diable!*'

*

The boat was packed as there were fewer crossings during the winter months, and inside its portholes were opaque with steam from heat and breathing – you had to wipe the panes to look out. The stale smell of fried food, beer and coffee mingled with human odours pervaded the trapped air; excited children ran around, noisily pursued by adults. On the wet deck a cold sea-wind sprayed with icy salt water those few passengers who ventured out, lashing the face and penetrating the bones, driving them back inside. Presently the lights of Calais harbour vanished behind a veil of mist, and the boat glided over dark greenish water swathed in grey clouds, like a phantom in a dream. Reality receded; the few remaining passengers went inside one by one, and I was left alone on deck numbly floating in my thoughts.

Although apprehensive about Persia, I was anxious to get there quickly, and almost regretted the diversion by way of England. But a week would pass quickly, I thought, and then I would see . . . I did not know that fate had other plans, and that its clock was ticking away towards an appointed hour.

The lights of Dover did not become visible until we were practically in the harbour, so dense was the fog. The train journey to London was similarly dark and has left little impression on my memory, but I recall the change of atmosphere as we disembarked in the new country: the pace seemed slower and more relaxed, porters, conductors, and passengers at once more courteous and aloof. Driving with my brother-in-law from Victoria to Kensington I looked out of the window to see the town, which was very different from Paris, and from what I had imagined by looking at posters.

It was a Saturday night, and my sister and her husband were invited to some official dinner, so I offered to baby-sit, since my two little nephews were the real reason for my detour to London.

After they were put to bed I settled down with a book, but I was too anxious and excited to read, and instead decided to ring up Christopher and Curtis's friends, although it was unlikely that any of them would be home on a Saturday night. There was no answer from the first two, but 'the Explorer' said that he had indeed received a letter from Curtis and was expecting my call, and that he could come over and see me, as he was going out of town for a few days in the morning.

'Let us go shopping for some presents for the family,' my sister suggested the next morning over breakfast.

'I'm not going home. I'm going to get married.'

'Whatever do you mean? Who to?'

'To an Englishman. I met him last night.'

'Where? Who is he? What does he do?'

'He came to see me here for a little while. I don't know very much about him, except that he has been an explorer and has written a book. He is now working on something else.'

'What does he do for a living? Has he got a job? Any money to live on?'

'I don't know, and it doesn't matter – I can always sing for our supper! He probably lives in an attic.'

My brother-in-law was laughing at his wife for falling for my joke, for surely I was not serious:

'I thought marriage was a bourgeois institution and that you would *never* marry!' my sister gibed.

'I've changed my mind.'

'How did he ask you? He must be crazy too!'

'Oh, he hasn't asked me. But he will. He is very handsome, and funny – you'll like him.'

'He is good-looking, so she'll marry him, never mind if he turns out to be Jack-the-Ripper!' my sister said to her husband, deciding to treat the whole subject as farce, or perhaps just giving up on me.

'I will have children too, boys and girls.'

'You said you only liked other people's kids; and that you would never inflict the burden of existence on anybody!'

'I've changed my mind about that too. Children of mixed blood are usually beautiful and clever. You know, I think I'll like it here – people seem so nice. At Dover the Immigration and Customs officers smiled and said welcome, and the porter called me love!'

I heard later that a similar scene had taken place between my future husband and his mother, except that she being an Edwardian romantic had not found what he told her strange, rather 'One of those nice things that sometimes happen'.

At this point in a movie the picture would freeze and the credits begin to roll, whilst the music would swell to the crescendo of happy ending: we never wonder what happens to the protagonists in the years that follow that closing kiss. But reality is different: time chips and corrodes everything, until 'The ship of love is wrecked against the rocks of daily life.' But the shipwreck does not make the voyage worthless. Rather, to have embarked upon it rashly at the heart's prompting, and to have reached some sort of haven in the end, even battered and bruised, is a cause for gratitude and abundant thanks to the Grace of God.

28

Epilogue

We shall not cease from exploration
And the end of all our exploring
Will be to arrive where we started
And know the place for the first time

T. S. ELIOT

A warm, sunny Saturday morning in mid-October – they say that Paris has never known a more splendid autumn 'in living memory' . . . But I remember similar seasons, when one bright mellow day followed another, with just the occasional night shower to refresh the air and wash the cobblestones, when the sky was always serene and everything vibrated, sparkled, dazzled, and the whole city seemed to float in a golden bubble.

Today the open-air terraces of cafés and restaurants are full of people in light clothes, and extra tables are laid on the pavements for lunch. At every crossroads the smell of vanilla and charcoal from the stands of sellers of caramel-almonds and chestnuts spreads all round, while here and there a barrel-organ or a busker's guitar fills the air with the strands of old popular tunes that set memories spinning.

Anne has come up from the south to see me, and we walk over the Pont Neuf to the island in the middle and pause to look at the *Vert Galant* below, strewn with leaves though its willows are still green. We watch the river traffic, the panoramic view in both directions, then on into the maze of narrow streets of 'our' district – Saint-Germain – with its bookshops and cafés. It is like seeing the remake of an old film: the same plot and location, but a different cast, with only one or two vaguely familiar faces, aged as if by make-up to indicate the passage of time. In one bookshop the central column is covered with old photographs of writers and poets, many already gone, others now decades older than when these pictures were taken but still productive, as evidenced by their latest books on display.

The Luxembourg Gardens are teeming with people of all ages, but a predominance of young children fill the air with the sounds of their gaiety. Here middle-aged men are intent on a card game, there another group play boules next to a line of spectators, and further away an oddly-hatted elderly couple doze on a bench, arms entwined. The lawns are covered with young people, in small groups or *à deux*, divested of outer garments to catch the sun before it hibernates. The chestnut trees are ablaze with burnished greens, russets, yellows and purples, all glowing, and dead leaves have been swept into mounds in the alleys, though the ground still crunches under-foot with a new crop, fallen with the night breeze. From the central path you have a view over the garden – it has the poignant beauty of the ends of things.

Conversation with old friends always turns to politics as well as personal matters, to the dramatic events in Eastern Europe above all: 'Who would have believed it possible?' everyone exclaims in awe. That monolithic Soviet edifice had been but a house of cards, and we spent part of our youth believing it was creating a paradise on earth! Inadvertently we had contributed to the suffering of the victims through our own illusions. Anne's had been shattered when she went to live in Russia, and my own short-lived 'commitment' had been born from the spectacle of poverty and sorrow to which I was exposed as a child. The intense pity it provoked, the searing desire to contribute my share, however small, to diminishing human misery. In truth I have not changed sides, though the sides themselves seem to have changed. Still, it is better to have erred on the side of Goodness, to have rebelled because the human condition is unfair, and to echo Sancho Panza: 'Since we cannot render a simple justice, let us at least appeal to mercy.'

Today French intellectuals are blamed for their 'apathetic'

attitude to politics, compared to their passionate involvement of the past. With the celebration of the 200th anniversary of the French Revolution, many have returned to an allegiance to the principles of Human Rights – denounced in the past as 'bourgeois' – because they are based on absolute values rather than partisan self-interest.

Nearly all my Persian friends from student days are back in Paris – exiles again, in restricted circumstances, because of a cataclysm not of their doing. But they have a community, a sense of belonging, to which I can lay no claim – my exile had different roots. We meet and reminisce, laugh a great deal, and sometimes even cry. Ours is a century of exile – from history, tyranny, famine, life, even love, and each exile today is different from the next.

Every autumn I find my way to Paris for a few days, to see friends, catch up with things. But now I know that the feeling of nostalgia that overwhelms me is not *for* anything, but is objectless and stems from the unassuageable longing for that original '*ailleurs*', whose genesis far back beyond memory is the loss of paradise. I am always happy to be back, to feel young again and lead the life of a carefree student, even briefly. Yet after a few days I want to go 'home', which now means England: the *terre d'asile* for generations of exiles, through centuries, in their quest for tolerance and kindness. Yet it is not the cities themselves but my feelings for certain individuals that draw me to Paris and then pull me back to London. For in truth it has always been other people – my love for them and theirs for me – which has driven my life. Love, that mysterious crucible wherein all Being has its origin, and which is our only redemption.